I0883589

FROM ROMANOV TO WINDSOR

FROM ROMANOV TO WINDSOR

KING CHARLES III'S ROMANOV BLOOD

CORYNE HALL

AMBERLEY

First published 2025

Amberley Publishing
The Hill, Stroud
Gloucestershire, GL5 4EP

www.amberley-books.com

British Library Cataloguing in Publication Data.
A catalogue record for this book is available from the British Library.

ISBN 978 1 3981 2297 0 (hardback)
ISBN 978 1 3981 2298 7 (ebook)

1 2 3 4 5 6 7 8 9 10

Typesetting by SJmagic DESIGN SERVICES, India.
Printed in the UK.

Appointed GPSR EU Representative: Easy Access System Europe Oü, 16879218
Address: Mustamäe tee 50, 10621, Tallinn, Estonia
Contact Details: gpsr.requests@easproject.com, +358 40 500 3575

To the memory of my parents Peggy and Ernie Bawcombe,
who never lived to see my books and who are always in my thoughts

and

to the memory of Charles and Matilda Woodcock, buried at
Novo-Saratov, Alexandrovskoe, St Petersburg

Contents

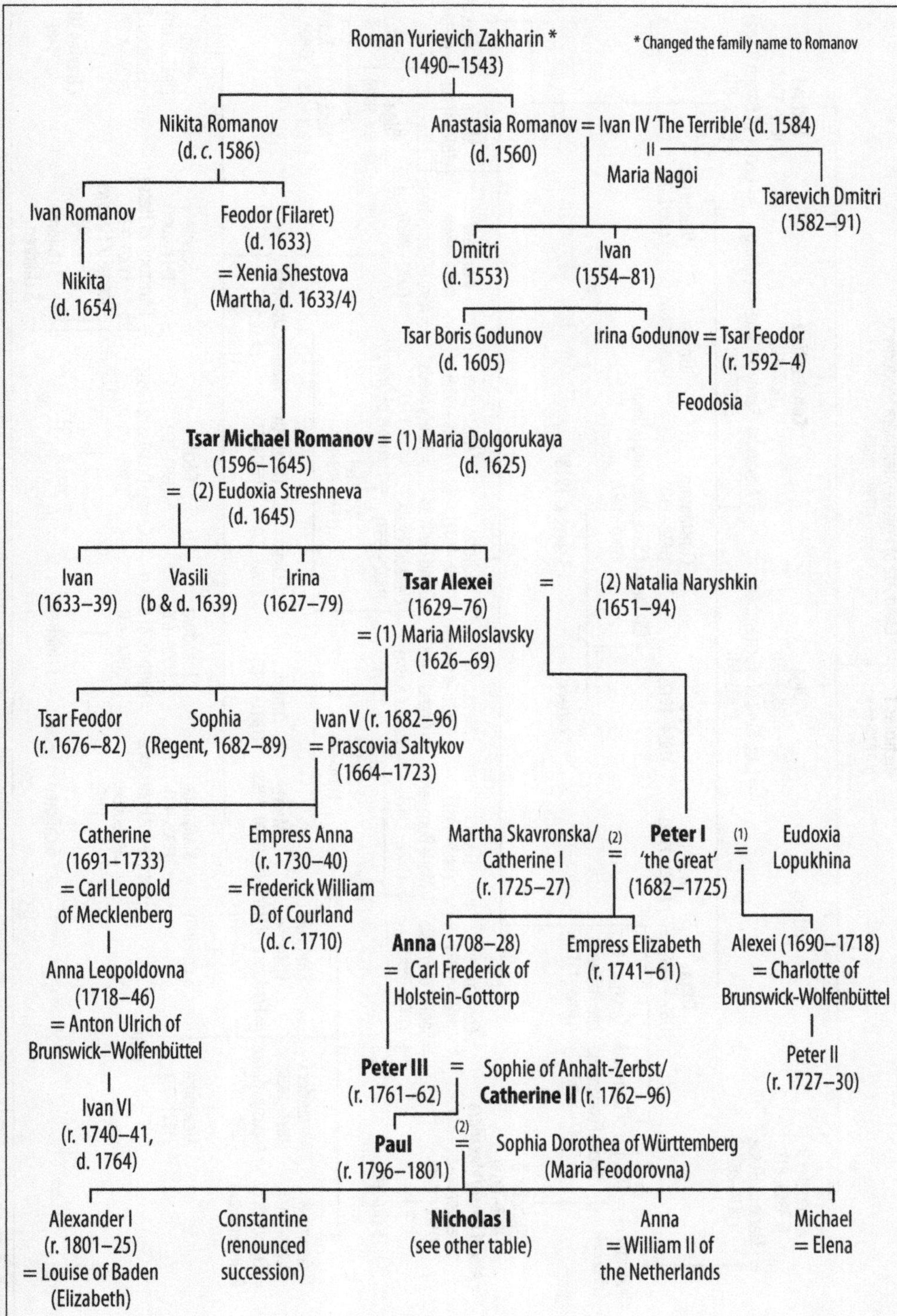

The Romanovs. (© Coryne Hall, 2025)

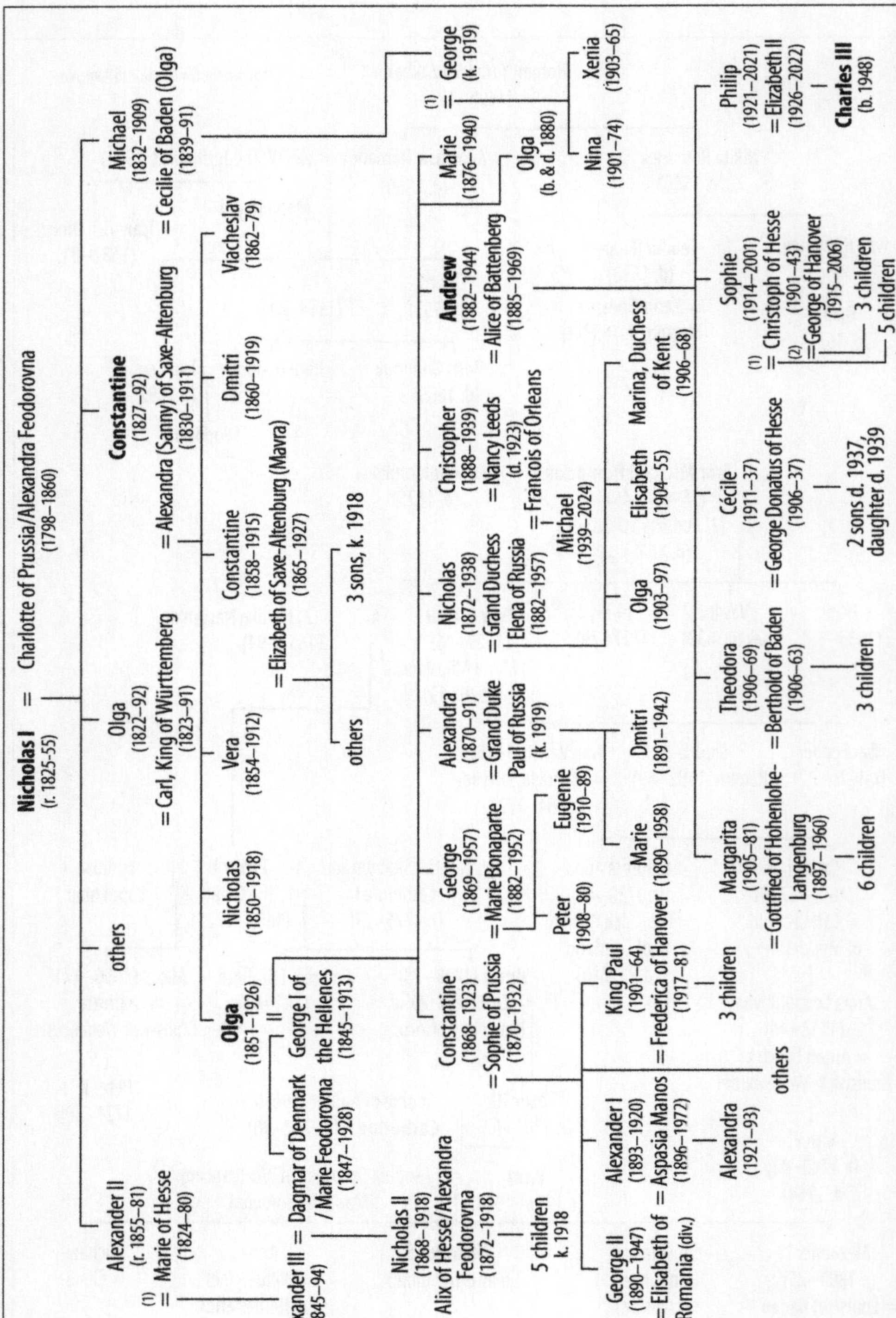

The Russian & Greek royal families. (© Coryne Hall, 2025)

A Note on Names, Dates and Titles

In December 1699 Peter the Great decreed that Russia would adopt the practice of numbering the years from the birth of Christ, rather than the creation of the world, bringing the country into line with the European nations. Henceforth the new year would begin on 1 January instead of 1 September. Russia also adopted the Old Style (OS) Julian calendar, which was used until 1 February 1918. This was eleven days behind the west in the eighteenth century, twelve days behind in the nineteenth century and thirteen days behind in the twentieth century. I have used the OS Julian calendar until 1 February 1918 for events inside Russia, and the NS Gregorian calendar thereafter. Many members of the imperial family continued to use the OS dating system after February 1918 and this has been noted where necessary.

Greece also used the OS calendar until 1923 and this is likewise reflected in the text. Events in Europe are according to the New Style Gregorian calendar, although occasionally it has been necessary to use both sets of dates to avoid confusion.

The title of tsar (tsaritsa for his wife) was correct until the time of Peter the Great, when it was changed to emperor and empress. The title of tsar is still used, however, especially in the media. Nicholas II preferred the older title of tsar to that of emperor.

The eldest son of the tsar was the tsarevich, while other sons were grand dukes. Daughters were grand duchesses. From 1886 the title of grand duke/duchess was limited by Alexander III to the sovereign's children and grandchildren in the male line only; great-grandchildren of the sovereign were princes or princesses.

Russians have three names – their Christian name, their patronymic (their father's name, which ended in 'vich' for males indicating 'son of', and 'ovna' or 'evna' for females indicating 'daughter of') and their surname. For instance, Nicholas I's sons were Alexander, Constantine, Nicholas and Michael Nicolaievich; his daughters were Marie, Olga and Alexandra Nicolaievna. Their surname, Romanov, was hardly used at all.

Readers might find the following glossary helpful:

Boyars	The top rank of the nobility until the reign of Peter the Great. Roughly the equivalent of the western aristocracy. The most elite among them formed the boyar council or duma.
Hetman	Military commander.
Maslenitsa	Carnival week.
Metropolitan	Orthodox bishop.
Panikhida	Orthodox prayer for the dead.
Ukaz	Decree.
Zemsky Sobor	Assembly of the Land.

List of Illustrations

Acknowledgements

The idea for this book began as an article for *Majesty* magazine shortly after the coronation of King Charles III, showing how he was the first British monarch to be directly descended from the Romanov tsars and emperors. I then realised that there was more to say on the subject and that it would make a much longer work. So my first thanks go to Joe Little, Managing Editor of *Majesty*, for encouraging me to expand the original article into a book.

It has come as no surprise to friends and relatives that I have written so many books and articles about imperial Russia, although my own link to Russia is more tenuous than the king's. My great-grandmother was born in St Petersburg and was an almost exact contemporary of Nicholas II. Although her parents were English, the story fired my interest and began a lifelong fascination with imperial Russia. It took many years of patient searching to find details of the family, including her brother and sister who died in childhood and were buried in the 'German colony' of Novo Saratov. Sadly, the graves are no longer there, although the cemetery was still in existence in 1998.

As always, the contributions of others have been invaluable. My grateful thanks therefore go to the following people for ideas, documents, photos, information and much-needed moral support: Arturo Beéche and the Eurohistory photo archive; Tatyana Bukharina, whose diligent research in the Crimea unearthed details of the little-recorded visits of the then Prince Charles and Prince Philip from local newspapers, and who then translated them all for me; Greg King and Penny Wilson, for pointing me in the direction of the *Atlantis* magazine Substack, a valuable aid to research; Marlene Eilers Koenig, who in the early 1990s sent me loads of American newspaper articles regarding the DNA tests, especially those on Anastasia Manahan's hair samples; Dr William Lee, for once again providing translations of the diary entries of Grand Duke Dmitri Pavlovich; Ove Mogensen; Karen Roth-Nicholls; Ian Shapiro; Vladimir Shavshin; the Tsarskoe Selo Museum and Heritage Site; Katrina Warne; Marion Wynn, whose travel journals of our trips to St Petersburg in 1998, the Crimea in 1999 and Moscow in 2001 proved such a valuable memory aid to the places and things we saw; Mikhail Yurlov; and Charlotte Zeepvat.

I would also like to thank the faceless people at the Ministry of Defence and the Defence Infrastructure Organisation for having absolutely no consideration for anybody when they sent no-fault eviction notices to all the civilian tenants in our road completely out of the blue. They left us all struggling to find other homes in an area where rental properties are scarce. Writing this book while coping with the problems of finding somewhere to live and the logistics of moving into it was a real nightmare, especially given the size of my library and archive. The MOD and the DIO provided no understanding or help whatever.

My thanks to everyone at Amberley, especially Connor Stait for commissioning the book and Alex Bennett for such a marvellous job as usual on the manuscript, family trees and photos.

Last, but by no means least, is my husband Colin. He proved a tower of strength when things were really tough and his help regarding the intricacies of the DNA testing of the Romanov bones was invaluable. As always, he read and corrected the final draft and this book would never have been finished without his support when I was near breaking point.

Introduction

On 11 July 1613 a sixteen-year-old youth was crowned grand prince, tsar and sovereign autocrat of Russia in the Uspensky Sobor (Dormition Cathedral) of the Moscow Kremlin. Four hundred and ten years later, on 6 May 2023, the Archbishop of Canterbury placed the historic St Edward's Crown on the head of a seventy-four-year-old British man in Westminster Abbey as the congregation shouted, 'God save the king.' Eleven generations in a direct line separate these monarchs.

When Charles III ascended the throne on 8 September 2022, he became the first British sovereign to be directly descended from the Romanov emperors who ruled Russia for 304 years from 1613. By the time of the 1917 revolution, they ruled one-sixth of the surface of the earth. Their story encompasses great wealth and unlimited power, palace coups and murders, as well as at least one heir allegedly killed by his own father, the emperor.

Most people realise that Charles descends from Queen Victoria, and some also know that he descends from King Christian IX of Denmark – but how many people realise that when Charles was born in 1948 the blood of the Romanovs entered the *direct* line of succession for the first time? Although he inherited the crown from his mother, Queen Elizabeth II, it was his father, Prince Philip, Duke of Edinburgh, who provided the direct line of descent from the Romanovs. Born Prince Philip of Greece and Denmark, his paternal line goes back through the Greek royal family into the heart of the Russian royal family, to Catherine the Great and beyond. In another link, through the family of Prince Philip's mother, King Charles is related to the last Empress of Russia, Alexandra Feodorovna, and her sister Grand Duchess Elisabeth, both of whom were killed by the Bolsheviks in 1918.

Prince Philip's first visit to Russia was in September 1973, in a semi-private capacity as president of the International Equestrian Federation to attend the three-day eventing competition in Kiev. Armed with briefing papers listing topics of conversation to avoid ('the fate of the Russian royal family, Soviet internal politics, nationalism, Soviet Jews, political prisoners and dissidents, the 1968 Soviet invasion of Czechoslovakia, Soviet spies in Britain'),[1] he piloted his own plane into Moscow's Vnukovo Airport and was greeted by the Soviet Vice President Fyodor A. Surganov and other officials. He was then driven to a villa reserved for prominent visitors overlooking Moscow's Lenin Hills (which reverted to their former name of the Sparrow Hills in 1999).

He visited the Tomb of the Unknown Soldier, had lunch with the president of the praesidium of the Supreme Soviet Nikolai V. Podgorny, attended an armoury meeting at the Kremlin, visited a stud farm and presented the prize at a horse race. He then flew to Kiev, where Princess Anne was already training for the European Horse Trials, which he then attended. During the cross-country event he gave his KGB minders the slip during yet another lengthy lunch and roared off in a Jeep. According to *The Guardian*, he left 'hordes of leaden-armpitted KGB and tubby *chinovniki* [apparatchiks] abandoning their lunches and panting over the tailboard of another Jeep ... in pursuit'.

The duke and the princess were the first members of the British royal family to visit the Soviet Union since the execution of Nicholas II in 1918.[2]

Prince Philip returned to Moscow in March 1979, again as president of the International Equestrian Federation, to help plan for a future Olympic Games. He rather surprised the KGB by saying that their security measures for the competitors were inadequate.

In the summer of 1995, as president of the World Wildlife Fund, Philip visited the republic of Sakha to inaugurate the Lena-Nordensheld Biological Station in the Artic delta of the Lena River.

In October 2004 the Duke of Edinburgh took part in the commemorations of the 150th anniversary of the Crimean War, which were also attended by members of British noble families whose ancestors took part in the battles.

After laying a wreath at the British memorial, Prince Philip visited the Panorama Museum (the Museum of the Defence of Sevastopol) and other sights of Sevastopol. The British had organised a camp at the nearby site of the battle of Balaklava, where members of the 13th Light Brigade regiment and the 17th Uhlan regiment performed mounted military exercises. Also present were members of the re-enactment club of the Vladimir Infantry Regiment, headed by Sergei Zhilyaev, and the Victoria Military History Club, headed by Captain Igor Frolov.

On the anniversary of the Charge of the Light Brigade, 25 October, a liturgy took place at which Lord Cardigan, great-grandson of the commander who had sent his troops towards the cannons of the Donetsk Cossack Battery, was present. A horn had been specially brought from Britain. Its poignant sound formed 'a mute witness of the Balaklava battle'.[3]

As for the events in 1918, Philip was quick to put them into context. 'You can't condemn a whole nation for what a few extremists do or did,' he told *The Daily Telegraph* in 1994.[4]

Yet there is another branch of the British royal family possessing significant Romanov blood.

The maternal grandfather of the Duke of Kent, Princess Alexandra the Hon. Lady Ogilvy and Prince Michael of Kent was Prince Nicholas of Greece and Denmark. He shared the same descent from the Romanovs as his nephew Prince Philip. Prince Nicholas's third daughter, Princess Marina, a first cousin of Prince Philip, married Prince George, Duke of Kent, in 1934 but as he was a *younger* son of King George V, their children the Duke of Kent, Princess Alexandra and Prince Michael are much further down the line of succession to the British throne.

Furthermore, Princess Marina's mother, Grand Duchess Elena, was the daughter of Grand Duke Vladimir of Russia, the third son of Emperor Alexander II. Nicholas and Elena's descendants therefore have a double Romanov lineage.

Prince Michael is the member of the Kent family with the strongest interest in Russia. He speaks fluent Russian, qualified as an interpreter and has visited the country many times. He is patron of the Russo-British Chamber of Commerce and, through the Prince Michael of Kent Foundation, has undertaken a considerable amount of charity work in Russia. In 2004 he visited Sevastopol in the Crimea and two years later attended the reburial of the Dowager Empress Marie Feodorovna in St Petersburg.

The focus of this book, however, is on the *direct* line of succession.

King Charles shares many interests with his Romanov ancestors. He has a love of art, as did Catherine the Great; he served in the navy, the service to which his Russian great-great-grandfather Grand Duke Constantine was devoted and which had been built up by another ancestor, Peter the Great. The king has a love of gardens and gardening, a passion shared by Empress Marie Feodorovna (wife of Emperor Paul), who had a professional interest in botany. There is also his interest in architecture, and nobody who has seen the magnificent palaces of the Romanovs can deny that they shared that.

This is not a history of the Romanov dynasty; it is about the people who form the direct link between Michael Romanov and King Charles. Some of them were Russian, some were Greek, at least one originally was German and owed her throne to a *coup d'etat*. Some were Russia's rulers, others were not. The rulers exercised absolute authority over what rapidly became a vast empire. As a Russian proverb has it, 'Everything that is mine belongs to the tsar.'

So how did King Charles get from Romanov to Windsor?

1

Game of Thrones

It is very high up to God! It is very far to the tsar!
Old Russian proverb

In March 1613, an invading Polish army and a group of hostile Cossacks scoured the Russian countryside near Kostroma searching for a sixteen-year-old boy. This was no ordinary youth. He was the newly elected Tsar of Russia, Michael Feodorovich Romanov. When they found him, the Poles intended to kill him.

They discovered that Michael was living near the village of Domnino, about 250 miles north-east of Moscow, but, unsure of the way, they asked a local elder called Ivan Susanin to direct them. Legend has it he led them into an impenetrable forest, promising that it was a shortcut. While the Poles were lost in the forest, Susanin sent his son-in-law to warn Michael and his mother of the danger and to tell them to take sanctuary in the Ipatiev Monastery at Kostroma. When the Poles realised his deception Ivan Susanin was tortured, but he still refused to reveal Michael's whereabouts. His loyal silence cost him his life.

The story, whether true or not, was later used by Michael Glinka for his opera *A Life for the Tsar*, which had its premiere in 1836 and opened the operatic season every year until the 1917 revolution. In 1838 a monument to Susanin was erected in Kostroma on the orders of Nicholas I. Susanin's descendants were invited to every coronation right up to the last one in 1896 and were honoured at the celebrations for the tercentenary of the Romanov dynasty in 1913.

Michael Romanov did not at first seem like ideal tsar material. He was a barely literate, pale, pious young man who had a nervous tic in his left eye and weak legs but, politically, his youth and inexperience were an asset. He would be a compromise candidate, the 'useful figurehead' the boyar council wanted.[1]

His claim to the throne was as weak as his health. Michael was born on 12 July 1596, according to legend at the house of the Romanov boyars which still stands on Varvarka Street, an ancient route out of Moscow not far from Red Square. Its low, vaulted ceilings and small rooms were typical of boyar homes at that time, with male and female quarters segregated.[2]

The Romanovs' boyar ancestors moved to Moscow in the mid-fourteenth century and became advisors to the Muscovite rulers. Fixed surnames were unknown and it was Roman Yurevich Zakharin (1490–1543) who transformed the family name into Romanov.[3] Roman had a son, Nikita, and a daughter, Anastasia, who became the first of the seven wives of Tsar Ivan IV (he was hoping to take an eighth wife, a relative of Queen Elizabeth I, making Henry VIII look like an amateur).

Ivan IV was the first Muscovite grand prince to be crowned tsar. Nikita Romanov, who died around 1586, became a privy councillor to Ivan IV and then to *his* son Tsar Feodor Ivanovich. The Romanov family obtained lucrative positions at court, giving them power and a comfortable lifestyle. Nikita had a son called Feodor. Tsar Michael was the fifth son of Feodor Romanov and his wife, Xenia Shestova, and the only one of their sons to survive to adulthood. He was also the great-nephew of Ivan IV's first wife, Anastasia Romanov.

When Anastasia Romanov died mysteriously in 1560 at the age of thirty, Ivan suspected that his beloved wife had been killed by poison or some other nefarious means. (Modern research into her bones has in fact found traces of poison.) His grief turned to rage, cruelty and almost madness, which earned him the name of Ivan the Terrible. In a fit of anger, in 1581 he hit his eldest (and favourite) son on the head with an iron-tipped staff, fracturing his skull and killing him.

Ivan the Terrible died in 1584 and was succeeded by his feeble-minded son Feodor Ivanovich, the last male member of the old Rurik dynasty who had reigned in Muscovy since the fourteenth century. He reigned for four years but on his death in 1598 the dynasty was extinct and there was no natural successor. What followed was like a plotline from *Game of Thrones*.

The two main contenders were Boris Godunov (the late Tsar Feodor's brother-in-law) and Feodor Romanov (nephew of Ivan IV's wife Anastasia). Boris Godunov was elected by the *Zemsky Sobor* – but although Feodor Romanov originally backed Godunov, he had hoped to seize the crown for himself.

In 1601, Boris Godunov accused the Romanov family of treason, sorcery and witchcraft. Three of Feodor Romanov's four brothers were exiled, believed killed; he was banished to the St Anthony Monastery at Sisky, in the bitterly cold Arctic region of northern Russia, where he was compelled to become a monk under the name of Filaret. This ensured he could never take part in secular politics and become a contender for the throne. His wife, Xenia, was forced to take the veil as the nun Martha – invalidating her marriage – and banished to a convent in the Onega region. Their Moscow house was seized by Tsar Boris, while five-year-old Michael and his only surviving sibling, Tatiana (who died in 1611), were sent to Beloozero (now Belozersk), a remote region to the north of Moscow, to live with their aunt. They remained there in frightening uncertainty for fifteen months before they were allowed to move to one of the Romanovs' smaller estates 50 miles north of Moscow.

After Boris Godunov died in 1605, Filaret returned to Moscow. He was appointed Metropolitan of Rostov, where he was finally reunited with ten-year-old Michael and the nun Martha, although they could no longer live as husband and wife.

There was no law of succession in Russia. This opened the way to the Time of Troubles, the eight years of lawlessness after the death of Boris Godunov when a horde of pretenders emerged to claim the crown. Three purported to be Dmitri, a long-dead son of Ivan IV by his seventh wife (which would have rendered him illegitimate, as canon law only recognised three marriages). When Rostov was attacked by supporters of the second false Dmitri, Michael and his mother fled as the city fell.

Vasili Shuisky, a prominent boyar, reigned from 1606 to 1610 when he was deposed in a *coup*. The throne was then offered to the King of Poland's son Wladislav. Filaret, who had travelled to Smolensk with a delegation to negotiate the settlement, ended up as a prisoner in Poland and a Polish garrison occupied Moscow. Meanwhile, King

Gustavus Adolphus of Sweden invaded north-west Russia in 1611 and advanced towards Novgorod.

The Poles burned much of Moscow and were soon entrenched in the Kremlin, where they looted the treasures and held out in a state of siege for eighteen months. These were dangerous years for Michael, who found himself a prisoner in the Kremlin with his uncle Ivan Romanov (his father's only surviving brother) and his mother. In October 1612, extreme famine forced the Poles to surrender to a national army under Prince Dmitri Pozharsky and Michael was freed.

By early 1613, there had been no tsar since 1610. The result was a chaotic interregnum. Villages were deserted, corpses lay everywhere, crops, livestock and houses were destroyed, and the Swedes and Poles were still on Russian territory. Russia needed peace and stability. The only way to ensure this was the election of a new ruler on whose candidature everyone could agree.

On 21 February 1613, a *Zemsky Sobor* of delegates representing all classes of the people was convened in what was left of the Kremlin to elect a suitable candidate as tsar. They did not want a mature, strong man. The only choice the warring factions could agree on was sixteen-year-old Michael Romanov. He had no real political training, had not been involved in all the feuding during the Time of Troubles and, above all, had a tenuous link to the old dynasty through his great-aunt Anastasia. The decision took two weeks – but the delegates had no idea where he was.

When the Polish invaders were driven from Moscow in the autumn of 1612, Michael and his mother went to the family estates at Domnino. By the time the delegation set out they were at the Ipatiev Monastery at Kostroma on the Volga River, 200 miles north-east of Moscow. Michael's father was still a prisoner of the Poles.

The delegation left Moscow on 2 March. It was led by Feodor Sheremetev, a leading member of the boyar council, and the Archbishop of Riazan (the Elder of the Trinity Monastery) and contained lesser nobles, Cossacks, government officials and representatives of all classes of people from Russia's towns. Their journey through the devasted countryside would take nearly two weeks.

Michael had no desire to rule Russia. When he was woken by his mother on the cold, windy night of 13 March, told the delegation had arrived and that he must return to the capital, he was not impressed. Nor was his mother, who pointed out that all previous tsars had found their subjects disloyal and, anyway, his father was still a captive of the Poles, held hostage by King Sigismund III. What would happen to him? Mother and son told the delegation to meet them outside at dawn the next morning.

At dawn on 14 March, in freezing cold weather, Michael, wearing 'formal fur-lined robes and a sable-trimmed hat', emerged from the monastery with his mother. As the delegation greeted him as their Sovereign Lord, Michael sobbed and insisted that he had no wish to become tsar. His mother added that she would not bless the undertaking. By now Feodor Sheremetev and his colleagues were almost pleading with Michael to take the throne and save Russia from further chaos and ruin. Still he refused.

It took almost six hours of pleas, arguments and prayers to change his mind. Finally, Michael kissed the cross 'and accepted the steel-tipped staff of tsardom'. As the members of the delegation crossed themselves and prostrated themselves at his feet, he knew that the road ahead would not be easy.[4] 'Few examples can be found in history when a new sovereign ascended the throne in conditions so extremely sad as those in which Michael ... a minor, was elected,' wrote the nineteenth-century historian Nikolai Kostomarov.[5]

Michael seemed in no hurry to reach Moscow. The journey took the tsar and his party over a month. He was met with devastation in every village. The peasants were dressed in rags, and food and accommodation were in short supply. Michael grumbled about the lack of transport (many of his musketeers and Cossacks were on foot) and the fact that many of his courtiers had not even arrived.

On 28 April he reached the fourteenth-century Troitsky Sergeieva Lavra at Sergiev Posad, about 45 miles north-east of Moscow. A centre of spiritual teaching, it was one of the greatest and most important religious houses in Russia, with thirteen churches surrounded by high walls. Here they halted for a little while.

Michael and his mother were horrified at what they had witnessed on their route. He also had no money to equip his retinue and had to resort to begging from some of the wealthy merchants like the Stroganovs.

Michael arrived in Moscow on 2 May. As bells rang from all the churches, people came out to meet him with the traditional greeting of bread and salt and the boyars received him outside the city carrying crosses. Moscow was the centre of the Orthodox Church, the Holy City whose hub was the Kremlin, 'a complex of forts, cathedrals, palaces, armouries and cloisters'.[6] Its high, thick, crenelated red-brick walls and towers (one of which had a secret underground passage to the river in case of siege) rose from the banks of the Moscow River with the 266-foot-high golden domed bell tower of Ivan III (the Great) rising from the centre. The tower's 65-ton bell was only rung three times a year.

Ivan III and his Italian-educated wife, Princess Zoe Paleologue, niece of the last Byzantine emperor, had rebuilt much of the Kremlin and the result was a mixture of 'red brick, white stone, rich marbles, varicoloured tiles and shining metals'. Bulging onion domes of silver and gold gleamed in the sunshine, roofs were 'decorated with fanciful steeples' and everywhere Oriental and Italian Renaissance styles mingled.[7] Sophia, as she became after her conversion, also introduced the elaborate ceremonial of Byzantine court etiquette and the emblem of the Byzantine emperors – the double-headed eagle.

Outside in Red Square (the Russian word for 'red' also meant 'beautiful') was the Cathedral of St Basil, a fantasy of multi-coloured domes and steeples of various shapes and sizes built for Ivan the Terrible in the sixteenth century. He was reputedly so delighted with it that he had the architects blinded so that they could never build another.

Yet the Kremlin was now in a sorry state. Roofs were burned, windows smashed and litter was strewn on the floors. There was no accommodation ready for the new tsar. 'Piles of rubble still littered the Kremlin's squares, the walls were stained with soot and ash, and several streets were physically blocked.' The gates of what was supposed to be a fortress were hanging loose, there were bricks missing and even some of the foundation stones were dislodged. 'The moat between the fortress and the public square was choked with rubble and carrion.' Anything wooden had been plundered for firewood and bodies were heaped everywhere. An urgent repair programme needed to be financed, and taxes were raised seven times to fund it.[8]

Michael proceeded to the Uspensky Sobor (Dormition Cathedral), where he received the oaths of allegiance.

Moscow was not the west. Travellers described it as a 'magic world, weird, sumptuous, colourful', like nothing they had seen before.

Princes, boyars and high officials wore long, flowing caftans studded with pearls and precious stones, with sleeves which hung down to the floor. In winter, when going outside, they were clothed in an extra fur-lined robe with a tall, fur-lined hat. They all sported beards. 'It was believed that allowing them to grow to natural length was mysteriously connected with getting into heaven.'[9] Their wives wore the sarafan, a long pinafore dress, usually with a belt, over a long linen shirt with full sleeves, and a crescent-shaped headdress known as a *kokoshnik*.

From Cathedral Square in the Kremlin the Red Staircase, used for ceremonial processions, rose to the Holy Vestibule. This led to the fifteenth-century Palace of Facets (the *Granovitaya*, named because of the diamond-shaped stone facings on its exterior), the Golden Chamber and the Terem Palace, the official residence of the tsars, which was then being repaired.[10]

The Terem (the name refers to the upper chambers of a palace) was a riot of oriental fantasy. 'The roof was gilded and the windows exquisitely glazed; each entrance and each architrave were sinuously curved, and most of the stone details were picked out in bright paints: blue, red, ochre, green and white.'[11] The tsar's rooms eventually consisted of the vestibule, council chamber, throne room and bedchamber, all leading into each other.

Royal women and their very young children lived secluded in a series of dark, low-ceilinged rooms on the upper storeys where candles and incense burned and they knelt before the icons in the Red Corner of each room to utter prayers. Men were seldom seen here. The Terem 'had its own chapel, exchequer, offices, kitchens and cellars'.[12] Mirrors were covered and only used for arranging one's hair.

The seclusion of highborn women was a Tatar practice adopted from the east by the Muscovite princes. These women were expected to be models of feminine virtue. They were never submitted to the public gaze, nor did they see any of the men who visited their husbands or male relatives in their own home. Their days were spent sewing, embroidering or praying. The tsar visited his family every day, usually with a select group of relatives. These women were shielded at all times from the public. In church they occupied curtained recesses and their carriages were closed when they went out. Doctors were only allowed to enter in extreme situations, and even then they had to undertake examinations in semi-darkness and take a woman's pulse through a veil.

The Romanovs were not royal, so it was now up to them to turn Michael's tenuous connection with Ivan the Terrible's first wife into something more concrete in order to provide their dynasty with some legitimacy.

The first step was a coronation. This needed to be carried out as soon as possible.

On 11 July 1613, people of all classes gathered in the vast Cathedral Square of the Kremlin while nobles and officials of state awaited Michael in the Palace of Facets.

Coronations were carried out according to the ancient Byzantine ritual first used by Ivan the Terrible in 1547. Michael was fortunate in that some of the royal regalia had escaped the hands of the looters when the Treasury was plundered by Polish troops, who took almost all the armour and weapons. A few items had been kept under the protection of the boyars in the occupied Kremlin, while the Polish Prince Wladislav had agreed to spare the historic regalia. However, several other items had to be made from scratch. Even then there was a lack of gold in the Treasury and the craftsmen had to hastily buy from local merchants.

At 3.30 p.m. the Kremlin bells pealed as the tsar's procession set off through the Red Porch, where they bowed three times to the people before walking down the imposing Red Staircase and across Cathedral Square. Michael, clad in heavy Byzantine-style golden robes which accentuated the frailty of his frame, was preceded by the regalia carried on red cushions by boyars and the archpriest sprinkling holy water in his path.

The ceremony took place in the fifteenth-century Uspensky Sobor, whose five golden domes dominated the skyline and where the tsars had been crowned since 1547. The anthem 'Many Years' echoed through the cathedral as Michael entered. This was the first official ceremony in which he had ever taken part, and he appeared 'small and alone'.[13]

Under the cathedral's great columns, frescoed walls and near the great golden Iconostasis (icon screen) which held Russia's most treasured icons, Metropolitan Efrem asked for God's blessing. He tied a reliquary with a splinter of the Cross around Michael's neck, blessed him and pronounced the benediction. The tsar spoke about the many trials Russia had faced during the last fifteen years and stressed the need for peace and national unity. Efrem then placed the crown upon his head.

The Crown (or Cap) of Monomakh had been used at all coronations since 1547 and may have come from Byzantium as a gift from the

Emperor Constantine IX Monomakh in the late thirteenth or early fourteenth century. Its actual origins are uncertain but its workmanship is believed to be oriental. The oldest section was the cone, eight triangular gold pieces adorned with spiral-shaped scrolls, pointed rosettes and lotus blossoms made from fine filigree wire and adorned with rubies and emeralds. It was 'rimmed with sable and surmounted by rubies and emeralds the size of pigeon's eggs'.[14] Michael was then given the diamond-studded orb and the golden sceptre topped with double-headed eagles and was seated on the exquisitely carved royal seat of Ivan the Terrible, known as Monomakh's Throne. Efrem then declared him to be 'grand prince, tsar and sovereign autocrat of Russia'.[15] The tsar divested himself of his regalia and, in a foretaste of the coronation of his descendant King Charles III, was anointed with holy oil by Efrem to bestow the sacred nature of his calling, and given Holy Communion. Afterwards the tsar went in procession to the Cathedral of the Archangel Michael, the traditional burial place of the grand princes and tsars, to pray at their tombs.

The ceremony was followed by a feast in the Chamber of Facets, which had been restored just in time after a herculean effort. This thirteenth-century room had a 70-foot vaulted interior with walls covered by colourful frescoes and supported by one massive central pillar. Around this were large buffet tables, groaning under the weight of the banquet.

The throne stood on the south wall under a multitude of icons and, high up, there was a secret gallery from which the royal women could watch the proceedings below.

Throughout the coronation ceremonies Michael's legs were so weak that he walked only with difficulty and at one point toppled over in public under the weight of the robes and the heavy royal regalia.

The following day Michael celebrated his seventeenth birthday, but there was little time for rejoicing. There were still marauding Polish and Swedish armies on Russian soil. King Gustavus Adolphus of Sweden laid siege to Pskov in 1615 but failed to capture it. His brother Carl Philip still claimed the Russian throne but finally, following mediation by King James I of England, in 1617 he was ordered to give up his claim. Sweden handed Novgorod back to Russia, recognised Michael as tsar and, in return, gained an indemnity payment from Russia (which Michael could ill afford) and control of the coastal towns on the Gulf of Finland conquered in previous reigns. That just left the Poles to deal with.

During the early years of his reign the young, inexperienced tsar ruled in close consultation with the *Zemsky Sobor*, which he kept in session for ten years, and the boyar duma. Six new departments were created. They included a masonry department in charge of rebuilding Moscow and other damaged towns, a brigand department to restore order, a special apothecary department to look after Michael's weak health and a Siberian department. As the task of centralising the government in a country the size of Russia was impossible, the tsar relied more and more on military governors and local officials, whose responsibilities soon included 'many administrative, judicial and financial affairs'.[16]

The Treasury was empty. Only a loan from the Stroganov family enabled the tsar to pay and feed his army. A census was then carried out to determine what taxes the population should pay.

To found a dynasty, the tsar needed to marry. The usual way of choosing a wife, given the difficulty of attracting a foreign bride to faraway Moscow, was a brideshow.

The tsars always married beneath themselves to avoid inciting the boyar factions, who would not want the chosen bride to be from a rival clan. In 1615 courtiers were sent around the kingdom to look for suitable teenaged virgins from the Russian provincial nobility. The selected girls were sent to Moscow to live either with relatives or in a suitably designated house. As many as five hundred girls were then reduced to sixty candidates, who were suitably groomed by their relatives. Doctors and courtiers ruled out the weakest before descriptions of the remainder were sent to the tsar. Good health and beauty were essential but secretly these provincial girls also needed ties, even remote, to any of the factions in the Kremlin. Their family trees were therefore of paramount importance.

The tsar then viewed the remaining contenders and whittled them down further. These were examined by the head of the Great Court office and also by doctors to ensure that there was no medical reason why they could not produce children. The rejected girls were sent home bearing gifts.

The final stage was in the hands of the tsar, who signalled his choice by giving his preferred bride a handkerchief and a gold ring. In 1615 the successful girl was Maria Khlopova, whose family had no friends or allies at court. She received the title of tsaritsa and changed her name to Anastasia before moving with her grandmother and aunt to the top floor of the Terem Palace.

Michael's selection of Maria aroused jealousy and was opposed by powerful people, including his mother, the nun Martha, and his cousins Boris and Michael Saltykov, the men under Martha's patronage who stood to lose a great deal of influence. They now worked to undermine the bride.

About six weeks later, Maria Khlopova 'vomited and fainted' at a banquet at which the whole court was present. It is most probable that she had been slipped poison and that the culprits were the Saltykovs, but this was not raised openly at the time. Her uncle Gabriel Khlopov made light of the episode, saying that she had eaten too many sweets, but questions began to be asked about her health. Did this possible food poisoning indicate that her family had concealed a disease? Was she strong enough to bear children? Unbelievably, Michael Saltykov was now ordered to supervise Maria's health – and he began giving her potions from the pharmacy which caused convulsions and vomiting. This had the desired effect on the court. 'How could the tsar marry this girl?' they asked. The Saltykovs, backed by the tsar's mother, then bribed the doctors into saying that Maria was incapable of having children because she suffered from an incurable disease. The wedding was off.[17]

Michael was not yet confident enough to overrule his mother and seek an investigation. The unfortunate fiancée and her family were exiled to Siberia, all ruined. Maria's father became governor of far-off Vologda.[18] Yet Michael refused to even consider marrying anyone else.

In 1619, the war with Poland was suspended in what would be a fourteen-year armistice. Under the Treaty of Deulino the Poles kept the territories they had conquered in western Russia, including Smolensk, but Prince Wladislav refused to give up his claim to the Russian throne.

A welcome result of the treaty was the release of Filaret from Polish captivity. Michael met him 5 miles outside Moscow on 14 June 1619. It was a poignant reunion. Filaret was now seventy and Michael had not seen him for nine years.

The following week, at a ceremony in the Golden Chamber of the Kremlin, Filaret was named as Patriarch of the Russian church. At his insistence, Michael also accorded him the title of Great Sovereign. This effectively made him co-tsar, and from then until his death in 1633, although they received ambassadors sitting enthroned side by side, Filaret was the real ruler of Russia. He kept the boyars firmly in check and was so overbearing that the weak, sickly Michael was afraid of him.

Filaret saw his task as mobilising Russia for vengeance against Poland. He reformed tax collection and the Orthodox Church and began laying the foundation for the dynasty's wealth. Yet he was thoroughly reactionary and a *ukaz* (decree) of 1634 forbade the sale of tobacco, which he called 'an abomination unto the Lord'.

Filaret was the brains behind both the ceremonies and the architectural improvements to the Kremlin which established the Romanovs. Every year the tsar and his subjects celebrated Easter. Michael and Filaret took part in the Donkey Walk on Palm Sunday when the tsar, wearing the Crown of Monomakh and his robes, led the patriarch, mounted on a donkey, from Red Square into the Kremlin in a re-enactment of Christ's entry into Jerusalem. The 'donkey' was usually a horse with false ears, but this did not detract from the ceremonial of the occasion, for which the patriarch gave the tsar 200 roubles in thanks.

On Easter Day, the end of their long fast, everyone carried eggs decorated in various colours. When people met on the street they greeted each other with kisses and the words '*Khristos voskrese*' (Christ is risen), to which they received the reply '*Voistinu voskrese*' (indeed he is risen). Tsar Michael distributed eggs to his courtiers and servants, a tradition that continued until the end of the Romanov empire. The night before Easter he went into the prisons, where he opened the cells and gave each of the many prisoners an egg and a sheepskin coat. 'Let them be happy. For Christ, who died for their sins, is indeed risen,' he said. Then the prison doors were shut and the tsar went off to morning prayers.[19]

Yet Michael still had no heir. Filaret tried to arrange his son's marriage with protestant princesses of Denmark, Sweden or one of the German principalities (Catholics were not even considered), only to be rebuffed. The Danish king refused even to receive Filaret's envoys, and they fared little better in Sweden. Michael, who was still dreaming of marrying Maria Khlopova, was relieved and persuaded his father to investigate what had happened to her.

Maria was in Nizhny Novgorod, so Filaret sent his doctors there. They reported that she was perfectly healthy and said she had only vomited once before she was given a potion by Michael Saltykov.

The furious tsar immediately banished Saltykov, who, had it not been for the favour of Martha, probably would have been executed for treasonably hindering the tsar's marriage. Yet even now Martha, angered by the revenge her son had taken against the Saltykovs, refused to agree to his marriage with Maria, who remained in exile, a spinster for the rest of her life.

Instead, Martha proposed he marry Princess Maria Dolgorukaya, whose family were related to some relatives of hers. At the brideshow Michael duly selected her and plans for the wedding went ahead.

To give the new Romanov dynasty legitimacy it was vital to construct an image and promote ritualised links to the old line. The official in charge of arrangements, Ivan Gramotin, looked at the records of past weddings and revised the ceremonial.

The couple were married on 19 September 1624 in the Cathedral of the Annunciation, the traditional place where the rulers wed. Filaret and Martha took centre stage in the proceedings, not only as the bridegroom's parents but because of their positions in the church. Between the blessings given by his father and mother, Michael went to pray at the Chudov Monastery, the Cathedral of Archangel Michael and the Ascension Convent. After the wedding there was a banquet in the vaulted hall of the Palace of Facets.

The ceremonies usually took place over three days, but Michael's wedding included a fourth day on which gifts were exchanged and a banquet with high members of the clergy was held. Gramotin also made sure to include an extra day of feasting for the people, as a popular gesture.

Four months later Maria died, probably having been poisoned. This was the beginning of a belief, which endured almost until the end of the dynasty, that any marriage between a Romanov and a Dolgoruky was cursed.

With no time to lose, another brideshow was arranged. Out of the sixty virgins eligible for presentation Michael chose Eudoxia Streshneva, a provincial nobleman's daughter. Between the brideshow and the wedding on 5 February 1626 she was closely guarded in the Terem Palace to avoid any chance of misfortune. After the ceremonies, they spent their wedding night in a bed surrounded by icons and with the traditional fertility symbols of wheat and rye bread beneath the covers.

With Filaret effectively running the country, Michael was able to enjoy some years of domestic happiness with Eudoxia without being burdened too much by the cares of state. In private he liked jesters and court dwarfs, sang folk songs and took pride in an organ which he had purchased from Holland. His public appearances were few.

Eudoxia duly did her duty, being almost constantly pregnant and giving Michael three sons and seven daughters between 1627 and 1639, all born in the bathhouse of the Terem Palace, as was traditional. Unfortunately, Michael's sons Ivan and Vasili both died in 1639 (Ivan was five, Vasili only a few weeks, or even days, old). Only Alexei grew to adulthood. It was not a propitious start to the founding of a new dynasty.

Michael's reign was a period of recovery after the Time of Troubles. Manufacturing and foreign trade were encouraged, and a rare period of calm enabled him to beautify the Kremlin. He rebuilt parts of the Terem Palace and the Palace of Facets, and ordered a new set of grand regalia. Among the items produced by the Kremlin workshops was the Golden Throne, made for Michael from 13 kilograms of gold, ornamented with rubies, chrysolites, turquoises, topazes and pearls.

He also commissioned the upper stories of the Saviour Tower above the Spassky Gate, which marked the royal entrance to the Kremlin. Michael had a passion for gadgets and clocks, so the tower was refashioned with a large clock face by Christopher Galloway. The 238-foot steeple also held a network of secret passageways. 'The tower's outline soon became the emblem of Moscow itself,' it was said, and it often remains so to this day.[20]

In 1632, King Sigismund III of Poland died. Ever watchful, Filaret saw his chance of revenge against the people who had imprisoned him. The newly elected king was Wladislav IV, who still laid claim to the throne of Russia. Filaret raised an army of 60,000 men but this obsolete crew was no match for a modern western army. The commanders argued while Wladislav marched on Moscow – but the advance stopped suddenly when the Polish king learned that Sultan Murad IV and his Ottoman troops were invading his kingdom. A treaty of perpetual peace was signed between Russia and Poland in May 1634. Russia paid another large indemnity which Michael could ill afford, but Wladislav recognised Michael as tsar and was permitted to keep Smolensk.

In October 1633, at the age of almost eighty, Filaret died. He was soon followed by Martha. Michael now reigned alone, aided by his boyar cousins Feodor Sheremetev and Ivan and Dmitri Cherkassky.

Michael was on the lookout for a foreign prince to marry his daughter Irina, who was reportedly a beauty. He knew that if anything happened to Alexei, his only surviving son, during his own lifetime Russia would again be plunged into chaos. He hoped to avoid that at all costs.

Prince Waldemar of Denmark, son of King Christian IV and Kirsten Munk, arrived in Russia in 1644. His one condition was that he would not convert to Orthodoxy. The tsar, eager for the marriage to take place, was prepared to accept this but the patriarch and other lords were not so tolerant. Michael could not send Waldemar back to Denmark unmarried without attracting universal ridicule, so he was held a virtual prisoner in Moscow while the discussions dragged on.

Then fate intervened.

In April 1645 Michael fell ill with scurvy and dropsy. The loss of both parents plus two of his sons in the last few years had taken its toll and he was also probably suffering from depression. Purgatives and other remedies were administered but there was no improvement. On 12 July, his forty-ninth birthday, he fainted during a church service. Suddenly the court realised with alarm that the tsar might be dying.

Tsar Michael I died of a stroke during the night of 12/13 July and was buried in the Cathedral of the Archangel Michael. His wife, Eudoxia, followed him to the grave on 18 August. They were survived by three daughters – Irina, Anna and Tatiana – and their son Alexei.

Michael's thirty-year reign had helped stabilise Russia after the Times of Troubles, but now, once again, Russia lay in the hands of a sixteen-year-old boy.

2

The Young Monk

Alexei was born on 16 March 1629 and spent his first five years cloistered with his mother, Eudoxia, in the Terem.

When Alexei was five, the nobleman Boris Morozov was appointed as his tutor. Alexei moved into a new stone palace, which was 'furnished in incredible luxury', with coffers 'filled with pearls, uncut emeralds, rubies and sapphires'. Yet although his clothes were covered in precious stones, his food was frugal and his simple toys, which included a cart with horses, were made of carved wood.[1]

Morozov provided more than the customary elementary education. Indeed, he stimulated Alexei's curiosity so that the young boy began to assemble his own small library. He collected books in Polish, Greek and Latin as well as translations of foreign works on military strategy. He began to find out more about the west and western culture. He was thus better prepared to rule than his father had been.

He grew to be 6 feet tall and athletic. One of his physicians described him as inclined to fat, with light-brown hair and a stern expression. In a harsh, cruel age he was said to be 'humane and kind'.[2] He was also deeply religious and was known as the young monk. He never missed a religious service and, according to his English doctor Samuel Collins, writing in 1671, 'On fast days he frequents midnight prayers, standing four, five, six hours together, prostrating himself to the ground, sometimes a thousand times and on great festivals 1,500 [times] … We may reckon he fasts eight months in twelve.' Yet when roused, his temper could match that of Ivan the Terrible.

Alexei was crowned on 28 September 1645, after which he set off on a pilgrimage to the Troitsky Sergeieva Lavra and other religious houses with Romanov connections. He then lived mainly at the country palace of Izmailovo or at one of his hunting estates. During these early years of his reign, affairs of state were left in the hands of Morozov.

Meanwhile, Alexei went in search of a wife.

In 1648 there was another brideshow in the Kremlin. The tsar's chosen girl was Theodosia (some sources say Efemia) Vsevolozhsky, but, in an echo of past events, she fainted during a public ceremony. Rival families spread the rumour that she was deliberately concealing a sickness, this time epilepsy, or even that witchcraft was at work. Like her unfortunate predecessor Maria Khlopova, she was sent into exile.

Alexei's second choice was Maria Miloslavsky, variously stated to be either nineteen or twenty-one, the daughter of the boyar Ilya Miloslavsky. They married on 16 January 1648 and afterwards dined on swan, goose, suckling pig and chicken in the Palace of Facets. Ten days later, the fifty-seven-year-old Boris Morozov married her younger sister Anna, thus allying himself with the tsar.

The following year Maria gave birth to a son, Dmitri, who died within a year. Between 1650 and 1669 she gave birth to four more sons and eight daughters, but of these sons only Feodor and the physically and mentally deficient Ivan would survive their father.

Trouble was not far away. Alexei had inherited a budget deficit, which Morozov began reducing by increasing some indirect taxes. In June 1648, as Alexei returned from a pilgrimage, he and his followers were stopped by a disorderly mob who forced him to listen to a litany of grievances against Morozov and other corrupt ministers who were feathering their own nests at the people's expense. Alexei calmed the throng by promising an enquiry and rode on, but the retainers of one of Morozov's allies began whipping the encroaching horde, provoking a riot.

The next day, violence erupted in Moscow. Morozov's house was sacked and some of his underlings were killed. The crowd demanded that Alexei surrender Morozov and other named advisers. He refused to deliver Morozov but was forced to surrender two other men, who were brutally murdered by the mob before his eyes. The situation was eventually calmed by Alexei who, accompanied by his popular cousin Nikita (son of Ivan Romanov), apologised and promised lower prices. The mob's leaders declared that they were rioting against the tsar's evil councillors and meant no harm to him. Riots also broke out in Pskov and Novgorod, but the Metropolitan of Novgorod advised against retaliating with violence. Amnesties were declared and punishments were few.

Boris Morozov was exiled to a remote Arctic monastery (although the tsar ensured he would be protected there), and in 1649 Alexei had a new code of laws drafted and took up the reins of government himself. Among these laws was one which stated that forging the Russian coat of arms used on tsarist seals was equivalent to a crime against the tsar himself. The penalty was death.

Alexei also legitimised serfdom.

Serfdom had developed in the fifteenth and sixteenth centuries under Ivan III and Ivan IV, when the nobility began to hold their estates on condition of their performance of service, which was normally military. Their estates, however, were worthless unless there were peasants to work on them, so the workforce had to be legally tied to them. These serfs were under the protection of the state; they owned small plots of land and paid taxes, thus providing income for the tsar. They were also obliged to serve in the army, providing manpower when needed. Serfdom was not slavery and did not exist everywhere in Russia. It was unknown in Siberia, for instance, and parts of the north and south of Russia. It has been said that 'serfdom was an estate, not a class'.[3]

During Alexei's reign, grants of land to members of the nobility were gradually made permanent, so that they owned the serfs who worked their land. These people were subject to the justice of their landlords and could not leave the estate. Those who lived on state land were tied to their place of residence but were able to organise their lives. However, 'the Crown could hand the land where they lived to a landlord, enserfing them overnight'.[4]

Alexei ruled as an autocrat. He imposed grisly death sentences for sixty-three crimes, fired his ministers and promoted his unprincipled, corrupt father-in-law Ilya Miloslavsky, who had built himself a large palace in Moscow on the profits obtained by his corruption. No subject could travel abroad without the tsar's permission, but he sent his own agents to Europe to obtain goods for him and allowed some countries to trade with Russia. He also began Russia's first postal system. His first trade expeditions to China encouraged tea caravans to arrive regularly in Moscow and the drink became a national beverage.

Foreign traders enjoyed privileges, but when news of the execution of Charles I reached Alexei in 1649 he was outraged. He immediately cancelled all of England's considerable trading privileges within the Russian empire. 'You English have done a great wickedness by killing your sovereign,' he said, 'for which evil deed you cannot be suffered to remain in the realm of Muscovy.' When an envoy from Lord Protector Oliver Cromwell arrived, he was given a lecture. Alexei then sent aid to the exiled heir, later King Charles II.[5]

In 1652, the office of patriarch became vacant. Alexei secured the appointment of Metropolitan Nikon of Novgorod, a reformer who was determined that the Russian church should conform to the practices of the Greek Orthodox Church, removing any deviations that had crept in, especially in prayer books and ritual. He was opposed by the Archpriest Avvakum, who believed that the Greek Orthodox Church was discredited because in the fifteenth century its leaders had considered reunion with the Catholic church in Rome. One of the things on which Nikon and Avvakum disagreed was whether the sign of the cross should be made with three fingers or two. Alexei supported Nikon. Finally, those who clung to the old practices, known as the Old Believers, 'formed a separate church in defiance of the patriarch and the tsar'.[6]

Poland remained a permanent thorn in Alexei's side. The elected kings of the Polish Commonwealth, which 'since 1569 comprised the Kingdom of Poland and the Grand Duchy of Lithuania, ruled regions to which the tsar held territorial "patrimonial" claim'. He also protected the Orthodox subjects in Catholic Poland.[7]

Matters came to a head in 1648 when the hetman (military commander) of the Zaporozhian Cossacks of Polish Ukraine, Bogdan Khmelnitsky, rebelled against the Polish king, publishing a whole list of grievances. He appealed to Alexei, hoping that the tsar would assist him to obtain an autonomous Orthodox state and expel the Poles from their land. Although the idea of expanding his kingdom appealed to Alexei, he realised that Russia was ill-prepared for war. Only in 1653, after three consultations with the *Zemsky Sobor*, did he agree.

As the price of war, the Cossack leaders had to swear allegiance to the tsar. Their lands – the area that was later known as Ukraine – were incorporated into Russia, although in the long term the Cossacks were unwilling to renounce their freedom.

The twenty-five-year-old tsar, complete with orb, sceptre and 'pearl encrusted robe', left Moscow in a gilded carriage with his army, having conferred the title of Great Sovereign on Patriarch Nikon and left him in charge in Moscow.[8] Smolensk was captured in 1654, with the tsar taking part in the siege. The capture of thirty other towns followed.

The war brought Russia into conflict with King Charles X of Sweden, who invaded Poland, claimed the crown and captured Warsaw. Worried about the possibility of a Swedish presence in Poland, Alexei then allied himself with the Poles, hoping that when King Jan-Casimir died the nobility would elect him as his successor.

In 1656 a ceasefire was agreed with Poland, but Alexei declared war on Sweden before the peace treaty was signed. His army occupied large areas of Latvia, Estonia and Finland but he was unable to capture Riga from the Swedes. Meanwhile, the Cossacks feared the end of their independence if Poland and Muscovy united, and when Khmelnitsky died in 1657 civil war broke out between those who favoured union and those who wanted independence. The ceasefire broke down in 1658 and Alexei, knowing he could only fight one enemy, signed a truce with King Charles of Sweden. In 1661 the Treaty of Kardis was signed and Alexei had to relinquish all the Swedish territory he had conquered.

The war with Poland dragged on until 1667, when King Jan-Casimir of Poland had to send some of his forces south to defend his country against a Turkish attack. In the Treaty of Andrussovo, Russia regained Smolensk and Kiev.

To fund this war, Alexei debased the coinage. 'Copper coins were minted to the same nominal value as silver coins.' Fraudulent copper coins began circulating, struck by officials from their own stocks of copper, and 'the inflation caused by the increase in money supply' led to riots in Moscow in 1662.[9] The rioters marched on Alexei's residence at Kolomenskoye to demand that he punish those responsible. He sent for troops from Moscow, in the meantime promising the crowd that he would deal with the situation.

The pacified rebels began the return march to Moscow but on the way they met a second, more militant mob who persuaded them to return to Kolomenskoye and demand that the traitors, who included the head of the Treasury (Alexei's father-in-law Ilya Miloslavsky), be handed over to them. At this moment the troops arrived from Moscow. Alexei, who was already mounted for the return to the Kremlin, was jostled and the crowd insulted Tsaritsa Maria. The tsar ordered his troops to attack. Many of the rebels were killed where they stood, some were drowned trying to escape across the river, and hundreds more were later executed or exiled. In 1663 a decree ordered the copper coins be melted down and the silver currency re-established.

Relations between the tsar and the patriarch had deteriorated by 1657, when Nikon refused to consecrate the new metropolitan appointed to Kiev by Alexei. The following year, the tsar forbade Nikon to use the title of Great Sovereign. Nikon denounced Alexei but did not resign as patriarch. He refused to carry out his duties in Moscow and retired to a monastery. Alexei was unable to overthrow him and neither could the bishops dismiss him. Nikon tried to make a comeback by taking control during a service at the Uspensky Sobor in 1664 but obeyed when the tsar ordered him to leave Moscow. Although he was exiled to a remote monastery in the north, the tsar sent him money and gifts. Nikon's reforms caused a schism in the Orthodox Church and the Old Believers were persecuted.

On 3 March 1669, Tsaritsa Maria died shortly after giving birth to her thirteenth child, a daughter who also did not survive. Her death was followed by that of the tsar's four-year-old son Simon in June. Then in January 1670 the tsar's promising eldest son, Alexei, fell ill and died shortly before his sixteenth birthday. This series of tragedies left only the sickly Feodor and the handicapped Ivan. Although the tsar had an illegitimate son, Ivan Musin-Pushkin, by his mistress Ariana, he needed more legitimate sons to secure the dynasty.

Another brideshow was quickly organised. The frontrunners were Ovdotia Beliaeva and Natalia Naryshkin. Ovdotia was the preferred candidate of the tsar's sister Irina (unmarried, despite the previous efforts of Tsar Michael to engineer a foreign marriage for her). Natalia was the daughter of Kirill Naryshkin, an obscure provincial nobleman. Just as the tsar seemed about to choose Ovdotia, two anonymous letters were found in the Kremlin. They accused Natalia of bewitching the tsar by unknown means and alleged that before she came to Moscow she had 'flirted with a Polish nobleman'. Ovdotia's uncle and female servants were tortured in a bid to find the writer of the letters, but the culprit was never found.[10]

On 22 January 1671, the forty-two-year-old tsar married dark-eyed, raven-haired Natalia Naryshkin who, at eighteen, was only a year younger than Alexei's eldest daughter, Eudoxia. Her wedding gown was 'so laden with pearls and precious stones that she could scarcely walk' and the small ceremony took place amid music from 'organ, pipes and drums'.[11]

The lively Natalia was fascinated by western technology, and fond of music, singing and sweets. She had been brought up by her guardian Artemon Matveev and his Scottish Catholic wife Mary Hamilton in Moscow, where she had been exposed to western influences in furniture, books and art. Although she was not terribly intelligent, Alexei hoped that this robust young woman would provide him with more sons.

Tsaritsa Natalia immediately began to change the strict regimen of the Terem. In contrast to Maria, who had been extremely devout and opposed modernisation, Natalia scandalised Muscovites by going out unveiled and opening the windows of her carriage. She refused to hide behind a screen in church and, during a feast for her name day, served small meat pastries to the boyars with her own hands.

Furthermore, the Miloslavsky family were ousted in favour of the arrogant Naryshkins and Matveev became head of the Foreign Office and the Royal Pharmacy. This situation displeased the tsar's daughters (especially the third girl, thirteen-year-old Sophia) and their spinster aunts, who were still secluded in the Terem. No attempt was made to find them husbands; there were no eligible Orthodox princes among foreign royal families and marriage into a Russian noble family would cause jealousy and all sorts of other problems, which were already exacerbated by the tsar's second marriage. They remained in their gilded cage.

The most serious threat during Alexei's reign came with a Don Cossack rebellion led by Stepan 'Stenka' Razin, who sailed up the Lower Volga slaughtering the upper classes and officials and proclaiming freedom, claiming to be acting on behalf of Tsarevich Alexei, the tsar's eldest son who had died in 1670. After 'some daring pirate raids on the Volga and Caspian' he set his sights on central Muscovy, promising to liberate the people from the heavy burdens which the government imposed upon them. He had a magnetic personality and attracted considerable support from the peasants. In his entourage was not only a young man claiming to be Tsarevich Alexei but also another man who claimed to be the deposed Patriarch Nikon. In October 1670 he and his army of 20,000 men were defeated outside Simbursk, but Razin escaped. He was finally captured by loyal Cossacks in 1671 and handed over to the authorities. The tsar questioned Razin personally and he was then gruesomely tortured on a platform in Red Square before being executed.[12]

In 1672, Turkish forces invaded the Polish part of Ukraine. Alexei, who was still hoping to be elected to the vacant Polish throne, attacked the Sultan's troops and their Cossack allies in a show of support for Poland. The Turks drove out the Russians and the Poles elected Jan Sobieski as their king.

On 30 May 1672, Tsaritsa Natalia gave birth to a sturdy son who was christened Peter. As was traditional, more than 120 gingerbread cakes (*pryaniki*), including one bearing the arms of Moscow and another made to resemble the Kremlin, were presented to the tsar in celebration. Alexei celebrated by commissioning theatre performances, having a special medal struck and promoting Kirill Naryshkin and Artemon Matveev to lords-in-waiting. Both rose to the rank of boyar. A daughter, Natalia, followed 1673 and another, Fedora, arrived in 1674.

Tsaritsa Natalia liked to have fun and brought music and the theatre into the tsar's court. Alexei sponsored theatres and schools in which the finest European artists helped nurture the best artists and pupils. The first court theatre was built in the Kremlin in 1672 and run by Johann Gregory, a German pastor. Amusements during trips to the tsar's summer palaces around Moscow included hunting, falconry (a childhood passion for Alexei, who owned more than 3,000 falcons) and bear-baiting.

Although the Russian government was far from affluent, the tsar's court oozed wealth in what was described as 'barbaric splendour'. They dined off gold and silver plate and drank from gem-studded goblets, the basins they used for washing were edged with semi-precious stones, their robes were studded with pearls and worn with caps edged with expensive furs. Tables and benches were covered with priceless fabrics, while mosaics decorated the walls and floors. The tsar's own finances were helped by the fact that his childless cousin, the enormously wealthy Nikita Romanov, named Alexei as his heir.[13]

In 1660 some Armenian merchants, anxious to obtain trading rights in Russia, presented Alexei with a diamond throne. Made by the court jewellers of the Shah of Persia, it contained over 800 different-sized diamonds, as well as rubies, emeralds, tourmalines and turquoises. On the back, two genies held a pearl crown while an embroidered inscription on black velvet said in Latin: 'This throne was made with great art for the most mighty and invincible Emperor of Muscovy Alexis [*sic*], who doth rule happily on earth, and may it be a token of future eternal bliss in Heaven...'[14]

During trips outside Russia, Alexei took notes about clothes, manners, furniture and different plants and trees. He imported cattle from the Low Countries and agricultural implements from England. On his return detailed instructions were sent to bailiffs about the administration of his estates.

He hired an official portrait painter, ordered a *Book of Titled Figures* to be produced (which represented other rulers, as well as the Russian tsars) and encouraged icon painters to experiment. During his reign the gold and silver icon frames, *oklady*, were more elaborate and the icons were covered in pearls and precious jewels. He had the Icon of the Redeemer, revered in all Russia for its legendary miraculous powers, placed above the Spassky Gate in the Kremlin and decreed that any man passing through it must remove his hat in respect, an edict that was respected right up until the First World War.

The armoury workshops in the Kremlin were expanded and specialised in various arts and crafts.

Court ceremonial became more elaborate, with Alexei sitting on a silver-gilt throne with a jewel-encrusted crown and sceptre, surrounded by ermine-clad boyars. To add magnificence to the Terem Palace he imported Flemish and Persian tapestries and oriental carpets, covered the walls with gilded leathers and had the ceiling of the dining room decorated with a mural of planets and stars in precious metal. He imported European furniture such as chairs, cupboards, beds, display cabinets for his growing collection of tropical shells and tusks, as well as bookshelves, which were not traditional in Russia at that time. From the Golden Chamber, his study, a box could be lowered on a rope from the petition window, allowing people to deliver petitions to their ruler. Responses were usually tardy, leading to the expression 'leaving your business in the long box' meaning infinite delay.[15]

Alexei adhered to all the strictures of the Orthodox Church but never let religious devotions interfere with his work as tsar. His secretaries accompanied him to church and often he would dictate important letters during less significant moments. As he had been anointed by God, he saw fit to conduct state business in the house of God.

In 1654 the tsar set up the Secret Department. Although originally intended to run his sizeable falconry establishment, in effect it became his private office. Responsible for the supervision of his personal finances and correspondence, it had the charge of the Crown Estates and became a training ground for officials.

Under Alexei the Crown Estates were improved. The hunting lodge Izmailovo, his favourite summer residence, was given a new baroque entrance and the gardens, another passion of his, were redesigned and tended by German experts. There were orchards, market gardens, a vineyard, and factories where Russian workers were trained in glassblowing and brickmaking by foreign craftsmen. He also set up the first zoo in Russia, which included some moose from North America.

He rebuilt the wooden summer palace of Kolomenskoye, 6 miles outside Moscow, which was an almost fantastical complex of interconnected dwellings. Alongside a hundred onion domes, tent roofs, horseshoe arches and spires, there were 'heart-shaped gables, arches, balconies and staircases', all brightly painted and gilded.[16] Its two hundred rooms boasted three thousand windows, western-style furniture and the mechanical devices so adored by Natalia, banishing the gloom of the Kremlin. Alexei built baths for members of his family and, even more unusually, there were three for the servants.

There was also a large, rambling hunting residence at Preobrazhenskoe, situated by the Yauza River west of the German settlement in Moscow. Here Alexei built a court theatre where German actors performed.

None of these changes affected the peasantry, who continued to till their fields and work the land as they had done for generations.

In 1674, a procession of churchmen and boyars made its way through the Kremlin carrying 'a precious icon of the Saviour'. Through a route lined with musketeers, they came out onto Red Square where, in a specially created ceremony, Alexei formally named his son Tsarevich Feodor as his heir. By this time Alexei was hunting less than previously and used a carriage rather than riding on horseback. He was obese, his blood pressure was high and he took a concoction of pills and potions which his foreign doctors administered without examining him. All this was done secretly 'because of superstition about the tsar's health'.[17]

Alexei died peacefully on 29 January 1676, possibly of kidney failure, at the age of forty-seven. He was buried in the Cathedral of the Archangel Michael. His heir, fourteen-year-old Feodor, was sickly and with legs so swollen that he had to be carried to his father's funeral on a stretcher. The future was not bright.

The dynasty now had two rival factions: the Miloslavskys, relatives of Alexei's first wife, and the Naryshkins, relatives of Natalia. The Naryshkins claimed that Feodor was too infirm to rule and was unlikely to live long, while Alexei's other son, Ivan, was profoundly disabled and should be passed over. Peter, the lusty child of Alexei's marriage to Natalia, was the logical heir.

The Miloslavskys were dismayed. This would mean Tsaritsa Natalia would rule as regent for her son. The patriarch came to the rescue, reminding the warring factions that Alexei had named Feodor as his heir and recalling the chaos caused by elected tsars.

The result was that Feodor was proclaimed tsar, Matveev was banished and Natalia and her children were more or less excluded from the court.

Alexei was almost the last of the old medieval rulers. It would not be long before Russia was drawn closer to Europe.

3

From Moscow to St Petersburg

Peter the Great and His Family

The block, the rope and poison – these are the true emblems of Russian autocracy.
Dmitri Merezhkovsky (1866–1941)

The accession of Tsar Feodor brought the Miloslavsky clan to the fore again. Tsaritsa Natalia and her children Peter, Natalia and Fedora remained in the Kremlin's private apartments or at Kolomenskoye.

When Peter was five, Nikita Zotov was appointed his tutor. He taught Peter to read and write, yet Peter wanted more and begged Zotov to tell him about Russian history and great battles. Books showing foreign places, ships, weapons and historical events were specially made for him and he was given a large globe. Zotov stimulated Peter's curiosity but, although he learned a little German, grammar remained a mystery to him. He preferred carpentry and warfare.

Peter's life continued in this vein until shortly before his tenth birthday. Then, on 27 April 1682, his half-brother Tsar Feodor died. Although Feodor had married twice, his infant son had died and he had not named an heir.

For the first time since the Romanovs came to power, the succession would not pass from father to son. The next heir was Feodor's sixteen-year-old brother Ivan, who suffered from scurvy, was mentally incapacitated and was described by the Austrian envoy as 'very infirm and congenitally blind with a growth of skin right over his eyes'.[1] Whoever became tsar, there would be a regency. The result was another struggle between the Miloslavskys and the Naryshkins.

Patriarch Joachim and the bishops went to the top of the Red Staircase and asked the crowd below to decide between Ivan and Peter. Gradually the shouts for Peter became louder and louder.

Peter would become tsar under the regency of Natalia, but the real ruler would be Natalia's former guardian, Artemon Matveev. Yet the situation was not that clear-cut.

The Streltsy were the simple Russian pikemen and musketeers who guarded the Kremlin. By 1682 their pay was well in arrears, and they also resented the way in which they were exploited as unskilled labour by their commanders. They needed no real encouragement from the Miloslavskys to revolt.

On 15 May a rumour spread through the ranks that Peter's half-brother Ivan, who had been passed over, had been murdered. A group of angry soldiers burst into the Kremlin demanding to know if it was true. Natalia immediately took Peter and Ivan out to the top of the Red Staircase to show the Streltsy that both were alive. So far, so good – but then the chief of the Streltsy Department, standing near Natalia, loudly condemned the men's mutinous behaviour. He was promptly dragged off and thrown onto the pikes of the men below, who hacked him to death under the eyes of Natalia, Ivan and Peter.

The men of the Streltsy then rampaged through the palace, killing Matveev (who they accused of plotting to kill Ivan) and anyone else they found from the Naryshkin faction. Most were thrown down the Red Staircase and impaled on the pikes. Over the next few days, the bloodshed continued as others were tortured and killed – but the man the Streltsy really wanted was Natalia's younger brother Ivan Naryshkin, who had been promoted to boyar and armourer and was now accused of sitting on the throne and trying on the crown.

Still living in the Kremlin was Peter's twenty-five-year-old half-sister Sophia, described by a contemporary as an 'ambitious and power-hungry princess'.[2] During the reign of her brother Feodor she had come out of the Terem, attended meetings of the boyar council, become involved in state affairs and acted as her brother's confidante and messenger. With pleas for Ivan's life falling on deaf ears, Sophia took charge of the situation, persuading Natalia that she had to give up her brother to save the lives of the rest of the royal family. Natalia had no choice but to submit.

Following Ivan Naryshkin's brutal torture and death, calm was restored fairly quickly. Natalia's father, Kirill, was forced to become a monk and sent to a monastery 400 miles north of Moscow. The Streltsy were given at least some of their arrears of pay (funded by an auction of the murdered boyars' properties) and much of the silver plate in the Kremlin was melted down.

With Natalia overwhelmed by the deaths of Matveev and her brother, Sophia took power. The Streltsy then made another demand. Unhappy that Peter's half-brother had been pushed aside, they now demanded that Ivan and Peter rule as co-tsars, with Ivan V as the senior ruler as he was the elder. On 29 May, Sophia was appointed regent. The following month, the only joint coronation of two tsars took place.

Dressed in long, golden robes embroidered with pearls, the two boys moved down the Red Staircase side by side and crossed the square to the Uspensky Sobor, where a double throne awaited them, made by the Kremlin workshops from 'partially gilded, chased, carved and engraved silver plates'. A later bill for repair shows the weight of the silver as 13 poods (208 kg). Its red velvet seat was divided in the middle by an armrest. Three steps led up to it and it was surmounted by an openwork canopy 'with chased representations of horsemen, birds and fantastic beasts' supported by columns. Double-headed eagles perched upon openwork posts at each corner. Behind the right-hand seat, screened by a curtain, was a hiding place for Sophia to sit and murmur instructions.

The Crown of Monomakh was used to crown Ivan, marking its last appearance in a coronation, while Peter was crowned with a specially made replica and invested with a newly made six-faceted sceptre made of gold and studded with rubies and diamonds, as well as a diamond and emerald cross.[3]

After the coronation, Peter began to hate Moscow and the Kremlin. The massacres he had witnessed, with the Streltsy running rampant through the palace, scarred him for life. He hated the 'dark rooms and maze of tiny apartments lit by flickering candles', the bearded priests and the women secluded in the Terem.[4]

Peter and his mother moved out of the Kremlin, and his formal education came to an end.

Throughout Sophia's regency, Peter saw his brother only on formal occasions such as state banquets, religious festivals or the reception of ambassadors. Even so, relations between them were excellent. Yet there would come a time when Peter would be old enough to rule alone and Sophia would have to step aside.

In 1684, Sophia arranged Ivan's marriage to Prascovia Saltykov in the hope that he would father an heir. Meanwhile, at Preobrazhenskoe, where he and his mother had settled, Peter formed squads of young servants and noblemen into play regiments, drilling them and fighting mock battles. One of the first recruits was Alexander Menshikov, a boy who worked in the stables and was said to be the son of a pie seller. Peter's first commander was fifty-year-old Prince Feodor Romodanovsky, a soldier and courtier who became devoted to him. Eventually, with the help of men from Moscow's nearby German quarter (where the foreign mercenaries and military experts lived), these play soldiers developed into the Preobrazhensky and Semenovsky Guards, the elite regiments of the Russian army.

Peter also learned to sail in an old ship of western design which he and a friend, the Dutch trader Franz Timmerman, found in a storehouse on the old royal estate of Izmailovo. Peter had already been given a sextant, which Timmerman showed him how to use, so he recruited more westerners to repair the boat for him. His sailing teacher was a Dutchman, Karl Brandt, and they soon had a boatyard on the shores of Lake Pleschev, 85 miles north-east of Moscow.

From then onwards Peter was obsessed with boats and the sea, desirous to learn all he could from westerners. This would have monumental consequences for Russia.

By 1688, Peter was sixteen and his mother had decided that it was time for him to marry. On 27 January 1689, after a brideshow, he selected the girl Natalia had chosen.

Eudoxia Lopukhina was the twenty-year-old daughter of a middle-ranking nobleman, described by a contemporary as 'fair of face, but of mediocre intellect and no match for her husband in character'.[5] The marriage was a disaster, but a few months after the wedding she was pregnant.

To almost universal amazement, Ivan's wife, Tsaritsa Prascovia, was also expecting her first child. Everything now depended on which of the two wives had a son.

When Prascovia gave birth on 21 March 1689, it was a girl, Maria.

In August 1689, seventeen-year-old Peter fled to the Troitsky Sergeieva Lavra at Sergiev Posad, a traditional site of sanctuary for the

Romanovs. The brutal scenes that he had witnessed in the Kremlin seven years earlier seemed about to be repeated and he was convinced that the Streltsy were coming to kill him.

The alarm had been sounded by two messengers who galloped into the courtyard of Preobrazhenskoe just after midnight. Someone in the Kremlin had mistaken an extra-large Streltsy escort assembling for Sophia's visit to a monastery as a possible attack on Peter; meanwhile, a messenger sent by Peter to the Kremlin with a routine dispatch was pulled from his horse and dragged inside by people who misinterpreted the message as a sign of attack by Peter's play army.

Consequently, when the messengers arrived at Preobrazhenskoe, Peter leapt from his bed and, still in his nightshirt, ran to the stables, mounted a horse and galloped to a nearby grove of trees. There he hid while he awaited the attendants bringing his clothes. He then dressed quickly and they all set off to the monastery, where they arrived at six o'clock in the morning. An exhausted Peter had to be lifted from his horse.

Later his pregnant wife arrived with his mother, accompanied by soldiers from the play regiments. They were joined by Patriarch Joachim. When Peter summoned the Streltsy to join him from Moscow, he had the power of the church and state behind him. The Scottish General Patrick Gordon, 'a foreign advisor in the pay of the Russian government', also joined Peter along with his elite unit of foreign officers. Gordon found an 'adept and admiring pupil' in the young tsar and became not only a hired general, but also a good friend.[6]

Peter was showing signs of taking power, and Sophia realised she would soon no longer be needed.

Sophia's regency had seen the renewal of the treaty with Sweden in 1684, a Russo-Polish Treaty of Permanent Peace two years later, and the first Crimean campaigns against the Tatars in 1687 and 1689, commanded by Sophia's lover and chief minister, Prince Vasili Golitsyn. The latter campaign had been disastrous, but Golitsyn tried to claim victories.

By the middle of September 1689, Golitsyn had been exiled to a remote Arctic region. Peter's brother Ivan had agreed to support his sibling, while Sophia, now powerless, accepted that she had lost. Peter banished her to the Novodevichy (New Maiden) Convent on the banks of the Moscow River, where she was confined for the remainder of her life. Ivan was permitted to keep his title of tsar and the half-brothers ruled together – on paper at least.

On 18 February 1690, Eudoxia gave birth to a son named Alexei. That same year, Prascovia gave birth to another girl, Feodosia – but with the birth of Tsarevich Alexei, Russia had an undisputed heir.

Peter was happy to leave the government in the hands of his mother Natalia and her boyar advisers, freeing him to follow his own interests, primarily shipbuilding and debauchery.

At 6 feet 7 inches tall, Peter was a giant in every sense. He was interested in the arts, sciences and war, fascinated by anything practical and could usually take mechanical objects apart and then reassemble them. His strength was enormous and, with his rather rough sense of humour, he often inadvertently inflicted physical pain on others. He could not bear incompetence or stupidity and was quick to anger, yet equally fast to forgive.

He hated both ritual and formality. He loved to drink (thanks to Zotov's influence), dance and engage in gargantuan feasts to satisfy his enormous appetite and had a taste for lusty foreign women. He was able to satisfy all those needs in the German quarter of Moscow, which by then housed Dutch, English and Scottish people. (To most Russians, who could not distinguish between the languages, all foreigners were German.) Tsar Alexei had permitted this new foreign settlement in 1652, with plots allotted to 'foreign officers, engineers, artists, doctors, apothecaries, merchants, schoolmasters and others in Russian service'.[7] They had western-style houses, worshipped in their own churches, wore western clothes, spoke their own languages and kept in touch with events in their native land. This was Peter's first introduction to life in western Europe.

Peter's excursions into this self-contained suburb increased after 1690. He revelled in the inhabitants' discussions about world affairs, stood godfather to their children and acted as best man at their weddings. One of the friends he made there was Andrew Vinius, son of a Dutch father and a Russian mother, who was now in charge of the post office. From him Peter learned Dutch and also some Latin.

Another prominent foreigner was Francois Lefort, the son of a prosperous merchant in Geneva. He eventually became a captain in the Russian army and married a cousin of the tsar's friend Patrick Gordon. Lefort, unequalled as 'a drinking companion and ballroom cavalier', was skilled at organising entertainments, loved to talk (especially about the west) and was frank, open and generous. He rapidly became Peter's boon companion. The tsar gave him a palace (ensuring also that he had the money to maintain it), and he soon became a full general, admiral and ambassador. 'My heart is wholly in Moscow,' Lefort told his Swiss friends when he visited them in Geneva.[8]

It was in the German quarter that Peter also found his first mistress. Anna Mons was the seventeen-year-old daughter of a Westphalian wine merchant, described as 'an exceedingly beautiful young woman, endowed with all the talents to please, except prudence and good sense',[9] who had already been the mistress of Lefort. She could be ill-tempered, especially when it came to money and power, and Peter was not her only lover. Peter gave her jewels, a country estate and a palace, and when he was in Moscow she almost fulfilled the duties of a tsaritsa, accompanying him everywhere. In fact, knowing that Peter was not in love with his wife, she hoped to replace her on the throne in due course. Peter, however, was satisfied with things as they were. Their liaison lasted for twelve years.

Peter's most notorious pastime was drinking. With Alexander Menshikov, Lefort, Gordon and others, the drinking bouts almost became drunken orgies. In around 1690, Peter created the Vastly Extravagant, Supremely Absurd, Omni-Intoxicated Synod (known as the Drunken Synod), which was a parody of the hierarchy and rituals of the church. It came complete with a prince-pope, twelve cardinals, bishops, archimandrites and other clerics who were all confirmed drunkards and gluttons. In their company Peter indulged in all the elaborate ritual that he usually hated, 'as if to proclaim that ceremony was only fit for drunken orgies, not for serious affairs of state'.[10] This blasphemy scandalised the Orthodox faithful.

After his mother's death in 1694, Peter took a more active role in government, ruling as an absolute autocrat. He was determined to enhance the international standing of Russia. He soon realised that, with Arkhangelsk in the north frozen for six months of every year, he needed an outlet on the Black Sea where he could build a navy to challenge the Ottoman empire and a foothold on the Baltic at Sweden's expense.

In 1695 he fought a war against Turkey with the aim of capturing the fortress of Azov at the mouth of the River Don. The siege was unsuccessful, and Russia withdrew, but Peter realised that Azov could be taken if Russia put a naval blockade in place. He created shipyards at Voronezh on the Upper Don and worked alongside the foreign shipbuilders and other conscripted unskilled workers, sleeping in a simple log hut next to the shipyard.

In July 1696, in a combination of a land assault and naval blockade, Peter took Azov from the Turks, marching with other naval commanders in the victory parade that October. Soon he began construction of a naval base just along the coast at Taganrog.

On 29 January 1696, Peter became the sole ruler of Russia when his half-brother Ivan V died without fathering a son. The births of Maria and Feodosia (both of whom died young) had been followed by three more daughters in quick succession, all of whom survived beyond infancy. Rumours circulated that the three girls' father was Prascovia's lover Vasili Yushkov, 'although the identity of the "real" father or fathers has never been established'.[11]

Ivan was buried in the Cathedral of the Archangel Michael next to his brother Tsar Feodor in what would be 'the last of the old-style royal funerals'.[12]

After achieving success against Turkey, Peter set out for western Europe in what became known as the Great Embassy of 1697–98. Travelling incognito as Peter Mikhailov, a humble carpenter, he was the first Russian ruler since the eleventh century to travel abroad in peace rather than at the head of an army. One thousand sledges, 'six pages, four dwarfs, about twenty liveried servants ... five trumpeters, musicians, a pastor, surgeons, physicians and a company of well-equipped soldiers'[13] were among the 250 people who accompanied him. There were also thirty-five 'volunteers' who would learn shipbuilding and navigation in Holland.

Francois Lefort was nominally in charge of the expedition but, with his sheer height and mannerisms, Peter's disguise fooled nobody. Travelling through Pskov, Riga, Konigsberg (where he had talks with the Elector of Brandenburg, who became King Frederick I of Prussia in 1688) and Berlin, Peter reached Amsterdam in August 1697.

His goal was to acquire technical knowledge and expertise so, with this in mind, he headed for the shipbuilding centre of Zaandam where by chance he met Gerrit Kist, a Dutch blacksmith who had worked for him at the shipyard in Voronezh. Staying at the humble home of one of Kist's neighbours, Peter spent a week dressed as a Dutch sailor labouring in the shipyards. In Amsterdam he gained more experience by working for three months in the shipyards of the Dutch East India Company, where he learnt how to build a frigate and obtained a certificate in shipbuilding. He visited workshops and factories where he acquired a knowledge of clockmaking, copper-engraving and even dentistry. He also delighted in watching anatomical dissections.

In January 1698 Peter headed to London, where he remained until May. He visited the Woolwich Arsenal and the Royal Observatory at Greenwich, studied shipbuilding at Deptford and had an affair with the actress Laetitia Cross. He lived at Sayes Court, a house in Deptford owned by the diarist John Evelyn, where he and his company did considerable damage. Three hundred panes of glass were broken, twenty-one pictures were destroyed, an explosion was caused on the kitchen floor and three wheelbarrows were driven through a hedge as a result of larking about in the garden. The total damage was estimated at £350.

King William III, with whom Peter spoke in Dutch, arranged for him to watch parliament while it was in session, commissioned his portrait from Sir Godfrey Kneller (which is now in Kensington Palace) and gave him a yacht, *The Royal Transport*. In return, Peter gave him an object wrapped in a grubby piece of paper. It proved to be a huge, uncut diamond. Peter also visited Oxford, where he was recognised. He was described by the curator of the Ashmolean Museum as 'a very uncouth fellow with a long black wig and dirty hands'.[14]

By July Peter was in Vienna, where he discovered that the Holy Roman Emperor, Leopold I, was more inclined to accept an offer of peace from Turkey than join the fight against the Ottomans. He was about to move on to Venice, where he hoped to learn more about the Venetian war galleys, when urgent news arrived from Russia.

Four Streltsy regiments had revolted and, instead of carrying out orders to march from Azov to the Polish frontier, were marching on Moscow. They were only 60 miles from the capital and loyal troops had been sent to block their path. The letter informing the tsar had taken a month to arrive. Peter had no idea whether the rebels had reached the Kremlin or if his half-sister Sophia (who had once been regent) had seized the throne and denounced him as a traitor. He decided to return immediately to Moscow.

He left Vienna on 19 July, travelling even through the night with only brief stops to eat and change horses. When he reached Krakov, better news arrived. The rebels had been vanquished, there were 1,860 prisoners and 130 men had been executed.

Much as he wanted to see Venice, Peter was halfway home and so decided to continue to Moscow, albeit at a more leisurely place. At Rawa in Galicia he met the new King of Poland, twenty-eight-year-old Augustus II of Saxony, whose candidature he had supported in the hope that he would keep Poland in the alliance against Turkey. The men had the same tastes – drinking bouts, women (it is said that Augustus had 354 illegitimate children) and military reviews. They got along well and laid the foundation for a joint attack on the Swedish Baltic provinces.

After eighteen months away, Peter reached Moscow in August 1698, bringing with him 260 chests 'filled with weapons, scientific and mathematical instruments, tools and a stuffed crocodile'. With him came many experts in military and technological matters who would teach their skills to Russians.[15]

Peter soon established a commission to investigate the Streltsy revolt and found that it had been motivated by the fear that his desire to westernize the army would see the Streltsy abolished. Peter believed that Sophia had encouraged the revolt in the hope of regaining power. His men made extensive use of torture, and Peter often questioned the Streltsy members himself. A total of 799 men were beheaded, broken on the wheel or hanged, many of the latter outside Sophia's windows at the Novodevichy Convent. The Moscow Streltsy were disbanded and their members exiled to the provinces. Although Peter found no proof of Sophia's involvement, he was taking no chances and she was forced to become a nun. His violent reaction to the Streltsy revolt probably had its roots in the events of 1682.

Peter's next step was to modernise Russia, dragging the country out of the old ways. He ordered the boyars to cut off their beards (even clipping some off himself with shears), imposed an annual tax on anyone wearing one and decreed that all men except the clergy and the peasants must shave. This edict was regarded with horror in Moscow. As the old proverb said, 'A beard is a mark of honour – even a cat has whiskers.'

He also decreed that they must cast off their impractical traditional long robes and wear western clothes. This delighted the women more than the men, especially his sister Natalia and widowed sister-in-law Prascovia, who immediately sent to Paris for samples of the gowns, shoes and hats worn at the court of Versailles. Yet the exemption of the clergy and the peasants (who resisted all change and retained their native traditions) from these reforms created a schism between them and the more westernised upper classes. This new division only grew with time.

In December 1699 Peter decreed that the New Year would begin on 1 January instead of 1 September and adopted the Julian Calendar (rather than the Gregorian Calendar, which was viewed in Russia as Catholic and heretical). In 1702 he abolished the custom of secluding women in the Terem and ordered them to appear at social functions alongside men.

He created the Order of St Andrew, used as a cheaper reward than the gift of vast estates and serfs. The first recipients of the order (Russia's equivalent of England's Order of the Garter) were his loyal supporters Menshikov and Sheremetev. Peter founded schools of 'navigation and mathematics, geography, philosophy and astronomy'. The potato was introduced to Russia, as was lacemaking and tapestry weaving. Native horses were bred, books and newspapers printed, and a theatre was built in Red Square where foreign actors and musicians performed.[16] His one failure concerned efforts to open the grammar schools to all classes, which was opposed by the boyars and the clergy.

The tsar took part in all the popular festivals and celebrations. At Christmas he went out around Moscow to join in the traditional carol singing, in which everyone participated. Riding in a sleigh led by drummers and surrounded by boyars and courtiers, he went from house to house to sing carols for the owners. They were expected to respond with gifts and treats but, typically of Peter, he kept a list of the boyars and nobles who attended. Those who did not turn up were punished.

Maslenitsa (Butter Week) was the last eight days of Lent. This was a carnival time, with masked figures and dancing bears in the streets, swings and huge ice slides. Peter would turn up in a public park with a group of his officers to 'whirl merrily' on the swings, a pastime which he loved.[17]

Peter also turned his attention to Sweden, where there was a young and inexperienced new king. Charles XII was born in 1682 and became king in 1697. He was a tall, thin and tough soldier who liked heavy drinking and womanising.

An alliance was formed between Russia, Augustus II of Saxony–Poland and Frederik IV of Denmark to attack Sweden's Baltic states. The war began in 1700 but went badly for the allies. The Swedish king was militarily gifted and forced the Danes to surrender just as Russia was entering the conflict. The month-long siege of Narva ended with a disastrous defeat for the Russians in November, despite their forces being numerically superior.

To Peter's relief, his fear that Charles would invade Russia failed to materialise. Instead, Sweden attacked Poland, which gave the Russians valuable breathing space as Charles became 'bogged down in a complex situation' with King Augustus.[18]

The poorly equipped and trained Russian army needed to modernise. In 1701 an artillery school was founded, new green cloth uniforms were introduced and the modern flintlock weapons Peter had brought back from England were used as models for a Russian version.

Much of the artillery had been lost at Narva, so Peter ordered bells from the churches and monasteries of the leading towns melted down to make guns and mortars. Soon Russia was producing more cannon than Sweden. Conscription – which was for life – was introduced, and the trained conscripts were formed into western-style regiments. In 1701 the Admiralty Department was established for the construction and equipping of warships.

All this activity paid off. Russia scored victories over the Swedes in 1702 and the following year captured the Neva Delta, which gave Peter access to the Gulf of Finland. Between 1704 and 1706 his troops moved on to Estonia, Livonia and Courland. Meanwhile, Charles defeated King Augustus, forcing him to relinquish the crown of Poland and make peace. This time, war-weary Sweden was too economically weakened to invade Russia.

The year 1703 was a pivotal one for Peter. He met the woman who would become his second wife and he founded Russia's new capital city.

His relationship with Anna Mons was breaking up and he had never loved his simple, uneducated wife Eudoxia. She was too cloying, too possessive and disliked the foreign influences which surrounded Peter. Of the children she had borne him, only Alexei survived. Soon after Peter returned from the west, he had her bundled off to a convent where ten months later she was forced to take the veil as a nun, which invalidated their marriage. Peter soon had someone else in mind.

Martha Skavronskaya was a nineteen-year-old buxom peasant girl who had fallen into Russian hands in Livonia. Her origins are obscure but she was most likely Lithuanian or Scandinavian. Orphaned as a child, she was taken in by a pastor and made herself useful in his household. One story says that she was married off to a Swedish dragoon in the summer of 1702 but, after his regiment had to evacuate Livonia soon afterwards, he disappeared and she never saw him again.

When the Russians moved in, it is said that she was captured and taken to the army camp with only a blanket over her naked body. For about six months she served in the household of Field Marshal

Count Boris Sheremetev, who used her as a laundry woman (and possibly as his mistress). Soon she came to the notice of Alexander Menshikov, who took her into his household in Moscow, where she may have become *his* mistress. Whether this is true or not, as outsiders from humble origins they shared an unbreakable bond and were both totally dependent on the favour of the tsar.

It was at Menshikov's house that the tsar spotted Martha.[19] Soon after, she left Menshikov and became Peter's mistress.

At some point Martha converted to Orthodoxy under the name of Catherine Alexeievna, 'the latter from her godfather', Peter's son Tsarevich Alexei, and the former 'from her patron St Catherine of Alexandria'.[20]

In the winter of 1704 she gave birth to the tsar's son, Peter Petrovich. Another son, Paul, followed in October 1705 and then a daughter Catherine in December 1706. All these children died before 1708. In all, the couple had ten children but only two reached adulthood.[21]

The tsar married Catherine secretly in November 1707. They went through a more public ceremony on 19 February 1712 in Menshikov's private chapel, despite that fact that Peter's first wife, Eudoxia, was still alive. Furthermore, with Alexei as Catherine's godfather she was Peter's spiritual granddaughter, so their marriage was incestuous according to Orthodox traditionalists.

Catherine was now the tsar's official consort. Two years later he created the Order of St Catherine in her honour.

The capture of the Neva Delta opened Russia up to the Baltic. In 1703 Peter decided to build a new capital out of the marshes where the mouth of the River Neva meets the Gulf of Finland.

These empty marshes were not a promising site. The word *neva* in Finnish means swamp. Peter chose Hare Island, in the centre of the river, where Finnish fishermen occupied huts in the summer before the water rose too high. Here he would build a fortification to defend the mouth of the river.

Folklore says that he cut two strips of earth from the ground and laid them down in the form of a cross. This would be the site of the SS Peter and Paul Fortress. According to another legend, St Petersburg owed its beauty on such an unpromising site to the fact that the city was built in the sky, then lowered down to earth in one piece.

It was to be a symbol of the new Russia, Peter's 'window on the west' as Pushkin later described it. Nineteen islands were linked together by a series of immense waterways spanned by 150 bridges. As building work began, Peter took up residence in a three-roomed, one-storey log house just outside the site of the new fortress. The labour required to construct the city was enormous. Carpenters, stonecutters, masons and unskilled labourers were soon summoned from all over Russia to lay out streets, build shipyards and houses and dig canals. Stone was almost wholly unavailable in the Neva Delta, so Peter forbade construction of masonry buildings elsewhere. All coachmen were obliged to deliver three paving stones when they arrived in the city, while ships had to deliver thirty quarry stones.

The human cost was appalling. Thousands died as bogs and marshes were transformed into parks and gardens while 'muddy streams' became 'majestic canals'.[22] It was deliberately planned as a great western city with wide, straight avenues and enormous squares. By 1714, there were said to be over 34,000 buildings in St Petersburg, although this was doubtless an exaggeration.

Eventually, along the 3-mile waterfront of the Neva arose splendid baroque palaces designed by Italian architects for the nobility, who were ordered to move there whether they wanted to or not. In 1712 the government offices were transferred from Moscow and it became Russia's new capital, 'the Venice of the North'.

Peter's own Winter Palace was a two-storey wooden structure with a central building and two wings, constructed near the Admiralty so that he could see the fleet from his window. The rooms were small and low-ceilinged in accordance with the tsar's preference. This building was demolished in 1721 and replaced by a larger stone structure.

He also had a fourteen-roomed summer palace, built in 1710 where the Fontanka Canal meets the Neva. Its wide windows looked out to the water on two sides and there was a dock for his boat. Peter lived in simply furnished rooms on the ground floor, which included a laboratory and a turning room where he worked on a carpenter's lathe, carving in bone, sometimes while discussing state business. Catherine's more lavish rooms (which included a throne room) were on the first floor and had Chinese silk wallpaper. The parquet floors were laid with mother-of-pearl and ivory. The dining room only seated a few people. If the tsar hosted a large banquet it was held in the palace of Prince Menshikov, St Petersburg's governor-general, on Vasilevsky Island, the largest in the delta.

Yet St Petersburg was threatened by the elements. In 1705 several feet of water flooded the city; the early wooden buildings were subject to devastating fires and at night wolves prowled the streets. Even in daylight nobody was safe. In 1715 a woman was devoured in daylight.

Nevertheless, in 1712, without any decree being issued, the city became Russia's new capital. Government functioned wherever the tsar was, and he preferred St Petersburg.

In 1708, Sweden invaded Russia. Peter's army retreated, laying waste to the countryside as they went, while Charles XII and his men were drawn further into Russia. Charles hoped to obtain the support of the Cossack hetman Mazepa, so he diverted his men towards Ukraine, but less than 2,000 men came with Mazepa and Charles's hopes of Turkish assistance also evaporated. After a particularly severe winter, with his army exhausted and depleted, Charles laid siege to Poltava in April 1709.

On 27 June Peter mounted a direct attack on the Swedes, whose king directed the battle from a litter because of a wounded foot. It was a decisive victory for Peter. 'Now with God's help the final stone has been laid in the foundation of St Petersburg,' he said.[23] King Charles escaped to Turkey, where he remained until 1714.

The tsar then helped Augustus II to regain the throne of Poland under Russian suzerainty. By 1710 he had control of Karelia, Livonia, Riga, Vyborg and Reval.

Charles XII was not finished, however. In November 1710 he persuaded Sultan Ahmed II of Turkey to declare war on Russia. Things came to a head on the banks of the River Prut in July 1711, when Peter found his army up against a much larger Turkish force. After two days of fighting, he decided to negotiate. The terms were harsh. Russia had to surrender Azov, Taganrog was to be destroyed and there must be no further interference in the affairs of Poland. The Swedish king was to be given free passage home.

In 1714 the Russian fleet won an impressive victory over the Swedish fleet off Cape Hangö in Finland. Russia was fast becoming the dominant power in the Baltic and, under pressure from other powers, Peter was forced to withdraw from Poland and give up his idea of a base at Mecklenburg in northern Germany from where he could attack Sweden.

The victory at Poltava changed the status of Russia. No longer snubbed by the European powers, Peter could now look further afield when it came to marriage matches for his relatives. He began negotiating with foreign courts.

First his niece Anna Ivanovna (daughter of his half-brother Ivan V and Tsaritsa Prascovia) married Duke Frederick William of Courland (the south-western part of what is now Latvia) in 1710, becoming the first Russian princess to marry a foreigner for more than 200 years. Unfortunately, her husband died while travelling back to Courland after the wedding, probably from indulging in too much drink at the bacchanalian feasts. Peter forbade Anna to return to St Petersburg. She lived in Courland as its duchess until 1730, when events took an unexpectedly different turn.

Peter also negotiated Tsarevich Alexei's marriage to Princess Charlotte, daughter of Duke Ludwig-Rudolf of Brunswick-Wolfenbüttel. Charlotte's sister was married to the Habsburg Emperor Charles VI, so this was an important union.

Alexei was a huge disappointment to his father. Having spent the first eight years of his life under his mother's influence, he preferred reading devotional books to the military life favoured by Peter. He was intelligent and linguistically gifted but lazy, the complete opposite of the tsar. Pious, inclined to moodiness and with a taste for drink, he had no love for, or interest in, Peter's western ideas.

Alexei and Charlotte were married on 14 October 1711 in the great hall of Torgau, the castle of the Queen of Poland. She was allowed to retain her protestant faith but had to agree that any children would be raised in the Orthodox religion.

The marriage was unhappy. Alexei neglected Charlotte, left her without money and flaunted his mistress in front of her. The boyars and clergy who surrounded Alexei, and who disapproved of the tsar's reforms, alarmed her. He grudgingly made love to her in the hope of securing the succession. In 1714 she gave birth to a daughter, Natalia, and on 12 October 1715 to a son, Peter Alexeievich. Shortly afterwards, poor, unhappy Charlotte died at the tender age of twenty-one.

Later that month Peter and Catherine had a son, another Peter Petrovich. He and Catherine began placing all their hopes on this boy, despite that fact that he proved to be rather backward. Now that the succession no longer depended on Alexei, the tsar wrote a long letter telling him to mend his ways, otherwise he would deprive him of his right to the crown. Three days later Alexei sent a submissive reply to his Most Gracious Sovereign Father, saying, 'I have nothing more to report except that, if you desire to deprive me of my right to the

Russian crown, let your will be done…'[24] He was willing to renounce his rights peacefully and live quietly on a country estate.

At this point the tsar became dangerously ill. For several days his condition was critical, and on 2 December the last rites were administered. Then, very slowly, he began to improve. He now worried about what would happen after his death and desired a son who would play an active role as heir to the throne. He gave Alexei an ultimatum – change and become worthy of the succession, or become a monk.

Advised that if he accepted a monk's habit he could always slip it off again later, Alexei sent a reply. 'I will embrace the monastical state and desire your gracious consent to it.'

This was not the answer Peter wanted. Perhaps he had been too harsh. He gave his son six months to think things over.[25]

In February 1716, Peter embarked on a second European visit. This time the destinations were Copenhagen, Amsterdam, Paris and Berlin.

On 26 August he sent a letter to Alexei from Copenhagen. It was a final ultimatum – Alexei was instructed to answer via the same courier. Peter once again offered him the choice of knuckling down and proving that he was a capable successor or retiring and becoming a monk.

Alexei followed neither course. He fled.

In the autumn of 1716, after borrowing some money, twenty-five-year-old Alexei absconded with his serf mistress Afrosina to the court of his brother-in-law Emperor Charles VI in Vienna, where he begged for asylum. Faced with this awkward situation, Emperor Charles kept Alexei in hiding and waited for Peter's next move.

As the tsar travelled round Europe, news of the disappearance of his son was both embarrassing and alarming. It was imperative that he be found. After a search in north Germany, it was thought he might be in the emperor's lands, so Peter's representative in Vienna was ordered to make enquiries. By the end of March he had been tracked down to the castle of Ehrenberg in the Tyrol. A letter was sent to Emperor Charles asking him to send Alexei back to Russia under armed escort.

The emperor hesitated and sent a messenger to inform Alexei. The tsarevich broke into hysterics, saying he would do anything rather than return. He was then informed that another place of refuge would be given to him inside the empire.

Early in May 1717, Alexei and his party reached the Castel Sant'Elmo in Naples, which had come into the Habsburg empire under the Treaty of Utrecht four years earlier. There he spent the next five months, with Afrosina masquerading as a pageboy despite the fact that she was now obviously pregnant.

This news reached Peter at Spa, where he was resting after the Paris leg of his trip. He wrote immediately to Emperor Charles, who had obviously deceived him, demanding the immediate return of his errant son.

Finally, his patience exhausted, the tsar sent Count Peter Tolstoy and Captain Alexander Rumiantsov to inform the emperor that if he did not send his son back 'he would take whatever further steps were necessary to obtain his return'.[26] Charles replied that Alexei was not a prisoner and was free to come and go wherever he liked.

Tolstoy and Rumiantsov finally arrived in Naples where, over the course of several interviews, Alexei was cajoled, bullied and threatened with the removal of Afrosina if he did not return. Afrosina was also bribed with promises and gifts to urge him to go back to Russia. Finally, emotionally and psychologically battered, Alexei agreed to their demands, on the promise of an unconditional pardon and the right to marry Afrosina.

In January 1718, Alexei arrived in Russia. Afrosina travelled separately because of her delicate condition. Despite Alexei's pleas to let him marry his beloved, when she finally arrived in Russia she was arrested and thrown into prison.

Naturally, as the heir, Alexei had become the focus of all serious opposition. The tsar's health was not good, and people looked to the future. Peter believed that Alexei was involved in a conspiracy to overthrow him. He confronted his son in the Kremlin, where he was forced publicly to renounce his rights to the throne in favour of his little half-brother Peter Petrovich. A manifesto to this effect was issued on 3 February.

He was then told that his pardon depended on him naming those who had helped and encouraged him. He gave the names of fifty people as his accomplices. One of them was his own mother, Eudoxia, now forty-four years old, who had discarded the veil long ago in her convent at Suzdal and even had a lover. She was brought to Moscow for questioning but no action was taken against her. Instead, she was packed off to a remote convent on Lake Ladoga under strict supervision.[27]

Despite the use of torture on the others named, no evidence of a conspiracy was found. Many of the accused were later exiled or executed.

The tsar returned to St Petersburg, where Alexei was heavily guarded. In the end, Alexei was doomed by Afrosina. When questioned by the tsar she maintained that Alexei 'had wished for his father's death, had plotted rebellions and hated everything his father stood for'.[28] Confronted by her testimony, Alexei confessed.

Peter questioned both at Monplaisir, his one-story Dutch-style cottage at Peterhof on the Gulf of Finland. His main concern was whether Alexei had planned to rebel during his father's lifetime. Alexei finally broke and admitted that he would have joined the rebels, even while his father was alive, if the army had mutinied.

This was treason. Alexei was arrested and thrown into the Trubetskoi Bastion of the SS Peter and Paul Fortress. On 14 June, proceedings against him commenced in the Senate Hall in St Petersburg in front of a tribunal of Russia's high dignitaries. He was interrogated under torture on 19 June, but after twenty-five lashes of the knout (a particularly severe form of flogging which flayed and shredded a man's back) Alexei offered no new confession. During more questioning under torture on 24 June, when another fifteen lashes were inflicted, then a further nine, Alexei confessed that he would have paid Charles VI to raise an army against his father. That night the Senate and civil officials sentenced him to death.

Peter sent an official to inform his son but hesitated about signing the authorisation. He visited Alexei early on the morning of 26 June, where he remained for half an hour. His entourage remained, only leaving at 11.00 a.m. By then Alexei was utterly broken by the lashes of the knout. He died at 6.00 p.m. that evening.

Although Peter wept during the funeral, rumours abounded that he had killed Alexei or had ordered him to be strangled. Most likely he died from the effects of the knout, which could kill a strong man with only forty lashes.

Peter had proved that he was an autocrat first and a father second.

The cottage of Monplaisir where Peter interrogated Alexei was the genesis of the opulent palace of Peterhof, 19 miles west of St Petersburg.

After his visit to Paris, Peter wanted something that would rival the Palace of Versailles. He instructed Alexandre LeBlond to build a two-storey palace on a small rise overlooking the Gulf of Finland to use for state functions or visiting dignitaries. It would later be enlarged by his daughter Elizabeth into the magnificent building we see today.

Peterhof's glory, however, was its fountains. A water stairway led to a huge ornamental lake and a long canal bordered by fountains which reached right down to the sea. The formal French gardens contained fountains and water cascades. Little pavilions were dotted around the park – the Hermitage, Marly and Monplaisir. Set right by the sea, Peterhof was Peter's favourite place.

While Catherine lived in the Grand Palace Peter usually stayed at Monplaisir, where he transacted state business. Here he had a study full of nautical instruments, a kitchen and dining room, and a bedroom from which he could look out over the sea from his bed and open the window to listen to the waves. Everywhere were blue and white Dutch tiles and pictures of Dutch ships and seascapes. Tulips grew in the garden. The little red-and-black lacquered Chinese room with its ninety delicate panels seemed almost out of place. He drew up a set of rules for guests, who were only allowed to remain overnight if they had an allocated bed number and must take off boots and shoes before lying down. Anyone who broke the rules had to drain 1.25 litres of fortified wine from the Great Eagle Cup – in one gulp.

He gave Catherine the estate of Tsarskoe Selo (the Tsar's Village), and commissioned Johann Braunstein to construct a small country palace for use as a private retreat. This would later be enlarged by their daughter Elizabeth, who added two further wings.[29]

LeBlond also designed a small wooden palace for Peter at Strelna, 6 miles further along the Gulf of Finland.

In 1718, the childless King Charles XII of Sweden was killed during a campaign in Norway, cutting short the peace negotiations with Russia. Sweden's new ruler, his sister Ulrika Eleanora (wife of Prince Frederick of Hesse), continued the war but could not gain support among the European powers for an anti-Russian coalition. Negotiations therefore resumed.

In August 1721, the war with Sweden ended after twenty-one years with the signing of the Peace of Nystad. It allowed Peter to retain most of his territorial gains, although he returned the Aaland Islands and most of Finland to Sweden. The Russian Baltic coastline now stretched from Riga to Vyborg.

Jubilation broke out all over Russia. Peter gave banquets (even dancing on the table during one) and a masquerade party that continued for several days. Russians in fancy dress danced, dined, strolled along the banks of the Neva and, after sleeping off the effects of all this, rose to begin celebrating again.

During his reign Peter had annexed Kamchatka and the Kurile Islands in the Far East but failed to establish protectorates over the khanates of Khiva and Bokhara. In 1722 and 1723, during a campaign against Persia, he gained Derbent and Baku, securing the western coast of the Caspian Sea.

Peter's reign saw many administrative reforms. Perhaps the most important was the Table of Ranks he issued in 1722, by which social status was now dependant on service. There were three categories – the armed forces, the court and administration – each having fourteen numbered ranks. Regardless of their background, anyone with a good education could apply to enter at rank fourteen, with the goal of reaching rank one. The title of boyar was abolished in favour of that of count and those who reached the eighth rank of service (equivalent to an army colonel or a navy captain) were entitled to a status equivalent to that of the ancient nobility. Rank thus became more important than pedigree.

The church was also subjected to increasing state control, with bishops having to take an oath of allegiance to the monarch. Peter abolished the patriarchate and placed the Holy Synod at the head of the church, with a chief procurator appointed by the tsar.

At the request of the Senate, on 22 October 1721 Peter assumed the title of Peter the Great, father of his country, Emperor of all Russia. Every ruler until 1917 'maintained the title of emperor', which appeared in all official documents.[30]

Father of his country he may have been, but he still had no heir. His and Catherine's only surviving legitimate son, Peter Petrovich, died in 1719 and he was reluctant to leave the crown to Peter Alexeievich, the son of Alexei and Charlotte.

He may have considered marrying the Greek princess Maria Cantemir, his latest mistress, in the hope of siring another legitimate son but instead he crowned Catherine as empress consort in May 1724. She was the first wife of a reigning Russian monarch to be crowned. As she knelt before him in the Uspensky Sobor, Catherine received the imperial crown 'adorned with pearls, diamonds, and a huge ruby of marvellous beauty larger than a dove's egg'. The ceremony was notable for its European flavour. Catherine wore a red dress embroidered with silver. Her embroidered purple robe trimmed with gold was sent over from Paris, while Peter's blue silk kaftan and breeches, trimmed with silver, had a matching hat with a large white feather.[31] Muscovite Russia had moved on.

For years Peter had suffered from convulsions which only Catherine was able to calm, putting his head on her lap and stroking it until he slept.

By the autumn of 1724 he was ill with an infection of the urinary tract. This was exacerbated in November when, while out sailing in his yacht, he spotted a small boat in trouble. The vessel had grounded on a shoal and the occupants seemed unable to save themselves. Peter sent his skiff to help but his sailors were unable to refloat the grounded boat. With the high waves making it impossible for him to move his boat closer, Peter jumped into the sea and, with the water waist high, waded over to the vessel. His arrival galvanised the desperate occupants, who caught lines thrown from the other boat. Other sailors jumped into the water and, together with the emperor, hauled the boat off the shoal.

Peter returned to his yacht, changed his wet clothes and at first seemed little affected by his spell in the icy water. However, chills and fever soon set in and an old stomach pain reappeared. He cancelled a planned trip and returned to St Petersburg.

For a while he appeared to recover and took part in the Christmas and New Year celebrations as well as the antics of his Drunken Synod.

On 6 January 1725, the Feast of Epiphany, the ceremony of Blessing of the Waters took place on the frozen River Neva near the Winter Palace. Peter presided as the metropolitan blessed the water three times with raised hands and then dipped a cross through a hole in the ice three times while a cannon salute was fired. Peter's participation on this bitter January day resulted in him catching another cold.

By 16 January, Peter was compelled to take to his bed. As European specialists were summoned, he appeared to rally and continued to work. On 23 January, however, he suffered a relapse. The last rites were administered but still he clung to life.

The end came on 27 January. Peter had passed a law authorising the sovereign to choose his or her own successor, but when he died he had done nothing about it. He called for his daughter Anna and asked her to take down his will. He was only able to murmur, 'Give all to…' before he lapsed into a coma and drew his last breath.[32] He was fifty-two.

Before Peter the Great, Russia's tsars were buried in the Cathedral of the Archangel Michael in the Moscow Kremlin. This tradition changed after 1712, when Russia's capital was transferred to St Petersburg. The wooden Church of SS Peter & Paul, situated inside the fortress of the same name, already held the remains of Peter's eighteen-month-old daughter Catherine who died in 1708. This wooden church was demolished when work began on the stone cathedral, built between 1712 and 1733. Tsarevich Alexei and his unfortunate wife Charlotte were buried in the cathedral while it was still under construction. It was perhaps significant that, when completed, this cathedral had a gilded spire instead of a traditional Russian dome.

Peter the Great died before work was completed, so Domenico Trezzini designed a temporary wooden chapel within its walls. On 10 March 1725 the bodies of Peter and his daughter Natalia (who had died of measles on 4 March) were conveyed to the fortress along a route lined by 1,250 grenadiers holding burning torches, while cannon salutes were fired from the Fortress and the Admiralty. The coffins were placed inside the cathedral 'under a canopy upholstered in golden cloth'. Peter the Great was finally interred on 29 May 1731.[33]

At Peter's death, Russia was a great European power. He had turned it towards the west, streamlined the government and begun the process of modernisation. It would be up to his successors to continue the work.

His death led to another crisis in the succession, with the court divided over who should succeed. Peter had left daughters, but no legitimate sons. Out of the ten children Catherine bore him, only Anna and Elizabeth lived beyond their seventh birthday.

Some of the boyars backed the son of the long-dead Tsarevich Alexei. Others, whose careers Peter had advanced, supported Catherine. She had already been crowned empress consort, and her claim was strengthened by the support of Prince Menshikov (who had been arraigned and suspended by Peter the Great on suspicion of corruption) and the elite Guards regiments. She had placed the succession question in the hands of the Senate, and any opposition was quashed when the Guards officers invaded the Senate building and proclaimed her empress.

The former peasant captured in Livonia became Empress Catherine I. Between the death of Peter the Great in 1725 and the accession of Catherine II in 1762, four female and three male Romanov monarchs ascended the throne.

As we shall see, it is from Peter and Catherine's elder daughter, Anna Petrovna, that King Charles descends.

4

The Heir from Holstein

King Charles's Descent from Peter the Great's Daughter

Anna Petrovna (Annushka) was born on 27 January 1708, before Peter and Catherine underwent their official marriage ceremony.

Her father publicly acknowledged her as a princess in 1710 and gave a court dinner in her honour, but, as Peter and Catherine did not publicly marry until 1712, technically Annushka was born out of wedlock. This ambiguous status affected her marriage prospects and also those of her younger sister Elizabeth, born at Kolomenskoye in 1709.

Peter wrote affectionate letters to his daughters and took a great interest in their education, often visiting them during lessons. He regretted the neglect that his own formal education had suffered, so they were educated like European princesses, also learning dancing and etiquette. Annushka was taught High Dutch, French, German, a little Italian and Swedish. She wrote to her mother in German although Catherine, who was illiterate, could only dictate her own letters. Annushka was 'intelligent, well-mannered and high spirited'[1] and liked to read historical and philosophical works.

While birthdays were celebrated with a modest reception, Annushka's name day, 3 February (the feast of St Anna), required a far more lavish celebration. Name days were important to Russians. After mass, there was a dinner and the launching of a ship, followed by a party complete with a firework display.

In 1717, Annushka and Elizabeth both fell ill. Smallpox was suspected but luckily both recovered with no disfigurement. That year Peter commissioned portraits of them to be painted by the French artist Louis Caravaque.

Peter had swept away restrictions on overseas marriages, and soon Annushka and Elizabeth were attracting the notice of foreign diplomats. One described Annushka as 'brunette, and as pretty as an angel with a charming complexion, arms and a figure very much like her father and rather tall for a girl, even inclined to be thin, and not as lively as her younger sister'. Three years later she was described by a contemporary as having a 'majestic beauty, ...so slender, so graceful'.[2]

In March 1721, when Annushka was thirteen, Peter and Catherine travelled to Riga to meet twenty-one-year-old Duke Charles Frederick of Holstein-Gottorp, son of Frederick IV of Holstein and Princess Hedwig Sophia of Sweden. A short, plain man who drank heavily and was 'indifferent to all intellectual interests', he was a Lutheran prince raised in the military style of Prussia.[3] By royal standards he was also very poor, but as the only nephew of Peter the Great's nemesis, the childless King Charles XII of Sweden, he had a claim to the Swedish throne. After this initial inspection Catherine encouraged him to remain in Russia. It was hoped that he would be a suitable bridegroom for one of her daughters.

The girls were close companions. Charles Frederick serenaded them with his private orchestra, and they went on picnics, attended parties in the Summer Garden and enjoyed excursions to Peterhof. The girls were admired everywhere and people said they were as 'lovely as angels'.[4]

On 23 November 1724, Charles Frederick and sixteen-year-old Annushka were betrothed. Even on the eve of the ceremony Charles Frederick did not know whether he was to marry Annushka or Elizabeth. It was said that he was more in love with blonde Elizabeth, but once the engagement was announced he was said to be passionately in love with taller, darker Annushka (or maybe with her dowry of 30,000 roubles). She reportedly also made a good impression on his entourage, though her own impressions of Charles Frederick were not recorded.

After a service at the Trinity Church Peter took rings from each of the couple and exchanged them with the other. He then kissed the couple and wished them a long life together before they were blessed by the Archbishop of Novgorod. A supper, ball and firework display featuring 'Venus in a carriage drawn by swans with the legend "Happy Concord"' followed.[5]

During the ceremonies it became obvious that the emperor was seriously ill. Before the wedding could take place, Peter the Great died in the Winter Palace.

The planning of Annushka's marriage to Charles Frederick was taken over by Menshikov, who supervised the construction of a pavilion made for the wedding, which was postponed until 21 May 1725. Annushka's mother, now Empress Catherine I, did not attend, remaining secluded in mourning while four hundred guests revelled in the great hall. Later, she appeared briefly at the wedding party to drink a toast with the young newlyweds.

During Catherine's two-year reign Annushka and her husband remained in St Petersburg and were given seats on the supreme privy council, although this was strictly for the sake of appearances.

The short reign of Catherine I was distinguished by debauchery. The French envoy described drinking bouts that 'lasted the entire night and into the next day'.[6] She summoned her peasant siblings from Livonia and set them up in luxury at Tsarskoe Selo, although they spoke no Russian.

Although the empress commanded the Senate to report to her every Friday, real power lay with Menshikov. He dominated the supreme privy council set up by Catherine, who lacked the discipline to attend the sessions. She preferred to eat and drink until three in the morning and then sleep until five in the evening and party again until the early hours. The council was little better. When Baron Osterman arrived late for the first session, which was preceded by a banquet, he found the five other members literally under the council table, drunk.

On 6 May 1727 Catherine died, probably from problems relating to drink. She was forty-three. Even before her death the question of the succession had raised its head again.

Count Peter Tolstoy, chief of the Secret Chancellery, backed Annushka and Elizabeth despite the fact that both were born out of wedlock. Menshikov then betrothed his daughter Maria to eleven-year-old Peter Alexeievich (son of the ill-fated Tsarevich Alexei and Charlotte of Brunswick-Wolfenbüttel) and persuaded Catherine to leave the throne to Peter. Her daughters pleaded with her not to back Menshikov and his faction, but their efforts were in vain.

On Catherine's death Peter II duly succeeded to the throne and moved the court back to Moscow – but he never married Maria. On 8 September 1727 an order for Menshikov's arrest was signed by his aristocratic enemies, who were tired of his lust for power, greed and arrogance. After a trial, Menshikov was exiled to Berzov in Siberia, where he died in 1729. His wife and daughter Maria also died in the bitter Siberian winter.

In 1729 Peter II was betrothed to Princess Catherine Dolgoruky, but on the day set for their wedding, 18 January 1730, Peter died of smallpox. The so-called curse of the Dolgorukys had struck again. Peter was the last Romanov in the direct male line.[7]

Having been expelled from Russia by Menshikov after Catherine's death, Annushka and Charles Frederick returned to Holstein where, on 10/21 February 1728, six months after her arrival at the thirteenth-century Kiel Castle, Annushka gave birth to a son who was christened Charles Peter Ulrich in the Lutheran Church in Kiel. He was named 'Charles' after his father and great-uncle King Charles XII of Sweden, 'Peter' after his grandfather Peter the Great, and 'Ulrich' after Queen Ulrika Eleanora, the current ruler of Sweden. Charles Frederick still considered himself heir to the Swedish crown and his lifestyle, aided by a large subsidy from St Petersburg, reflected this.

The marriage contract between Annushka and Charles Frederick stipulated that the couple must renounce their rights to the Russian throne, but this did not apply to any children of the marriage. Little Charles Peter Ulrich therefore had claims to both the Swedish and Russian crowns.[8]

Shortly after the birth of Annushka's son, a ball was given in celebration. Although the weather was cold and damp, Annushka insisted on standing at the window to watch the firework display that followed, saying she had been used to a much harsher climate in Russia. She caught a chill and died in May from consumption, just two years after her wedding. She was twenty.

In accordance with Annushka's will, her body was brought by ship to St Petersburg, where it arrived on 20 October. The coffin then lay in state in the Winter Palace for twenty days before on 12 November she was buried beside her parents in the wooden chapel in the SS Peter and Paul Cathedral.[9]

After Annushka's death Charles Frederick took very little interest in their son. Charles Peter Ulrich was handed first to nurses, then to a French governess and at the age of seven began military training, proving totally at home in this environment. He liked nothing more than wearing a soldier's uniform on the parade ground or watching the soldiers drilling in the courtyard, even if it meant interrupting his lessons. Yet he was a puny, sickly child who was often ill and took to playing with toy soldiers in his bed. He had no contact with children of his own age and his education was patchy. Thanks to his governess, he was reasonable in French and later he mastered Swedish, which he was able to translate into German. He loved music, especially the violin, although he struggled to play it without proper lessons.

In 1739, after Charles Frederick's death, Charles Peter Ulrich became Duke of Holstein-Gottorp and inherited his father's claim to the crown of Sweden. His uncle Prince Adolphus Frederick, Prince Bishop of Lübeck, was appointed his guardian but instead of supervising his charge he delegated these duties to officers and tutors who worked under the grand marshal of the ducal court, Otto Brümmer. He was a sadistic former cavalry officer who assaulted, beat, mocked, humiliated and starved the young boy – especially, as often happened, when he performed poorly at his lessons. If Brümmer hoped to toughen up the sickly boy, the result was the opposite. It would have enormous consequences in the years to come.

After Peter II's death in 1730 the crown of Russia was held by Anna Ivanovna (daughter of Peter the Great's half-brother and co-tsar Ivan V). On Empress Anna's death in 1740 it passed to the grandson of her sister Catherine, Duchess of Mecklenburg, two-month-old Ivan VI. His mother Anna Leopoldovna acted as regent. These people are not direct ancestors of King Charles III.

Then, on 25 November 1741, Peter the Great's thirty-two-year-old daughter Elizabeth staged a midnight palace coup with the help of the Guards regiments and overthrew the 'German party'. She arrested Anna Leopoldovna and her husband, deposed Ivan VI and seized power.[10]

Elizabeth has been described as the Russian Venus, 'the eternal debutante'[11] who loved jewels, clothes, parties, dancing and entertainment, particularly masquerade balls in which men had to dress as women, and women as men. Elizabeth attended dressed in masculine clothes, often as a Dutch sailor in homage to her father. After her death, 15,000 dresses and other outfits were found in her wardrobes. On cold winter days there was tobogganing down ice slides or sleigh rides, while at night there was ice skating in the palace galleries with open windows and water poured on the rapidly freezing floor.

Elizabeth was indolent but very religious. Devotional works were probably the only books she ever read. Like her sister Annushka, the Duchess of Holstein-Gottorp, she was a great beauty, yet despite a liaison with Alexei Razumovsky, a lowborn Ukrainian Cossack whom she may or may not have married morganatically, Empress Elizabeth was childless. There were rumours that they married on 14 November 1742, but if there was any proof it has never surfaced or has been destroyed. They are even rumoured to have had children, all of whom died. Again, there is no proof.[12]

One of Empress Elizabeth's first acts was to secretly summon her fourteen-year-old nephew Charles Peter Ulrich, Duke of Holstein-Gottorp, to St Petersburg and designate him as her heir.

It is from him that King Charles descends.

Peter, as he was known in Russia, arrived in St Petersburg in January 1742. With him was his grand marshal, the hated Otto Brümmer. Peter and his aunt Empress Elizabeth had never met before, but she gave him a warm welcome, promising to cherish her beloved sister's only son and become a second mother to him.

His appearance was unprepossessing. Pale, thin, with lank blond hair combed down to his shoulders, 'an awkward posture, a protruding lower lip, and a receding chin',[13] he also had a shrill, high-pitched voice. Believing the problems were caused by poor health, Elizabeth entrusted him to Dr Struve, a fashionable specialist. It did little to help.

Nevertheless, he accompanied Elizabeth to her coronation, travelling in the procession of carriages into Moscow in February. Elizabeth, who loved to dance, embarked on two months of religious devotions and entertainment before the climax took place in Moscow on 25 April. In the Uspensky Sobor, wearing a dress of gold brocade, Elizabeth took the crown and placed it on her own head.

Professor Staehlin from the Imperial Academy of Sciences was appointed as Peter's tutor. It quickly became apparent that the boy was ignorant about everything and uninterested unless the subject concerned soldiers or warfare. He was extremely idle. Nevertheless, the tutor was kindly and tried to find ways of stimulating his interest, and it is telling that Peter remained friendly with him for the rest of his life.

He had lessons in Russian and instruction in the Orthodox religion. Dancing lessons proved a disaster and Peter remained a comical dancer all his life. Noticing his liking for all things military, the empress made him a colonel of the Preobrazhensky Guards. Peter sneered. He preferred the tight-fitting German uniforms of Holstein and Prussia to the loose-fitting bottle-green uniforms introduced by Peter the Great and worn by the Russians.

On 18 November he was baptised into the Orthodox Church as Grand Duke Peter Feodorovich and proclaimed heir to the throne. The court then took the oath of allegiance to him. Yet despite all the coaching he was nervous, confused about the ritual and uncertain about the Russian language. Elizabeth had to prompt him at every step, whispering instructions. 'He spoke with his customary petulance,' an ambassador noted of the Orthodox service, and 'one may conclude he will not be a fanatical believer'.[14] Afterwards there was a public audience at which Peter continued his sullen demeanour. As a condition of becoming heir to the empress, Peter had to renounce his claim to the throne of Sweden.

Brümmer had remained in Russia, and the empress allowed him to stay even though he continued to torment the boy and did not shirk from violence towards him. Peter had no interest in the future of this vast, primitive empire. He preferred all things German to everything Russian, a fact that grieved Elizabeth. Whenever he could, he escaped to converse in German with officials from Holstein, the state of which he was still nominally grand duke. His idol was Frederick of Prussia, not Peter the Great, and he had no interest in ruling the Russian empire.

His sickly health worried Elizabeth. He was the future hope of the Romanov dynasty and her only heir. When he became seriously ill in October 1743 and did not leave his bed for weeks, the empress knew she had to act.

Peter was now fifteen, and it was time to find him a wife. Elizabeth knew just where to look.

After Peter the Great's death in 1725, with the prospect of a grand marriage for seventeen-year-old Elizabeth looking increasingly remote, Annushka's husband Duke Charles Frederick of Holstein-Gottorp suggested that his twenty-year-old cousin Charles Augustus might make a good match. Empress Catherine agreed to invite the young man to Russia, where he made a good impression.

Just before the betrothal was due to be announced, Empress Catherine was taken ill. The ceremony was postponed to allow her to recover, but on 6 May she died.

Elizabeth decided to go ahead, but on the eve of the announcement Charles Augustus was stricken with smallpox. He died four days later, on 31 May 1727. Elizabeth was devastated. She never entirely overcame her grief and always treasured his memory.

Charles Augustus's sister Johanna had married Prince Christian Augustus of Anhalt-Zerbst in 1727. Their elder daughter, fourteen-year-old Sophia, was now of marriageable age. Elizabeth summoned mother and daughter to Russia, sending them 10,000 roubles for expenses on the journey.

The empress was in Moscow. Sophia and her mother arrived there on 9 February 1744, having travelled incognito in heavy carriages on primitive frozen roads. Only when they reached Riga and it began to snow were they able to decamp to a magnificent imperial sledge drawn by ten horses. So large was this sledge that it was possible for them to stretch out on luxurious beds.

She had met Peter before when, at the age of ten, she and her mother visited his guardian Adolphus Frederick, the Prince Bishop of Lübeck. Sophia then described eleven-year-old Peter as 'agreeable and well-bred, although his liking for drink was very noticeable'.[15]

Peter and Sophia were second cousins on her mother's side and both were Germans, uprooted to Russia. He was now pleased to see her. At fourteen Sophia was slender, with lovely dark chestnut hair, a good complexion and dark eyes. She was intelligent enough to realise that the person she had to please was the empress and she seemed to make a good impression.

Elizabeth sent a professor to teach her the Russian language, a priest to instruct her in the Orthodox religion and a dancing master. To the empress's delight, she proved a much more diligent student than Peter and within a fortnight was able to speak a few sentences in Russian.

During the first few days Sophia listened carefully, gaining Peter's confidence and learning a lot a about him. She soon found that he cared little for Russia, 'remained a convinced Lutheran, did not like his entourage, and was very childish'. He thought of her as a playmate, not his soon-to-be betrothed, and confessed he was in love with another girl whom the empress would not permit him to marry. He would marry Sophia, he said, 'because his aunt wished it'.[16]

Then, in March 1744, Sophia fell ill with pneumonia and for a while appeared to be at death's door. Hearing the news at the monastery where she was on a pilgrimage, the empress hurried back and prescribed repeated bleeding. She then barred Sophia's troublesome mother, Johanna, from the sickroom and nursed her personally, pouring out all her maternal love in gestures of obvious affection. Several weeks later, to celebrate Sophia's recovery, Elizabeth gave her a diamond necklace and earrings, while Peter gave her a ruby-encrusted watch.

On 28 June 1744, Sophia publicly disavowed her Lutheran faith and was baptised into the Orthodox Church. At Elizabeth's insistence, she took the name of Catherine after the empress's own mother. Catherine later admitted that she learned the creed in Russian parrot-fashion. After the service the empress gave her another diamond necklace and a brooch.

The following day Catherine and Peter were betrothed at a ceremony in the Uspensky Sobor in the Kremlin. The four-hour service was conducted by the Archbishop of Novgorod and the empress handed the betrothal rings to the couple. From Peter, Catherine received a ring worth 12,000 roubles, though she noted that the one she gave him was worth 14,000. Afterwards there was a banquet in the Palace of Facets, followed by a ball.

By imperial decree she was now Her Imperial Highness Grand Duchess Catherine and she was given her own court. Yet there was still no sign of a wedding. The doctors declared that sixteen-year-old Peter was immature and that it would be at least another year before he was capable of fathering a child.

The court of Grand Duke Peter and Grand Duchess Catherine was juvenile to say the least. They played games such as blind man's bluff, ran around laughing and used the lid of a big harpsicord to slide along the floor on a pillow. Catherine was trying to please her future husband by never correcting him as others did; Peter for his part remained friendly to her, knowing that this would please his aunt the empress.

Johanna was still at court but now found if she wanted to see her daughter she had to be announced. She was forced to walk behind Catherine, who blushed each time this happened. Johanna gradually became more distant.

In November 1744, Peter contracted measles. When he recovered Elizabeth decided that the court should return to St Petersburg.

They had reached Khotolovo when one night Peter developed a high fever. Smallpox was suspected. Catherine and Johanna were sent on to St Petersburg while the empress, who had gone ahead, was alerted by messenger. She immediately hurried back and personally nursed Peter for the next six weeks, despite the danger of catching the disease herself.

Peter recovered but his face was badly pockmarked and with a swollen, puffy look. His head had to be shaved, so he wore a huge, ungainly wig which made him look ridiculous.

In February he returned to St Petersburg with the empress. Catherine met them in a dimly lit hall of the Winter Palace (at that time a temporary palace built for Elizabeth on the site of the old one). She described him as almost unrecognisable, hideous. This disfigurement badly affected Peter's psychological balance and his mental health suffered. He remained in his rooms as much as possible, conducting indoor military parades with his costumed servants as he had done with the toy soldiers as a child.

Catherine, meanwhile, was blossoming into an attractive young woman.

By imperial decree, the wedding took place on 21 August 1745. The sixteen-year-old Catherine was dressed in a shimmering silver brocade gown and train with embroidered silver roses that sparkled in the light. A lace cloak, so heavy that she could barely move, was attached to her shoulders. She wore splendid bracelets, earrings, brooches and rings, and on her head Elizabeth placed the diamond crown of a grand duchess.

Seventeen-year-old Peter wore a suit of the same material as his bride's dress with the buttons encrusted with diamonds. His shoe buckles and the hilt of his sword were similarly bejewelled.

Preceded by trumpets and drums, the procession of twenty-four carriages left the Winter Palace for the Church of the Nativity of the Theotokos (also known as the Kazan Cathedral) on the Nevsky Prospekt.[17] A three-hour service conducted by the Bishop of Novgorod would make them man and wife.

Catherine found the whole occasion an ordeal. Not only was she physically repulsed by Peter but the weight of her magnificent silver gown, plus all the jewels and the crown, was too much to bear. After the ceremony she asked the empress's permission to remove the crown as it was giving her a headache. Elizabeth said no. Only when her headache worsened just before the wedding ball did Catherine receive the empress's reluctant consent to remove it for a few minutes. Elizabeth, anxious to get the newlyweds to bed so that they could conceive the long-awaited heir, cut the ball short and escorted them to the bridal chamber.

Neither of them knew anything about sex. When Catherine asked her mother what would happen, Johanna refused to answer. Peter had been given a few facts by his servants but he was left bewildered and had little idea of what was expected of him.

The result was that when Peter finally joined Catherine in the marital bed some hours later, after drinking with his German friends, he fell asleep. The marriage remained unconsummated.

When Madame Krause, the chief lady-in-waiting, questioned Catherine in the morning, she received no reply. On the following mornings Madame Krause's questions remained unanswered. Whether the reason for Peter's coldness was physical or psychological is unknown.

With the wedding over, Elizabeth was free to get rid of Catherine's mother. She believed that Johanna had been spying for Frederick II (the Great) of Prussia, with whom Russian relations were extremely strained. Her letters had been intercepted and various improprieties were uncovered. Johanna had been warned about her intrigues and the empress feared that if she remained in Russia she would gain a dangerous influence over Peter and Catherine. Despite Johanna's plea for forgiveness, Elizabeth sent her packing with a gift of 60,000 roubles and countless presents.

Eight months after the wedding there was still no sign of a baby. The empress's Chancellor of Foreign Affairs, Count Alexei Bestuzhev-Riumin, recommended that a senior governess be appointed as Catherine's chaperone. She would ensure that the grand duchess had no familiarity with members of the court, had no private conversations with foreign diplomats and wrote no letters to them. In other words, the governess would be a watchdog to ensure Catherine's fidelity and political harmlessness.

The woman chosen was the empress's cousin on her mother's side, twenty-four-year-old Maria Choglokova. She remained at her post for the next seven years, providing nothing but 'harassment, oppression and misery'.[18] Catherine hated her.

The empress blamed Catherine for the couple's failure to consummate the marriage, accusing her of acting on her mother's instructions to betray Russia to the king of Prussia and of loving another man than her husband. None of it was true. During her time in Russia Catherine had been at pains to learn the language (although she never really mastered it) and the culture. She was discreet, obedient and submissive. Her only failure was in not producing a son.

Elizabeth decided to isolate the young couple so they would be reduced to each other's company and conceive an heir. Peter's German friends and attendants were sent packing and Maria Choglokova's husband was appointed Peter's governor. In her memoirs Catherine called him 'an arrogant, brutal fool; a malicious, pompous, secretive and silent man who never smiled; a man to be despised as well as feared'.[19] None of the attendants were permitted to enter the couple's private rooms without the permission of the governor and governess. This harsh treatment brought out paranoia in Peter, and cunning in Catherine.

Peter and Catherine were now thrown together, but she found him difficult to live with. To her dismay, he kept his forbidden dogs behind a partition in the bedroom where the stench became intolerable. He scraped at his violin, torturing her ear drums. He hanged a rat for eating two of his stuffed soldiers. While he took solace in books about knights and battles, Catherine's reading tastes were more serious and intellectual. Although she had learnt Russian, French was her preferred language.

Their only ally was Madame Krause, another native of Holstein, who smuggled toy soldiers, cannons and miniature fortresses to Peter. He concealed them in the bed and played with them until two o'clock in the morning. There was nothing Catherine could do but watch. Although all this was hidden from Maria Choglokova, she was criticised by the empress for failing to ensure that the couple did their duty.

Finally Madame Groot, the young widow of a painter, was assigned to seduce Peter and initiate him into the pleasures of the bedroom. He then began a series of affairs with other women, but none of these resulted in him fathering children, even though they had children by other men. Catherine intimated that their marriage was consummated at this time, after five years, but in the final version of her memoirs (which she was continually revising until her death and which were not published in Russia until 1907) she insinuated that consummation had never taken place. Of course, she had every reason to blacken Peter's reputation in the light of what would happen in 1762.[20]

Catherine's seeming inability to attract her husband's interest while he encouraged her to flirt with other men was humiliating for her. Was it her rejection of him when she saw his pockmarked face that had affected him? Everyone knew he was pursuing other women, but did she reject his advances, repulsed by his appearance? Did his feelings of inferiority in her company make him impotent with her? Illnesses such as measles and smallpox could also have made him sterile. We will probably never know.

Elizabeth had given Orianienbaum (Orange Tree), Menshikov's former estate on the Gulf of Finland, to Peter. Here everyone from Peter himself down to the lowest gardener walked around with muskets on their shoulder, took part in parade ground drill and stood watch at night in what became almost a military camp.

Catherine, dressed in men's clothing and accompanied by an old huntsman who provided the guns, went along the shore by boat to hunt ducks. Riding was also one of her passions. She designed a special saddle which permitted her to ride off side-saddle and then, when she was out of sight of Maria Choglokova, move the pommel and swing her leg across to ride like a man. If the grooms were questioned, they could say truthfully that she rode on a woman's saddle as the empress had commanded.

By 1751, Peter and Catherine had been married for six years. That September three young noblemen joined the household as Peter's gentlemen-in-waiting. They were Lev Naryshkin, Peter Saltykov and his twenty-six-year-old brother Sergei, who came from one of Russia's oldest noble families. Both the Naryshkins and the Saltykovs had married into the Romanov family – Natalia Naryshkin was the second wife of Tsar Alexei, while Prascovia Saltykov had married Ivan V.

Peter Saltykov was a ruffian and a notorious gossip. Twenty-six-year-old Sergei was handsome, with a dark complexion. He was also married. His wife, Matriona Balk, was one of the empress's ladies-in-waiting, although he had quickly tired of her. According to Catherine, he loved intrigue and lacked principles. He also liked a challenge. A closely guarded grand duchess who was reputedly a virgin certainly provided that.

Catherine, who was undoubtedly attracted to Sergei, usually encountered him during evenings in the apartments of Maria Choglokova. This access was facilitated by the empress, who had decided to take matters in hand and saw the potential affair as a means of getting Catherine pregnant.

Choglokova told Catherine that she was free to choose Lev Naryshkin or Sergei Saltykov. Unhesitatingly she chose the latter, who had already made numerous advances.

After two miscarriages, on 20 September 1754 Catherine gave birth to a son, Grand Duke Paul, in the Summer Palace in St Petersburg. Elizabeth delightedly swept up the baby and went off with him, leaving Catherine lying exhausted on a bed with dirty linen. More than three hours passed before anyone attended to her.

Immediately rumours circulated that the father was Sergei Saltykov. At this point Catherine had nothing at all to gain by denying that Peter was the father. The birth of a male heir had made her own position more secure. 'So she keeps us guessing, perhaps because she herself did not know for sure.'[21] Certainly, as he grew, contemporaries noted that the boy resembled Peter in both looks and mannerisms.

Peter celebrated the birth by getting drunk. More and more he took refuge at Orianienbaum, drilling his little army of Holsteiners and other retainers and wearing a Prussian general's uniform. He also took a mistress, Elizabeth Vorontzov, niece of Vice Chancellor Count Michael Vorontzov.

Paul was raised under the supervision of the empress. He was installed in Elizabeth's bedroom, where she rushed to him whenever he cried. She behaved as if the baby was her own, probably out of jealousy that at the age of forty-four she had never borne a child herself.

To reward Catherine for her efforts, the empress gave her one hundred thousand roubles from the Treasury. Peter complained that nothing had been given to him. The cabinet secretary then had to ask Catherine to return the money so that it could be paid to her husband. Saltykov was sent abroad on a mission.

Denied any role in the upbringing of her son, whom she saw about once a month, Catherine concentrated on filling in the gaps in her education. She became a voracious reader and, even if she was no scholar, it broadened her horizons and prepared her for the future. Chancellor Count Alexei Bestuzhev-Riumin now became her friend and wider liberties were accorded to her, such as speaking to ambassadors.

In June 1756, Elizabeth suffered a stroke. As the empress's health began to worsen it became clear that all knew Peter was not fit to reign, and it was rumoured that she intended to disinherit him in favour of Paul. Using her jeweller as a trusted go-between, Catherine began secret discussions with Bestuzhev-Riumin to explore how she could take power for herself and Paul after the empress died. The chancellor proposed that Peter and Catherine reign jointly, while he would run the government. Although Peter hated Catherine and she feared his accession, she remined non-committal.

On 8 March 1757 Catherine gave birth to a daughter, named Anna after Peter's mother. The father was believed to be Count Stanislas Poniatowski, the tall, dashing Polish-born secretary of the new British Ambassador Plenipotentiary Sir Charles Hanbury-Williams. 'Gentle, cultivated', educated in Paris and 'something of an innocent', Poniatowski was totally infatuated with Catherine, who was three years his senior. 'God knows where my wife gets her pregnancies,' Peter exclaimed. 'I have no idea whether this child is mine and whether I ought to take responsibility for it.'[22] Catherine challenged him to swear on oath that the child was not his, but he would not provoke an official enquiry or risk social ridicule.

Baby Anna died on 8 March 1759 and was buried in the Church of the Annunciation in the Alexander Nevsky Monastery in St Petersburg.[23]

Poniatowski was sent to Poland.

In August 1757 Prussia, funded by the British, invaded Saxony. Elizabeth entered into an alliance with France and Austria and joined the Seven Years War against Prussia. Her troops invaded Prussia in the summer of 1757, but Russia's commander-in-chief, Field Marshal Stephen Apraxin, was anxious to avoid any major battles as he knew the empress was not at all well. It was common knowledge that Peter, who could succeed to the throne at any moment, was strongly pro-Prussian and idolised Frederick the Great. A victory was gained that August, but Apraxin failed to follow up the advantage and was dismissed.

Elizabeth, who had suffered a second stroke, was now convinced that the fault lay with Bestuzhev-Riumin and that he was in the pay of the British and Prussians. Early in 1758 he was arrested, along with Catherine's jeweller who had acted as courier in their secret negotiations about the future. Luckily for Catherine, Bestuzhev-Riumin had managed to burn all his papers beforehand and there was no evidence incriminating her.

Bestuzhev-Riumin's exile led to the promotion of Count Michael Vorontzov to the post of chancellor. Catherine was now in a very precarious position. She had protested her innocence to the empress, which allayed Elizabeth's suspicions, but she was afraid that Peter might denounce her so that he could marry his mistress. According to Elizabeth Vorontzov, Peter had said that he would marry her if he could get rid of his wife. She was already openly installed in his apartments. Her sister Princess Catherine Dashkova formed part of another group, keen to install Catherine as regent for Paul as soon as the empress was dead.

Even Empress Elizabeth was now thinking of bypassing Peter.

In April 1759, the handsome Gregory Orlov arrived at court as escort to Count Kurt von Schwerin, a Prussian prisoner of war who served as an adjutant of Frederick the Great. While Peter was delighted to meet someone who was so close to his idol, Catherine fell in love with the magnificently endowed Orlov.

Aged twenty-five to Catherine's thirty, Orlov was a lieutenant in the Izmailovsky Guards. The son of a provincial governor, he had been heroic on the battlefield and wounded three times. Orlov and his four brothers were popular with their comrades.

While Peter was talking to Schwerin, Catherine had clandestine meetings with Orlov in a small house on Vasilevsky Island. As well as offering sensual pleasures, he harboured political ambitions. Soon Catherine was pregnant again, but this time she was careful to hide her condition.

By 1761 Prussia was almost defeated, but at this moment circumstances in Russia changed dramatically. At three o'clock on Christmas Day, after suffering another stroke, Empress Elizabeth died.

At the age of thirty-four, Peter III was Emperor of Russia and Catherine was his consort – but not for long.

5

Exit Peter III – Enter Catherine II

'There is no evil, but that it brings some good.'
Russian proverb

On 5 January 1762, the great officials congregated in the palace to hear the metropolitan invite Peter III to occupy the throne, 'the rightful possession of which all Europe and Asia acknowledge to be thine'. The new monarch was pleasantly surprised as, wearing the green uniform of the Preobrazhensky Guards with the blue ribbon of the Order of St Andrew, he rode through the assembled troops in the courtyard to their lusty cheers. 'I did not think they loved me so much,' he remarked later.[1]

That evening there was a supper for 150 people, followed by a banquet the next evening. On both occasions the guests were ordered to wear light-coloured clothes instead of the customary mourning.

Catherine, now empress, was treated with all due ceremony and friendliness. Her estates were increased and her debts were paid. Yet, although during the last few weeks she had kept herself secluded to hide her pregnancy, she knew how to play her part.

Elizabeth's open coffin had been moved to the Kazan Cathedral, where she lay surrounded by candles. The emperor refused to stand vigil or kneel before the bier; he paced around the cathedral laughing, pointing and sticking his tongue out at the priests.

In contrast, as a stream of mourners filed past to pay their respects, they saw a heavily veiled figure dressed in black and without any adornment kneeling by the bier apparently lost in grief. Everyone realised this was Empress Catherine. She came partly out of respect but also because she knew that this apparent demonstration of humility and reverence would be the best way of appealing to the common people. 'More and more she captured the heart of the Russians,' reported the French ambassador.

On the day of the funeral, Peter walked alone behind the coffin as it crossed the Neva to the Fortress of SS Peter and Paul. Although he wore a long black robe, his conduct was not in keeping with the occasion. He often stopped, waited until the coffin was around 30 feet in front of him, then took long strides in an apparent hurry to catch up. His long train billowed out behind him as the elderly noblemen who carried it were unable to match his pace. Peter was delighted by this prank, which he repeated several times. Those watching were less impressed by this childish conduct of a thirty-four-year-old man who owed his position to the late Empress Elizabeth.

In January, Peter made several administrative changes. He reduced the government tax on salt, ended the compulsory service to the state for noblemen and landowners instituted by Peter the Great and granted them freedom to travel abroad. He abolished the notorious Secret Chancellery, which investigated cases of sedition or treason, and permitted religious dissenters to return with full freedom of worship.

He also went to the Schlüsselburg Fortress to visit the deposed Emperor Ivan VI. It will be recalled that this great-grandson of Peter the Great's half-brother Ivan V had been deposed by Empress Elizabeth in 1741 when he was a baby. He and his mother, the regent Anna Leopoldovna, had been banished to the north of Russia, where Anna died in childbirth in 1746. Little Ivan, separated from his family and kept in solitary confinement, grew up more or less an imbecile. In 1756 he was moved to Schlüsselburg Fortress, on an island where the Neva meets Lake Ladoga. He was now a tall, illiterate twenty-two-year-old man with torn, dirty clothes whose hair reached down to his waist. Peter confirmed Empress Elizabeth's order that he should be killed if anyone tried to liberate him.

Peter also ordered an immediate cessation of hostilities with Prussia. Before his accession he had openly stated his intention of ending the war against Frederick the Great and then changing sides to support him against Austria and France. Now he did just that. Frederick was ecstatic; Elizabeth's death had saved him and his kingdom from ruin. Nearly a third of his lands were in the hands of the enemy, and Frederick himself was on the verge of suicide. Hearing news of the ceasefire, he ordered the release of all Russian prisoners and sent an officer to negotiate peace.

To the dismay of Austria and France, Peter said he was willing to sacrifice all the conquests made by Russia. Worse was to come. On 3 March Baron von Goltz, the new Prussian envoy, arrived in Russia to settle the peace terms and detach Russia from her allies. He informed Peter that King Frederick would cede East Prussia to him permanently, but this was something the emperor did not require, eager as he was to please his idol. The text of the peace treaty was settled privately between Peter and von Goltz and signed on 24 April without witnesses, merely being sent to Chancellor Michael Vorontzov for confirmation. It not only restored all the territory seized during the war but stated that Peter had contracted an 'eternal' alliance with Prussia. It was ratified by Frederick in June 1762.

Peter issued other decrees. Women were ordered to curtsey, as was done at the French court, rather than give the customary Russian bow. When their early attempts proved awkward Peter mocked them. His enthusiasms were taken to extremes. He maintained a near obsession with correct military uniform and drill and turned his estate of Orianienbaum into a military camp. The elite Guards regiments were ordered to wear Prussian uniforms in place of their Russian ones.

As a monarch Peter was energetic but childish. He never commanded loyalty. Count Stanislaus Poniatowski summed him up. 'He was not stupid, but mad, and as he loved to drink, this helped scramble his poor brains even further.'[2]

Peter had no liking for the Orthodox Church and its rituals. He had a Lutheran chapel built in his palace, ordered priests to wear short gowns and shave their beards like Lutheran pastors, and decreed that all private chapels were to be closed. A rumour soon circulated that he intended to convert Russia to Lutheranism.

The greatest mistake made by what one author called 'this rabid Prussophile of limited intellect'[3] was to act on his earlier stated intention of coming out in support of Holstein-Gottorp. He would go to war with Denmark to recover Schleswig, the territory the Danes had taken from his duchy in 1721. Vorontzov could not believe that such an anti-Russian programme would be carried out, but Peter made no secret of the fact that his heart lay in Holstein.

This alienated the Guards regiments. Catherine and her supporters now saw their chance.

Catherine had managed to keep her pregnancy a secret, using mourning for Elizabeth as an excuse to remain secluded in her apartments. On 11 April 1762, she gave birth to a son, Alexei Bobrinsky. The child was hidden in the house of her faithful valet, who during the birth set fire to his own house as a diversion, knowing that Peter and his mistress would rush to see the blaze.

By now she and Peter saw each other most mornings and they retained civility but that was all. They inspected the new apartments when the Winter Palace was finished and moved in during the spring. Catherine occupied a wing which overlooked the Neva and the Admiralty, while Elizabeth Vorontzov was allotted a lavish apartment directly below Peter's. By now Peter detested his wife so much that he refused to utter her name, referring to her as 'she'.[4] As Catherine was increasingly snubbed at court, the foreign ambassadors who had once been so eager to gain her favour ignored her.

Peter had already stated his intention of marrying Elizabeth Vorontzov and making her empress, a move that would spell danger for Catherine.

The one thing that he had not organised was his coronation. Instead, he intended to go to war.

On 9 June, four hundred guests were invited to a dinner in the newly finished Winter Palace to celebrate the signing of the peace with Prussia. When Peter proposed a toast to the imperial family, Catherine failed to stand. Peter sent a retainer to her end of the table to ask why. The reply came back that she was one of the three members of the imperial family so did not see the need. The adjutant was sent back to say that Peter's two Holstein uncles were also members and it was *them* he was honouring. Then Peter shouted down the length of the table calling her a fool. Catherine burst into tears but managed to retain her composure enough to ask her neighbour to tell her a funny story.

Later that night Peter ordered her arrest. The order was received by Prince Feodor Bariatinsky, the emperor's adjutant, who was sympathetic to Catherine and a friend of her lover Gregory Orlov. Bariatinsky informed Peter's uncle Prince George of Holstein, who managed to get the arrest order cancelled.

Three days later, Peter left for Orianienbaum to drill his soldiers before they all left for war against Denmark to regain Schleswig. Catherine was left in St Petersburg. Rumours then reached Peter that there was restlessness in the capital. Even Frederick the Great heard that something was afoot and tried to warn him. Peter just shrugged it off, saying, 'If the Russians had wanted to do me harm they could have done it a long time ago, seeing that I take no particular precautions....'[5] He ordered Catherine to leave the capital and go to Peterhof.

Leaving Paul behind in the care of his governor, Nikita Panin, on 17 June Catherine moved to Monplaisir where plans for a coup began to take shape. It was organised by the Orlov brothers, who by now had subverted several Guards units.

There were five Orlov brothers: Ivan, Gregory, Alexei, Feodor and Vladimir. It was Alexei (known as Scarface), Gregory and Feodor who participated in what happened next.

The urgency increased when one of the minor conspirators was arrested and during questioning implicated Captain Passek of the Guards. Passek was arrested on 27 June. So far Catherine had managed to cover her tracks when involved in intrigues, but this time her supporters feared her life was in danger.

When Gregory Orlov heard the news he hurried to see Panin, who still had charge of little Paul. Knowing that Passek would reveal the conspiracy if he was tortured, it was decided there was no time to lose. Catherine must immediately return to St Petersburg and be proclaimed empress, without waiting for Peter to be arrested and deposed.

In the middle of their meeting, Alexei Orlov (Scarface) arrived. Without delay he went outside and hailed a shabby carriage on the street. In this unpromising vehicle, accompanied by Bariatinsky and with Sergeant Gregory Potemkin on the running board, he travelled through the night on the 20-mile journey to Peterhof.

Failure would mean disgrace, exile and maybe even death.

At five o'clock in the morning of 28 June, a maid woke Catherine at Monplaisir. Minutes later Alexei Orlov entered and informed her of Passek's arrest.

Catherine jumped up, put on a simple black dress and, with her maid (wearing bedroom slippers) and her servant Shkurin, accompanied Orlov to his carriage. She was still wearing her nightcap. As they rushed along, they met up with the carriage of the empress's French hairdresser Michel, who arranged her tresses as they rode. Nearer St Petersburg, Catherine and Scarface changed to a carriage containing

Gregory Orlov, so she arrived at the barracks of the Izmailovsky Regiment with her lover. The Guards enthusiastically swore allegiance to Catherine as empress. They followed her to the next stop, the Semenovsky Guards' barracks, where the scene was repeated.

Catherine decided to enter St Petersburg immediately. At the Kazan Cathedral, the Bishop of Novgorod proclaimed her the sovereign autocrat Catherine II and her son Paul heir to the throne.

As church bells rang throughout the city, the empress walked to the Winter Palace where the leading courtiers, officials and army officers swore oaths of allegiance. Later she appeared on the balcony, holding Paul in her arms. But were the cheers for Catherine as empress, or as the mother of Paul?

As the soldiers exchanged the hated Prussian tunics for their old Russian ones, Catherine changed into a borrowed uniform coat of the Preobrazhensky Guards. She ordered them all to congregate in Palace Square, ready to march to Peterhof.

Meanwhile, at Orianienbaum, Peter was asleep. When he finally woke he had a terrible hangover. After reviewing the Holstein battalion stationed at the palace he set out with a sizeable retinue for Peterhof, where he was to attend a dinner with Catherine to celebrate his name day, the feast of SS Peter and Paul.

To Peter's surprise, Monplaisir was deserted. He was told that Catherine had left early that morning. Rushing in, he discovered the gala dress she was due to wear strewn across the bed.

Eventually realising what had happened, Peter sent for his Holstein troops from Orianienbaum, who arrived with only their parade ground rifles, unaware that they might have to fight. He was advised to take command of the considerable force he had assembled at Narva for the war against Denmark and march with them to St Petersburg. The rebellion would then be crushed in short order.

Peter ignored this sage advice, instead sending an adjutant to the Kronstadt naval fortress at the mouth of the Neva to take command of the garrison there and bring his warships to attack St Petersburg. Half an hour later he countermanded this order and sent Prince Ivan Bariatinsky to Kronstadt with orders to prepare for his arrival. The commander of the fortress, unaware of the coup, said that it was always ready to welcome the emperor. As Bariatinsky sailed away, orders arrived that nobody should be allowed in or out of Kronstadt. The garrison swore allegiance to Catherine.

By that evening Peter was distraught. He had sent several messengers to St Petersburg but almost none had returned. From the few who did, he discovered that Catherine had proclaimed herself empress with the backing of the church, the Guards regiments and senior officials. He ordered his Holstein troops to take up defensive positions in the park but they had no cannon balls to fire. He was unable to flee, as everyone had come by carriage and there were no horses available.

At that point Ivan Bariatinsky arrived and said that Kronstadt, with its 3,000-man garrison, was still loyal. Peter seized on this, deciding they would sail to Kronstadt and use the fortress as a base. However, when they arrived after midnight the guard refused them permission to enter.

'I am your emperor!' Peter protested.

'We no longer have an emperor,' the guard replied. 'Long live the Empress Catherine II.'[6]

Instead of escaping by sea to Revel and going from there to Holstein, he returned to Orianienbaum with Elizabeth Vorontsov, her ladies and a few attendants. On arrival, he heard that Catherine was approaching with a large contingent of soldiers. At this news, Peter gave up. He dismissed his followers, lay down on the couch weeping and asked for a pen and paper. In French, he wrote to Catherine. He apologised for his recent behaviour and offered her a share in the government as joint ruler.

The letter was given to Prince Alexander Golitsyn to deliver.

Thirty-three-year-old Catherine mounted her grey horse Brilliant and, wearing the green and red tunic of the Preobrazhensky Guards and a fetching broad-brimmed hat, prepared to ride off from Palace Square at the head of 12,000 troops. As she rode through the ranks, she realised that her sabre was missing its sword knot. Immediately Gregory Potemkin rode up and offered his. She could not fail to notice the tall, slim young man with a shock of auburn hair who had taken part in the coup the night before. When he tried to return to the ranks his fresh horse refused to do so; it was trained to ride as part of a squadron. In what Potemkin later called 'a happy chance', she began talking to him.[7]

They had stopped to rest in a small tavern on the Peterhof–Orianienbaum road when she was handed Peter's letter. His offer to share the throne with her was not enough for Catherine, and she realised other measures would have to be taken. Prince Golitsyn swore allegiance to her and said that Scarface and his Hussars had sealed all the entrances to Orianienbaum.

Meanwhile, Peter, having received no reply to the letter, wrote again. This time he said he would abdicate and go to Holstein if he could take Elizabeth Vorontzov with him.

When the second messenger reached Catherine she accepted his proposal but insisted that the abdication must be in writing. Peter then copied and signed an abject document sent by Catherine, declaring that he would renounce the throne of his own free will and not seek to recover it during the rest of his life. He was advised to go to Peterhof and throw himself on Catherine's mercy.

At Peterhof, he and his companions Elizabeth Vorontzov and General Gudovich were arrested. Peter was obliged to surrender his sword and decorations. Scarface was ordered to take him under escort to Ropsha, a country estate about 28 miles south-west of St Petersburg, where he remained under house arrest. As Frederick the Great later said, Peter 'allowed himself to be overthrown like a child being sent off to bed'.[8]

Peter's continued existence posed a threat to Catherine. She had no right to the throne; the true heir was her seven-year-old son Paul.

Peter died on 6 July 1762, officially of a 'haemorrhoidal colic', an explanation so absurd that it became a euphemism for political murder. People joked that piles was 'a very dangerous condition in Russia'.[9]

Other, more sinister causes were immediately suspected.

A note to Catherine from Scarface mentioned a quarrel, followed by a brawl during a drinking bout which ended with Peter being strangled. Scarface begged Catherine's mercy for 'this misfortune',[10] but it was certainly convenient for her. After all, the deposed Ivan VI was still languishing in a fortress after seventeen years.

Peter was buried in the Alexander Nevsky Monastery, wearing his beloved uniform of the Holstein Dragoons, as he had not been crowned.

Catherine would not make the same mistake. She immediately arranged her coronation.

6

Catherine II and the Expansion of Empire

Seven inland seas and seven mighty rivers
From the Nile to the Neva
From the Elbe to China
From the Volga to the Euphrates
From the Ganges to the Danube
Such is our Empire to be.
Feodor Tyutchev, 1844

King Charles's five-times-great-grandmother Catherine II was crowned in Moscow on 22 September 1762 in a magnificent ceremony which outdid anything arranged for any previous ruler.

The empress's dress was of golden silk, its skirt embroidered with double-headed eagles. Four thousand ermine skins were used to make her mantle. The new crown with which she crowned herself was so spectacular that it was used for every subsequent coronation until the fall of the monarchy. The commission was given to the Swiss jeweller Jerémié Posier, who selected from the imperial treasury 5,012 diamonds, 76 perfectly matched pearls (which formed two arcs curving over the top surmounted by a cross of diamonds) and an enormous 415-carat ruby bought by Tsar Alexei from a Manchu emperor in 1676. Despite his efforts to make the crown as light as possible, it still weighed 5 lbs. A band of diamonds was added to the solid gold orb and there was a gold sceptre in three sections divided by double bands of diamonds.[1]

The Orlov brothers were well rewarded and each raised to the rank of count, as was Nikita Panin. Gregory Orlov became adjutant-general (the official status given to Catherine's lovers) and moved into rooms with a staircase leading directly to the empress's apartments below. Gregory Potemkin was made gentleman of the bedchamber and given 400 serfs.

Catherine bore no animosity to those who supported Peter. Elizabeth Vorontzov was sent to Moscow, where she was given a house. After she married, the empress became godmother to her baby.

With the coronation over, Catherine got down to work. Although the coup had been masterminded by the Orlovs, she had no intention of becoming a puppet ruler. Yet Russia was in penury. Both Elizabeth and Peter had hoarded money rather than use it for the benefit of the empire. Catherine did the opposite, declaring that she belonged to the state, as did everything she owned.

She rose early every morning, wrote numerous letters, received ministers and drafted decrees. At eleven o'clock she dressed, received Orlov and went for a walk, often just with him, her ladies-in-waiting and her dogs. After dining at around one o'clock she sewed and read, then continued working until six o'clock. Orlov was received again before she dressed for the evening. Sunday was the court day, Monday and Thursdays were theatre performances and on Saturdays there was a masquerade ball. She liked to be in bed (usually with Orlov) by eleven o'clock.

Catherine was intelligent as well as being a born administrator and politician. Peter's army reorganisations were scrapped and a military commission devised a series of reforms. She established a medical college and in 1768 took the risk of having herself and her son Paul inoculated against smallpox by the English physician Thomas Dimsdale. There had already been one scare, when Paul went down with a fever soon after the coronation. She could not afford for him to die.

Catherine's new legal code, the *Bolshoi Nakaz* (Great Instruction), was to be unveiled in Moscow in 1767 and she intended to open the Legislative Commission herself. To stress the fact that this was intended to serve both the old and the new Russia, she decided to take a trip into the heartland of old Russia.

On 28 April 1767, a flotilla of large boats set off from Tver on the Upper Volga. Over a thousand people accompanied the empress on a voyage that stopped at Yaroslavl, Kostroma, Nizhny Novgorod,

Kazan and Simbirsk. She enjoyed river travel and marvelled at the nature along the riverbanks. 'Here the people along the Volga are rich and extremely well fed,' she wrote to Nikita Panin, 'and although prices are high everywhere, yet everybody eats grain and nobody complains or suffers want.'[2]

From Simbirsk, Catherine returned overland to Moscow, where in the Kremlin she opened the Legislative Commission wearing a small crown and the imperial mantle. After a service in the Uspensky Sobor, five hundred delegates assembled in the Palace of Facets to launch the *Bolshoi Nakaz*, which defined Russia as 'an absolute monarchy with fundamental laws'.[3]

The delegates then debated what title they should give Catherine in gratitude for her bringing them together. After much deliberation it was decided on the title of 'the Great'. This pleased her enormously. It had taken Peter the Great forty years to receive such an accolade. Her position strengthened, there would be no further talk of her merely being regent for Paul, nor any discussion about him taking the throne when he reached the age of eighteen.

Catherine kept her public and private lives separate. At the Great Palace at Tsarskoe Selo (now the Catherine Palace), the rooms designed for her by the Scottish architect Charles Cameron were small. He attached the Agate Pavilion onto an unfinished portion of the building, giving the empress six more rooms – including a library – all decorated with lapis lazuli, alabaster, agate, malachite and other semi-precious stones, along with coloured marble from Karelia, Finland and Siberia. Underneath the pavilion were Roman-style baths and a covered gallery where Catherine could walk in inclement weather or, in summer, take her meals. The busts of thirty of her favourite philosophers were placed there. So impressed was she by Cameron's work that the philosophers' gallery was renamed the Cameron Gallery.

A patron of learning, Catherine led Russia into the political and cultural life of Europe. She wrote satires and works on Russian history, encouraged the translation into Russian of foreign works and subsidised the public performances of plays. The first Russian dictionary was published by the Russian Academy of Languages, founded by the empress in 1783. She read Montesquieu and corresponded with Voltaire (always with a lot of flattery on his part). She subscribed to the cultural newsletter *Correspondance Littérraire*, edited by Friedrich Melchior Grimm and sent to Europe's crowned heads via their embassies, thus avoiding censorship. Catherine met Grimm in St Petersburg in 1774, and after he left they began a correspondence which lasted until her death.

The empress was also a noted collector of art, so much so that she had a new three-storey wing built onto the Winter Palace to house her growing collection of paintings, as well as her library. The Small Hermitage (a name which later referred to a whole complex of buildings adjoining the original Winter Palace) was designed in the 1760s by Vallin de la Mothe. It was private and more intimate than the main Winter Palace and she used it as a townhouse. In her salon, where 'silver serving trays of food were laid out, alongside brimming crystal decanters of wine and vodka', selected guests gathered every evening for philosophical discussion, music, poetry and general conversation. The empress liked to gamble at whist, bridge and other games of chance, although she usually lost. Giacomo Quarenghi was responsible for adding the Hermitage Theatre in the 1780s. Catherine even wrote some plays and had them performed there.[4]

She liked to show off her latest art purchases. In 1772 she acquired 158 Italian, Flemish and Dutch masterpieces sold by the family of Pierre Crozat, financial agent of Louis XIV's nephew Philippe, Duc d'Orleans. In 1778 she paid the exorbitant sum of £40,550 for more than two hundred paintings collected by the late Sir Robert Walpole of Houghton Hall in Norfolk, to the annoyance of the British. Her last large acquisition was 119 paintings of the French Comte de Baudouin, including nine Rembrandts, for which she paid 50,000 roubles.[5]

These purchases helped to make up for a great loss. In June 1771, the Dutch merchant and art collector Gerrit Braamcamp died. Catherine purchased some of the most significant works at the subsequent auction and arrangements were made to ship them to St Petersburg. They left Amsterdam on the *Vrouw Maria* on 5 September but in the Baltic the ship ran into bad weather and was caught in an Arctic hurricane. It ran aground, had to be abandoned and by 9 October had sunk near Åbo (Turku) in Finland (at that time part of Sweden) with its precious cargo lost. Although efforts were made to salvage the paintings, the ship was never recovered. 'The *Vrouw Maria* has been taken by the sea,' Catherine wrote dejectedly to Gustav III of Sweden. 'It is lost and I will have to deal with it.'[6]

Yet her large collection of Old Masters in one single place inspired London to found the National Gallery and Paris to open the Louvre. 'Catherine's compulsion to collect and obsession to outbid inadvertently helped to redefine the relationship between art, power and people in the modern world.'[7]

In order to establish herself as the successor to Peter the Great, one of Russia's greatest rulers, she had an equestrian statue of him erected in Senate Square. Sculpted by Etienne Falconet, it took eleven years to complete. It was mounted on a huge block of granite which took hundreds of men nearly two years to laboriously move from Finland to St Petersburg by road and then by sea. The finished statue became known as the *Bronze Horseman* and was later immortalised in a poem by Pushkin. The Latin inscription on the base is inscribed, 'To Peter the First from Catherine the Second 1782.' Excitement about this huge granite rock, which weighed 1,600 tons even when reduced to half its original size, was so intense that small fragments of it were used to make earrings. Catherine had a pair made for herself and also sent a pair to Queen Charlotte in England.

With no family, the empress relied on a few close friends. Chief among these was her lady-in-waiting Countess Prascovia Bruce. Their relationship was so close that the countess has often been credited with testing and approving potential lovers for Catherine. Whatever the truth, she remained loyal and discrete.

Catherine had at least twelve lovers, beginning with Sergei Saltykov. The most famous were Stanislas Poniatowski (who was probably the father of her daughter Anna), Gregory Orlov (whose liaison with her lasted eleven years) and Gregory Potemkin.

In September 1762, Augustus III of Poland died. Even though he had a son, Catherine wanted to control Poland and she decided that her former lover Stanislas Poniatowski would make for a malleable candidate. The idea was backed by Frederick the Great of Prussia who, in return for Catherine's support, signed an alliance of mutual support with Russia in 1764. Poniatowski was related to Polish magnates and he still dreamed of marrying Catherine – but she was having none of it. In August, Poland's national assembly elected him King Stanislas-Augustus.

She refused to marry Orlov, even though she was on the throne because he had helped put her there and he was the father of her son Alexei. He now wanted her all the time, not just at night. As compensation, he was given titles, jewels and land. The Italian architect Antonio Rinaldi built the Marble Palace in St Petersburg for him, but it was not enough. Orlov wanted marriage. Catherine saw that such a union would jeopardise Paul's rights of succession. Nikita Panin told her with honesty, 'A Madame Orlov could never be empress of all the Russias.'[8]

While he lived she could also be endangered by Ivan VI, who was still languishing in Schlüsselburg Fortress. In 1764 some disgruntled army offices attempted to release him. Acting on the empress's orders, his guards stabbed him to death.

The mutual assistance alliance with Frederick the Great was an attempt to find allies against Turkey, Russia's most dangerous neighbour. Catherine tried to create a northern system of alliances with Prussia, Poland, the Scandinavian countries and Britain. In 1768, Poland's Catholic nobles rebelled against King Stanislas-Augustus, angered by Catherine's attempt to secure civil rights for non-Catholic people. The empress sent in Russian troops, who then clashed with Turkish forces on the Polish–Turkish border. In 1769, Turkey declared war.

At the battle of Chesme in 1770, the Turkish fleet was defeated in a great victory. Russian forces occupied Moldavia, Wallachia and the Crimea, the lush peninsula with its mainly Tatar population on the shores of the Black Sea which had been ruled by elected khans since 1441. In 1772 the Crimea 'accepted the Russian offer of nominal independence in return for Russia's occupation of most of its ports'.[9] This proved problematic for Prussia and Austria, who demanded compensation for Russian expansion. In 1772 the three powers agreed the first partition of Poland, where Catherine gained Belorussia but Poland lost one-third of its lands.

By now Catherine's relationship with Orlov was strained and she began a brief affair with Alexander Vasilchikov, a young Guards lieutenant who was, in her words, 'an excellent but very boring citizen'.[10] Gregory Orlov was sent to handle negotiations with the Turks. Catherine never forgot that she owed her throne to the Orlovs and she was generous, as she was to all her former lovers. As well as the Marble Palace he received 150,000 roubles annually, a large further sum to help set up his household and the title of Prince of the Holy Roman Empire.

Meanwhile, she had given Gregory Potemkin the appointment of court chamberlain. He had lost his left eye, some said after a beating by the Orlovs.[11] He was an admirable administrator but insisted on going to war against Turkey, where he distinguished himself as a cavalry general. Catherine encouraged him to write to her privately, but he was slow to take up the offer. She enjoyed his sense of humour and his gifts as a mimic but when he returned to court he found Vasilchikov still there. Potemkin decided to force the issue. He retired to the Alexander Nevsky Monastery in St Petersburg, declaring he would become a monk.

While at war with Turkey, Catherine faced rebellion at home. In September 1773 the Don Cossack Emelyan Pugachev claimed to be Peter III and started a revolt, drawing considerable support after he promised to free the serfs and restore Cossack privileges. Alarm grew when he besieged Orenburg and captured several towns on the Volga. By the winter his rebel army was only 100 miles from Moscow. Anti-landlord hatred became widespread and the rebels killed at least 1,500 noblemen and their families and over 1,000 government officials. Even priests were not safe. Most of the nobles panicked and fled rather than stay and fight. 'Hurry up and exterminate these criminals who disgrace us in the eyes of the world,' Catherine wrote to her generals.[12]

The end of the Turkish war released the Russian army to deal with Pugachev. General Suvorov and his mounted infantrymen finally tracked down Pugachev and brought him back to Moscow, chained and in a cage. He was tried, sentenced to death and executed in January 1775.

The Pugachev revolt reminded Catherine that her empire was multinational and that a large part of the population was made up of serfs or peasants eking out a living as best they could. Mass executions followed in revenge for murdered landlords and priests, and the nobility returned to their estates as before. The real winners were the Don Cossacks, who were given 'a special status in which they incurred military service in return for lands and other privileges'.[13]

Nevertheless, the empress refused to hear any talk of freeing the serfs.

Catherine then faced another problem. In September 1772, Paul reached the age of eighteen. He could now expect to have his own court and play a political role, preferably as the rightful Emperor of Russia. Catherine was well aware that his claim on the throne was infinitely stronger than hers and that if he challenged her and won it would spell disaster. She decided to find him a wife. She invited the younger daughters of the Landgrave of Hesse-Darmstadt to Russia with their mother and let her son choose.

Paul's eye fell on seventeen-year-old Princess Wilhelmina. Despite her hesitation at the prospect of the marriage, she took the name Natalia on her conversion to Orthodoxy. The couple were married on 29 September 1773.

Paul had already become involved in a plot to make him joint ruler with his mother. Catherine decided not to give the newlyweds a separate court. He was now her rival, as well as her son.

Alarmed at Potemkin's disappearance from court, Catherine despatched Countess Bruce to the Alexander Nevsky Monastery to speak with him. Convinced both by the rank of the messenger and the content of the message, which promised the empress's favour, Potemkin flung off his monastic robes, shaved his beard and joined Catherine first at Tsarskoe Selo and then at the Winter Palace. At Potemkin's insistence, Vasilchikov was sent packing.

Potemkin, the scion of minor gentry from Smolensk, was the love of Catherine's life. He was now thirty-four (ten years Catherine's junior) and no longer slim but even with the loss of an eye she still thought him handsome. They shared a passion for 'literature, neo-classicist architecture and English gardens'.[14] Like Catherine, Potemkin collected art and jewels almost obsessively. Like her, he also loved power, but he was not content just to take the usual rewards of the empress's favourite.

In March 1774 he was promoted to lieutenant-colonel of the Preobrazhensky Guards and decided that Russia needed a further offensive against the Ottomans. Catherine appointed him governor-general of the newly conquered parts of southern Ukraine (New Russia) and acceded to his demand to join her war council. At the end of May she promoted him to general-in-chief and vice president of the War Collegium.

Peace was signed with Turkey in July. This gave Catherine further important territories including the port of Kerch, part of the Black Sea coastline, an 'independent' Crimea under Shagin Giray, whom the Russians imposed as khan (ruler) of the region, and freedom of passage through the Straits and into the Mediterranean for merchant shipping. Russia also gained a general protectorate of the Ottoman Christians, which would have huge consequences eighty years later.

Potemkin was both Catherine's lover and her political partner, even though they worked in different parts of the palace. Little notes flew between them exchanging news, gossip and declarations of love. They did not sleep in the same room; one or other of them would ascend and descend the connecting staircase. There is no doubt that Catherine was desperately in love with him, even standing outside his door on the coldest night waiting for him to be alone. There were tears and tantrums, and jealousy on both sides. She called him 'dear husband' and referred to herself as 'your devoted wife'. She never referred to any other lover in this way. But were they married?

If they were, it is believed that the most probable time would be in June 1774. Simon Sebag Montefiore believes 4 or 8 June while Robert Massie quotes 8 June, but both agree on the St Samponsovsky Church on the Vyborg side of St Petersburg as the location. Legend has it that the witnesses were the chamberlain Evgraf Cherkov and Potemkin's nephew Alexander Samoilov, who held the traditional crowns over the pair's heads. So far there is no concrete proof. The marriage certificates have disappeared. Yet for the remainder of his life Potemkin wielded a unique authority in Russia.[15]

In April 1776, Paul's young wife Grand Duchess Natalia died after giving birth to a stillborn son. Paul had been deeply in love with her and went into a frenzy of grief, refusing ever to think of marrying again. With no heir after three years of marriage, this was disastrous for the empire.

The empress was long since disillusioned with her frivolous daughter-in-law, who had been running up colossal debts. She now acted quickly. She had heard rumours that Natalia's relationship with Paul's best friend, Andrei Razumovsky, had been extremely close so she decided to break into Natalia's desk. There she found love letters exchanged between the couple and took them to Paul. When he discovered that the people he loved best had betrayed him, he exploded in fury. Razumovsky was ordered to leave the capital and Paul declared himself ready to marry again immediately.

Princess Sophia Dorothea of Württemberg was a niece of Paul's hero, Frederick the Great. Three years earlier Catherine had wanted Sophia as a bride for her son but at that time she was only fourteen. Now seventeen, she was the ideal candidate.

King Frederick helped by convincing Sophia Dorothea's parents about the advantages of the match. The princess's previous engagement to the handsome Prince Louis of Hesse was broken off and a meeting with Paul arranged.

Catherine organised a powerful incentive for Paul. The meeting would take place in Berlin at the court of Frederick the Great. Paul, who had never been abroad, travelled in a large comfortable carriage alongside Frederick's brother Prince Henry of Prussia. In Berlin, Frederick laid on a grand reception with triumphal arches, cannons and lines of soldiers. Paul was feted at balls, banquets and receptions as befitted the heir to a great throne. Accustomed to an insignificant role at his mother's court, he was suitably flattered. He also took an instant liking to the tall, blonde Sophia Dorothea, who came with Frederick's recommendation. The princess accepted the situation with good grace. 'The grand duke is exceedingly amiable,' she told her mother. 'He has every charm.'[16]

The empress was delighted at the outcome, sending a diamond necklace and earrings to Sophia Dorothea, stressing that the marriage must take place as soon as possible. She also insisted that her mother remain in Berlin. Recollections of her own mother's meddling were surely on her mind.

Sophia Dorothea and Paul were received with great ceremony at Tsarskoe Selo on 31 August. A few days later the princess was confirmed into the Orthodox Church as Grand Duchess Maria Feodorovna.

On 26 September 1776, Paul and Maria were married in the Winter Palace in a ceremony witnessed by the entire court. By 1779 they had two sons, Alexander and Constantine. The elder son was destined for the Russian throne, but Constantine was given this Greek name because Catherine hoped that he would be the ruler of a 'new Orthodox Greek empire based on Constantinople'.[17] Both boys would be raised under Catherine's direct supervision, as Paul had been under the auspices of Empress Elizabeth.

While she was working on the drafts of a local government reform document, Catherine fell in love with Count Peter Zavodovsky, a dark, good-looking young Ukrainian army officer and bureaucrat. Yet Potemkin remained as both her political partner and her 'husband'.

They had decided to live apart. He was setting up home in the Shepilev Mansion, which adjoined the Winter Palace (and which gave him access to Catherine's apartments via a covered passageway from beside the chapel), so while he was doing so she gave him the Anichkov

Palace on the Nevsky Prospekt as well as money to decorate it. Although he no longer lived in the apartments allocated to Catherine's favourite, he never lost his access to her bedroom. He was created a Prince of the Holy Roman Empire with the title of Serenissimus – but none of this stopped either of them from sleeping with other partners.

Zavadovsky acted as a convenient buffer, shielding Catherine from Potemkin's moods and demands and giving Potemkin security in the knowledge that he would keep his power without fear of being replaced.

Yet trouble was not far away. Zavadovsky complained about Potemkin's continued presence and influence, refusing to accept Catherine's explanations. He wanted nothing less than exclusivity. When Potemkin left for Novgorod in June he had it, but he soon became bored with court life, especially as his poor French prevented him from taking part in conversations.

Potemkin returned in July, complaining that he now had nowhere to go. 'My dear and beloved husband come to me. You will be received with open arms,' Catherine wrote.[18] He discovered that Zavadovsky was still a threat and the empress had to cope with the jealousy of both men. Potemkin retreated to a country estate instead of being present at the empress's birthday celebrations. From there, he demanded Zavadovsky's dismissal. He refused to relent.

Zavadovsky returned to Ukraine in the summer of 1777, having been given generous financial rewards by Catherine. In this way Catherine and Potemkin managed to preserve their mutual affection as well as their close working relationship.

Catherine instituted a series of charters which defined privileges and obligations for various social groups who would willingly undertake state service. She placed urban local government in the hands of elected councils under her 1785 Charter to the Towns, while in the same year the Charter to the Nobility ensured that only those who gave state service could take part in elections to local offices and local assemblies of the nobility. It also confirmed their right to own property (which was confirmed as their legal property) and serfs, and exempted them from corporal punishment and personal taxation.

To encourage education she founded the Smolny Institute, a St Petersburg boarding school for daughters of the nobility. She appointed a Commission on National Education in 1782 and founded a teacher training college the following year. By the end of the century her 1786 Statute of National Schools, offering free education for boys and girls, had led to the founding of over 300 schools, yet children of serfs were barred from this free education and the vast majority of Russia's population remained illiterate.

Under Catherine's rule the Russian empire also expanded.

The peace signed between Russia and Turkey in 1774 was precarious. Catherine wished to annexe the Crimea; Turkey wanted the region back. The empress also had dreams of conquering the European part of the Turkish empire, including Constantinople, which she hoped would provide a throne for her grandson Constantine. Potemkin and Catherine's other advisers knew that to do this they would need the support of Austria. Catherine therefore went out of her way to be friendly to Emperor Joseph II, and in 1780 they met at Mogilev, the emperor travelling incognito as Count Falkenstein. The following year a secret agreement was reached whereby Austria would provide Russia with military assistance if Turkey broke the peace treaty.

In 1777, Potemkin was ruling as viceroy over Catherine's southern empire. He built Kherson on the lower Dnieper River, constructed docks and a shipyard and began laying down warships. Seizing the opportunity of a war between Britain and France in the early 1780s, Catherine ordered the annexation of the Crimea, which was achieved by Potemkin in 1783.

He established a naval base at Sevastopol and encouraged economic development. In 1786 he began building Ekaterinoslav to serve as the capital. He also founded Nikolaev and began plans to build what eventually (after his death) became Odessa. In 1784 he was promoted to the rank of field marshal and president of the College of War, where he introduced practical reforms in army uniforms. By 1785 he had control of the staff of the Black Sea Fleet and oversaw relations with Turkey. The only thing he could not do was declare war.

In late 1786, Catherine finally yielded to persuasion and accepted Potemkin's invitation to come and see what he had achieved. The mammoth journey would last six months and cover over 4,000 miles by carriage, river galley and sledge. There were also diplomatic reasons for going. Catherine intended to meet her old lover King Stanislas-Augustus of Poland on the Russian–Polish border, and Emperor Joseph of Austria at Kherson.

In early January 1787, an immense cavalcade left Tsarskoe Selo in luxurious carriages, gliding over the snow-covered landscape on runners which turned them into sledges. Along with Catherine travelled foreign ambassadors, courtiers, government officials and members of her staff. No members of her family were present, nor did the empress delegate any power to Paul while she was away.

They reached Kiev on 29 January, where the party was joined by Potemkin and welcomed by cannon salutes and pealing bells. After a stay of six weeks on the banks of the Dnieper they boarded seven large, luxurious Roman-style galleys painted in red and gold. As they sailed down the river, crowds of people turned out to see this unusual spectacle, waving as Catherine's little fleet went by. Guests were ferried from one galley to another by small boats so that those who were not working with the empress could gossip or play card games. At noon, those chosen to dine with Catherine were rowed along to her own galley or, if it was a large company, to the special dining galley where musicians played while they ate.

After six days they arrived in Kaniev, the Russian–Polish border town where King Stanislas-Augustus awaited them. He and Catherine had not met since 1759 and both were aware that age had taken its toll. He was rowed out to the empress's galley but, because the Polish constitution forbade the king to leave Polish soil, he arrived as Count Poniatowski, a temporary incognito.

'It was thirty years since I had seen him and you can imagine that we found each other changed,' the empress wrote to Grimm.[19] Their private talk was strained and the king failed to persuade Catherine to remain for a few days. She was due to meet Emperor Joseph and insisted that the schedule could not be changed. Both Stanislas-Augustus and Potemkin were annoyed, the latter telling the empress that her refusal would undermine the king's position in Poland. To mollify them, her guests were permitted to attend that evening's ball in the palace which the king had built specially for her visit. Catherine remained on her galley and watched the firework display from the deck, declaring to Potemkin that Stanislas-Augustus bored her.

Emperor Joseph, again travelling incognito as Count Falkenstein, had decided not to wait at Kherson. Instead he waited at Kaidek, where Catherine's fleet would encounter the first of the Dnieper rapids. Receiving this news, Catherine quickly disembarked and rushed to intercept him in her carriage. They travelled back to Kaidek together, with Joseph insisting on maintaining his incognito. After twenty-four hours they travelled to the site of Potemkin's new city of Ekaterinoslav, where the empress laid the foundation stone of the cathedral. They then re-embarked on the galleys, which had successfully shot the rapids, and headed for Kherson by water.

At the entrance to the town Potemkin had erected a sign saying in Greek, 'This is the way to Byzantium.' Kherson had grown into a thriving fortified city, with a flourishing shipyard, warehouses and many Russian ships anchored nearby. On 15 May, Catherine and Joseph launched three new warships.

The Ottoman empire's reluctance to accept Russia's presence in the Crimea soon became apparent. Catherine's plans to sail all the way along the Dnieper to the Black Sea were abandoned when Turkey sent warships to the mouth of the river. Instead, Catherine, Joseph and the foreign ambassadors travelled overland where, on the Steppe, they were greeted by 1,200 mounted Tatar tribesmen who, although recently conquered, formed a guard of honour.

They passed through the Perekop Isthmus, the gateway connecting the Crimea to Ukraine and Russia. The Crimean climate was mild and the scenery spectacular. Many years later Prince Serge Obolensky described 'the blue waters of the Black Sea stretching away into the horizon. To the north, beyond the mountain slopes, were clean little villages of flat-roofed, white-plastered Tatar houses, each village with its mosque...' The magnificent dark-skinned men wore traditional 'black hats, short embroidered coats and tight white trousers'. The women 'dyed their hair bright red and wore floating veils to hide their faces'.[20]

The Crimean Peninsula had formerly been ruled from the ancient capital of Bakhchisaray. The khan's palace was a mixture of Moorish, Arabian, Chinese and Turkish styles based on the Ottoman palaces in Constantinople, with low white buildings, thick walls and elaborately decorated door and window surrounds. Inside, eastern carpets lay on the marble floors and divans lined the walls. There was a mosque, courtyards and fountains, including the Fountain of Tears later immortalised by Pushkin.[21] It was like something from the *Arabian Nights*.

They spent three days at Bakhchisaray Palace before moving on to Inkerman. Before them lay Sevastopol Bay, where ships belonging to the Black Sea Fleet – which Potemkin considered his greatest achievement – thundered a cannon salute. Catherine and Joseph then went on a carriage tour of the harbour and thriving city. The emperor was greatly impressed, although the massive firework display with 20,000 rockets terrified the Tatars in the crowd.

Abandoning plans to travel to Taganrog on the Sea of Azov, they returned to the Dnieper where Catherine and Joseph parted. The empress went to Poltava, where Potemkin staged a re-enactment of Peter the Great's famous 1709 battle, before they went their separate ways at Kharkov. As a parting gift, he presented her with a magnificent pearl necklace brought from Vienna; she gave him the title Prince of Taurus. 'I beg of you most humbly do me the favour of looking after your health,' she wrote to him later, 'for God's sake and our sake, and be as pleased with me as I am with you.'[22]

The journey gave rise to the myth of the Potemkin Villages, hastily constructed dwellings peopled by prosperous-looking peasants who greeted the empress all along the route. In fact, the dwellings and the peasants in their holiday clothes were real – it was only that the 'infirm, the village idiots, the raggle-taggle, were to be kept out of sight'.[23] There were no sham villages.

Catherine intended her Crimean journey to intimidate the Turks. Instead, it provoked them. In the summer of 1787 the sultan declared war, determined to take back the Crimea from Russia and eradicate their fleet. This triggered Emperor Joseph's agreement to come to Russia's aid, and in February 1788 the Austrian empire declared war on Turkey.

Potemkin, as viceroy and commander-in-chief, was placed in charge of the Russian forces but the effort proved to be both protracted and costly. In 1788 Gustav III of Sweden, hoping to gain territory lost to Peter the Great, also declared war on Russia but this ended in stalemate with the Treaty of Verela in 1790 and all borders left as they were. Further complications ensued with the French Revolution and then the death of Joseph II in February 1790. His brother and successor, Leopold, had no interest in pursuing the war and signed a separate peace with Turkey.

This Russo-Turkish war ended with the Treaty of Jassy in December 1791, by which Turkey accepted Russia's annexation of the Crimea and conceded Odessa and other Black Sea territories. Catherine's Russia could now become a naval power on the Black Sea.

In May 1791, revolution broke out in Poland. After forewarning Prussia and Austria of her intentions, Catherine sent in troops to crush the revolt in May 1792. The following January the three powers agreed on the Second Partition of Poland, but another revolt in 1794 provoked a further reaction from Catherine and Russian troops massacred over 20,000 Polish citizens. In 1795, the Third Partition was agreed.

On 25 November 1795, King Stanislas-Augustus abdicated. Poland had ceased to exist.

In 1783, the architect Yegorovich Starov had begun constructing the Tauride Palace in St Petersburg for Gregory Potemkin. On 28 April 1791, Potemkin staged an evening of entertainment there on a scale so elaborate that nothing like it had been seen before in Russia. The three thousand guests had already assembled when Catherine arrived, to be greeted by Potemkin wearing a scarlet tailcoat, whose solid gold buttons each encased a large diamond, and a diamond-ornamented cloak. His hat contained so many jewels that it was too heavy to wear and was carried on a cushion by a lackey.

Entertainments followed in which Catherine's grandsons Alexander and Constantine took part. As Potemkin led the empress on a tour of the palace, different performances were given in each room – dancing, poetry, choirs singing, a French comedy. Potemkin took her into the Winter Garden. He was jealous of Catherine's latest young lover, Platon Zubov (the only one he did not personally choose), but when he mentioned this rival for her affections the empress remained silent. She remained until two o'clock in the morning and both shed tears as she said goodbye.

Less than six months later, Potemkin was dead. He had been ill, probably from bronchial pneumonia, when he left Tsarskoe Selo in July but he refused to take any medicine. He died in a field on the road to Nikolaev, inland from the Black Sea, on 5 October 1791, covered with a silk dressing gown sent to him by Catherine. He was just fifty-two.

A courier reached the desperately worried empress in the Winter Palace a week later. Catherine collapsed, distraught. Days later her secretary reported 'tears' and 'tears again'.[24]

After Potemkin's death, Catherine's own health deteriorated. She gained weight, while rheumatism and ulcers on her legs restricted her mobility. She was sixty-two and began to feel her age. News that Louis XVI of France had met his end on the guillotine further depressed her.

One of Catherine's main concerns was the succession. She was determined that Paul would be by-passed in favour of his eldest son, but to do this she needed to find Alexander a wife. The daughters of Charles, Margrave of Baden seemed promising, so Catherine invited them to St Petersburg. Fifteen-year-old Alexander chose pretty fourteen-year-old Louise, who had blue eyes, fair hair and an 'indescribable grace' according to Countess Golovina. Louise for her part thought Alexander 'rather handsome'.[25]

The couple were married on 9 November 1793 after Louise had converted to Orthodoxy as Grand Duchess Elizabeth Alexeievna.

In 1795 the process was repeated for sixteen-year-old Grand Duke Constantine, when Hereditary Prince Francis of Saxe-Coburg-Saalfeld was commanded to send his eldest daughters – Sophie, Antoinette and Juliane – to St Petersburg. Fair-skinned, auburn-haired Juliane, described as pretty, vivacious and friendly, was certainly considered by the empress to be the best choice for her grandson. After only six days' acquaintance the grand duke was ordered to choose a bride. Constantine said that if he had to marry then he would take fourteen-year-old Juliane, because he liked her sense of humour. Countess Golovina thought that he did not want to marry at all. The wedding took place on 15 February 1796, after Juliane's conversion to Orthodoxy as Grand Duchess Anna Feodorovna.[26]

Catherine had ruled Russia for thirty-five years. Now there was one final humiliation.

She wanted a marriage between her eldest granddaughter, thirteen-year-old Grand Duchess Alexandra Pavlovna, and the young King Gustavus IV Adolphus of Sweden, eldest son of the late Gustav III. Catherine believed that such a union would decrease the hostility between Sweden and Russia while securing Russia's position on the upper Baltic; it would also generate a huge subsidy for the Swedish treasury. First, however, the king's engagement to Princess Louise of Mecklenburg-Schwerin had to be broken, which Catherine achieved by 'blandishments, veiled threats and multiple intrigues'.[27]

She then invited the as yet uncrowned seventeen-year-old king and his uncle on a private visit. They arrived incognito as Count Haga and Count Vasa on 15 August. Many entertainments were staged in their honour, and Count Haga was given every opportunity to be alone with Alexandra. One evening after dinner in the Tauride Palace he told the empress that he would like to marry her granddaughter.

The formal betrothal was arranged for 11 September 1796. There was just one problem: Gustavus insisted that Alexandra become a Lutheran. Catherine insisted that her granddaughter remain Orthodox, especially as she would be providing large subsidies to Sweden. The clause was entered into the marriage contract but Gustavus said the matter was still under discussion. Finally, under pressure from his uncle, he agreed to amend the contract in his own hand. The details were left to the current adjutant-general, Platon Zubov.

When the dignitaries gathered for the signing, they found the king had removed the clause for further discussion with Catherine. When pressed, he refused to go beyond an oral assurance that Alexandra would be able to practise her faith. Confident that he meant that Alexandra would be allowed to remain Orthodox, Catherine assembled the family and the court in the Winter Palace for the formal betrothal ceremony.

The empress sat on her throne with Alexandra standing beside her, but three hours later there was still no sign of the Swedish king. Finally, Zubov was handed a message. Gustavus had changed his mind again. He would put nothing in writing while Catherine's clause remained in the contract. The marriage was off.

Catherine rose, her speech unintelligible due to what some thought was a mild stroke. A few minutes later she recovered, announced that the king was unwell and that consequently the ceremony was postponed. Shaken, she left on the arm of her grandson Alexander.

On 5 November, Catherine rose at six o'clock as usual, drank some coffee, wrote for a while and then disappeared into her water closet.

Some time later, when she had not emerged, her valet tried the door. It was partially jammed. After fetching the empress's maid, the door was forced open and they found Catherine lying on the floor against the door, her eyes closed, her face purple. When the valet tried to move her, she uttered a low groan and sank into a coma. With the help of other servants, the empress was carried with difficulty into her bedroom where, unable to lift her up onto the bed, they placed her on a mattress on the floor. She was unable to speak.

The doctor was summoned and a messenger was sent to inform Grand Duke Paul. It was thought that the empress had suffered a stroke.

Paul and Maria arrived to find their sons Alexander and Constantine already present with their wives. Catherine lay on the mattress surrounded by tearful retainers. The vigil lasted all night, everyone wondering whether Catherine would recover. If she did, would she disinherit Paul in favour of Alexander?

Paul's retainers began to arrive, wearing Prussian uniforms. Alexander also went to change. His wife Elizabeth was disgusted. 'His mother still breathed and the emperor [Paul] had nothing better to do than make his sons put on uniforms,' she wrote later. 'The pettiness!'[28]

By dawn there was no more hope. Paul ordered an accession manifesto to be drafted and his mother's papers to be sorted and sealed under the supervision of Alexander and Constantine. The study door was then to be locked and the key given to Paul. No document disinheriting him was discovered, much to his relief. He was believed to have been shown an unsigned letter from Maria agreeing with Catherine that Paul should be disinherited, plus a decree from Catherine changing the succession. These were torn into small pieces by one of his staff.

By five o'clock that evening, the end was near. Surrounded by her family and loyal retainers, the empress was given the last rites.

At 9.45 p.m. on 6 November, having never regained consciousness, Catherine died.

By her own calculation in 1779, she had built 144 cities, won 78 victories, concluded 30 treaties and issued 123 edicts to improve the lot of the people. This list was lengthened further by the time of her death.[29] Although she never realised her dream of an empire based on Constantinople, she incorporated the Crimea and the Caucasus as protectorates, gained parts of what had been Poland and Lithuania, and added large swathes of Turkey to her territories. The army and navy were doubled.

She had truly become Catherine the Great.

7

Murder in the Castle

Paul and Maria, King Charles's 4x Great-grandparents

With the accession of Emperor Paul, everything changed.

On 7 November 1796, the emperor and his elder sons appeared in the Guards' new Prussian unform. In his accession manifesto Paul proclaimed that he had ascended 'the throne of our forefathers, which we inherited', laying the stress very much on the word father.

It was no secret that Paul hated his mother, this hostility fuelled by the suspicious death of the father he never really knew but whose memory he worshipped. Determined that the unfortunate Peter should not be forgotten, one of his first acts was to order the exhumation of his body from the Alexander Nevsky Monastery. Peter III had not been embalmed, and when the coffin was opened it contained only his bones and the remnants of his clothes. Claiming that his mother had been too busy to arrange his father's last rites, Paul decided to remedy the situation. He ordered that Peter and Catherine would be buried together.

In early December, the new emperor walked behind Peter's coffin in procession down the Nevsky Prospekt followed by his family, members of the court and the diplomatic corps. Eighty-year-old Alexei Orlov (Scarface), the sole survivor from the events at Ropsha in 1762 and the man Paul blamed for his father's death, was ordered to carry Peter's crown on a cushion behind the casket. At the Winter Palace, Peter's coffin was placed beside Catherine's for a lying-in-state. Grand Duke Alexander's wife Elizabeth was shocked by the emperor's lack of grief for his mother; he acted as if it was his father who had just died. A few days later they were buried side by side in the Cathedral of SS Peter and Paul, where their sarcophagi can still be seen.

Paul was also critical of what he saw as Catherine's luxurious and corrupt court. All Catherine's associates were dismissed or banished; contacts with the west were closed. Platon Zubov, Catherine's last favourite, was dismissed and retired to his palace in Courland. The Tauride Palace was turned into a barracks for the Horse Guards and the hated Potemkin's tomb in Kherson was vandalised, his bones scattered. Thousands of Polish prisoners were released and the rehabilitated King Stanislas-Augustus received an invitation to Paul's coronation. Catherine's son by Orlov, Alexei Bobrinsky, was created a count. In short, Paul undid everything he could of his mother's reign.

The newborn Paul had been prevented from bonding with Catherine when, soon after his birth, Empress Elizabeth swept him away to her own rooms. It was forty days before mother and son saw each other again and then their meetings were infrequent. When Elizabeth's interest waned, Paul was cared for by a succession of nannies who showed no real tenderness for him.

When he was six his education was entrusted to Count Nikita Panin, who crammed into him mathematics, history and modern languages such as French and German. (Panin later became Catherine's advisor and confidant.) Metropolitan Platon of Moscow instructed Paul in religion, and he genuinely became pious.

Peter the Great's 1722 Act of Succession only specified that the worthiest successor should be nominated by the ruler; there was no requirement for a blood link.[1] Catherine had realised she would be under pressure to merely act as regent until her son came of age, and also that Paul was popular with the Russian people. She treated him with a mixture of affection and cold indifference, ensuring he was kept away from government business. When he begged to fight in the Turkish war of 1788 she refused. Paul grew up 'nervous, tense and suspicious', sensing danger in every corner and extremely sensitive to anything that felt like a slight.[2] Although Catherine was happy to spend thousands of roubles on a painting, she was miserly with her son.

The one happy thing in Paul's life was his marriage. Maria Feodorovna came from a happy family and she was determined to replicate that in her own life. At first this was not easy. Paul and Maria were forbidden by Catherine to see their elder sons, Alexander and Constantine, more than a few times a year; even then, she specified how long the meetings would last.

Yet the birth of Alexander in 1777 so delighted Catherine that she gave the young couple a piece of land along the Slavyanka River about 3 miles from Tsarskoe Selo. In the forest there, where Paul had once hunted, were two lodges called Krik and Krak. Gradually Paul and Maria began to build other houses on the site – the small wooden Pallust and the two-storey Dutch-style Marienthal, as well as a Chinese kiosk and some fake ruins.

In 1780, Catherine generously allowed the couple to borrow Charles Cameron to build them a new stone palace. The finished result, Pavlovsk, is still one of the loveliest in Russia.

While construction was underway, Paul and Maria left on a European grand tour that proved decisive in opening up their cultural tastes. Travelling as the Count and Countess of the North, they left St Petersburg in September 1781. While abroad, they took every opportunity to meet artists, craftsmen, sculptors, bronzesmiths and furniture makers from whom they commissioned works for Pavlovsk.

They went first via Poland to Vienna, where Maria had a joyful reunion with her family. Then they continued to Turin, Rome (where they acquired a large group of marbles), Venice and Florence.

In May 1782 they arrived at Versailles, where they made a grand entry at Europe's most glittering court. Maria wore 'magnificent jewels and a dress of silver brocade embroidered with pearls' with a skirt that measured 21 feet in circumference. Paul, whose French was excellent, made a superb impression. They got on well, with twenty-eight-year-old Louis XVI and twenty-seven-year-old Marie Antoinette, who organised a dizzying round of balls, banquets, opera and theatre performances, as well as visits to hospitals and prisons.[3]

All the while, letters flew back and forth between Paris and St Petersburg with instructions for interiors, gardens and furnishings for Pavlovsk, much to the dismay of Cameron, who was used to exercising full control over everything.

They left Paris with an abundance of gifts from the French monarchs. These included Gobelins tapestries, a magnificent set of Sèvres vases and a porcelain toilette set decorated in gold and enamel with more than sixty items displaying Maria Feodorovna's coat of arms, the latter commissioned by Marie Antoinette for her guest.

They travelled through the Loire Valley, where they saw some of the lovely castles, then on to Britanny. After visiting Belgium and Holland they spent a month with Maria's family at the Württemberg family's residences of Montbéliard (now in western France) and Etupes.

By the time they returned to Russia in early November, the foundation stone of Pavlovsk was laid and building had begun.

Cameron had designed a three-storey Palladian villa crowned with a dome and decorated with columns, linked to two wings by semicircular open galleries enclosing a large, open piazza in front of the building. He worked on the construction from 1782 to 1796 and was followed by the Italian Vincenzo Brenna. Later work was undertaken by Giacomo Quarenghi, Andrei Voronikhin and Carlo Rossi.

On their return from Europe, Catherine gave Paul the magnificently isolated palace of Gatchina, 30 miles south-west of St Petersburg. Originally built for Gregory Orlov, it looked like a barracks with towers, battlements, high walls, octagonal towers and a moat. Imposing iron gates admitted, or excluded, visitors. Paul ran it like a Prussian military encampment but he also built a school, hospital, churches and even glass and china factories.

Maria furnished the state apartments with exquisite taste and the galleries housed the great art collections – enormous Chinese vases of porcelain and jade and, in the Chesmi Gallery, magnificent tapestries commemorating victory over the Turks in 1768. There were statues from Italy and sixteen sets of furniture from Paris. Outside, formal gardens were created and the terrace looked out across the large park and the islands in the lake. There were grottoes, summerhouses, a river and a boathouse. In the private garden there was a secret exit accessed behind the panelling of one of Gatchina's nine hundred rooms. Other hidden staircases led to underground dungeons, and a long tunnel led from the palace to the Silver Lake.

While Paul and his troops strutted around at Gatchina, Maria's domain was Pavlovsk, where she collected fine art and indulged her passion for gardens and flowers. Maria was a talented artist who drew, painted, embroidered and created objects in amber and ivory which she often presented as gifts. Some of her work was unfortunately lost during the Second World War.

By the time Paul came to the throne the couple had a growing family and there was no shortage of heirs. Alexander and Constantine were followed by Alexandra (whose betrothal to the King of Sweden had gone so spectacularly wrong) in 1783, then Elena (1784), Maria (1786), Catherine (1788), Olga (1792–95), Anna (1795) and Nicholas (1796). Two years later Michael completed the family. Catherine the Great attended the births and loved to receive drawings of the children from Maria.

After his mother's funeral, Paul announced that his coronation would take place on Easter Day, 5 April 1797. In contrast with Catherine's crowning, which had 'glorified Russian tradition', this was to be an event filled with Prussian military ceremonial. 'Everything [in Moscow] was according to the German style to please the taste of the new Tsar,' wrote a contemporary. When Paul went to the altar to take communion he strode up like a soldier, with a sabre still hanging at his side.[4]

In 1797 Paul set out the law of succession, so that Russia would never be without an heir. From now on, the throne would pass only through the male line of the imperial family in strict order of primogeniture. In the unlikely event that the male line failed, 'the succession would revert to a male of the female line'. If there was a female ruler, her husband would not be entitled to become sovereign. Candidates were precluded from inheriting by illegitimacy, morganatic marriage (an unequal union) or not belonging to the Orthodox faith. Furthermore, the grand dukes were barred from marrying Russian nobles or commoners (although as junior branches of the family became more prolific in the nineteenth century these marriages increased).[5] Paul also decreed that a dowager empress should always have precedence over the reigning empress.

He set up a department of appanages (estates), which set out the incomes of the family according to the rules of succession and blood relationships. The heir was known as the tsarevich. He and the sovereign's other sons and daughters were addressed as imperial highness. This title also applied to grandsons, great-grandsons, granddaughters and great-granddaughters of the emperor. After that, male descendants were princes of the imperial blood with the title of highness, while females used the title of their father or husband.[6] There were also edicts about who could wear the imperial Orders and when. All this was enshrined in law.

A new military manual based on the Prussian model was issued and the uniforms introduced by Potemkin were thrown out. Only Prussian uniforms were to be worn, which was apparent in the daily military parade, led by Paul strutting along in high boots and Prussian uniform. This caused a lot of resentment.

In 1797 alone, Paul issued 48,000 separate orders and reversed many of his mother's decisions. He restored compulsory state service for the nobility, reduced their local representation and reintroduced corporal punishment and confiscation of their property. He decreed that peasants were not to work on their lords' lands for more than three days a week. Sunday was to be a day of rest. This was unpopular with the nobles.

Everything French was now banned, especially the frockcoat, and this really annoyed the upper classes. In 1800 Paul banned the importation of books and music, and forbade the use of revolutionary terms such as 'citizen' and 'society'. Military discipline was ruthlessly enforced in every walk of life. He reinstated the old Muscovite custom, abolished by Peter the Great, by which people should prostrate themselves before him. He ordered that when passing an imperial palace or seeing the emperor or any member of his family, people must alight from their carriages and bow. Ladies were forced to curtsey to the emperor in the street, even if it meant dragging their fine clothes through the mud.

Paul was 'obsessive, volatile and prone to violent, irrational rages'. He once told the Swedish ambassador that 'in Russia only the man with whom I am speaking is important and only while I am speaking with him'.[7]

As a child Paul had been fascinated by the stories of knights. To the bafflement of his staff, he financed the Catholic Order of the Knights of St John of Malta, allowing them to re-establish their Grand Priory in areas which had been taken from Poland by Catherine the Great. This went against the championship of Orthodoxy that the Romanovs had always epitomised. In November 1797, Alexander and Constantine became knights of the Order in a convention in St Petersburg overseen by the emperor.

Paul was horrified by Napoleon's occupation of Malta in 1798. He saw himself as the Order's saviour and aspired to reestablish its former glory. When the grand master surrendered to Napoleon, Paul accused him of cowardice and at the end of the year accepted the invitation to become grand master himself. Determined to oppose Napoleon and include Russian knights in the Order, he opened a priory and even had himself painted wearing the Order's red and gold regalia in 1800.

Paul dreamed of liberating Malta from the French, so he joined the second anti-French coalition of Austria, Britain and Naples. He also entered into an alliance with Turkey in 1798 to stop France's expansion in the eastern Mediterranean, which threatened Russia's growing Black Sea trade. Together they drove the French from the Ionian Islands, which were then occupied by Russia.

He also wanted the legitimate rulers restored in Italy but, although his forces performed well in the Italian campaign, Paul withdrew from the coalition when he found that Austria was more intent on taking Italian territory than restoring the rightful rulers.

In November 1799, Napoleon Bonaparte seized power in France. This caused Paul to consider negotiating with what he considered an anti-revolutionary French government, but his terms (the restoration of pre-war governments in Italy, Germany and Malta) were unacceptable. Britain had occupied Malta in 1800 and now refused to return it to the Order of the Knights of St John. Britain supported Austria, so relations between Britain and Russia deteriorated.

However, many of the Russian nobility favoured a pro-British policy and their opposition was intensified by Paul's irrational behaviour and the danger that his erratic policies could bring. A plan to send Russian troops to challenge the British in India aroused fears that Britain would attack St Petersburg in retaliation.

In 1799, Paul and Maria's daughter Elena married Grand Duke Frederick Ludwig of Mecklenburg-Schwerin.[8] Also in that year the unfortunate Grand Duchess Alexandra, who had been so humiliated by the King of Sweden, married. Her husband was Archduke Joseph, son of the Emperor of Austria, but there was to be no happy ending. After an unhappy marriage, Alexandra died in childbirth aged seventeen.

The birth of Paul's last child, Grand Duke Michael, in 1798 proved traumatic for Maria and the doctors advised the couple to cease marital relations. Paul had already formed a relationship with Catherine Nelidova, one of the empress's ladies-in-waiting, which although passionate was probably platonic. Maria sensibly became friends with her rival and together they were able to moderate some of Paul's irrational behaviour.

Then, in 1798, he distanced himself from both women when he became involved with Anna Lopukhina, a sixteen-year-old virgin with black hair and a bad figure, who was related to the first wife of Peter the Great. When Paul told Maria not to interfere in politics again, Tsarevich Alexander took his mother's side.

Anna Lopukhina resisted the emperor's advances, protesting that she was in love with Prince Paul Gagarin. Paul ordered them to be married immediately. Now known as Princess Gagarin, Anna was ill-treated by her husband and soon ceased to resist the emperor. Paul gave her a palace, changed the colour of the Guards' uniforms to her favourite scarlet and lifted the ban on the waltz because it was her favourite dance. She was the only woman on whom he conferred the Order of Malta.

Paranoid about security, in 1797 Paul commissioned a secure fortified residence in St Petersburg. It was built on the site of Empress's Elizabeth's Summer Palace, where Paul was born and which he demolished. The Michaelovsky Castle had a moat, five drawbridges, an inner courtyard which served as a parade ground, cannons and a chapel dedicated to the Archangel Michael. It also had secret staircases to enable him to escape from any perceived danger. Its walls were painted red like the robes of the Order of Malta and a portrait of Frederick the Great and prints of Guards uniforms hung in the emperor's bedroom.

Five thousand men were employed on the construction and, such was Paul's urgency, 'iron plates were heated and applied to the walls to dry the mortar more quickly'.[9]

It did him no good.

For some time, a conspiracy to overthrow Paul had been hatching. The original initiators were Vice Chancellor Count Nikita Panin (nephew of Catherine the Great's minister) and Admiral José Ribas.

Tsarevich Alexander was approached by Panin, who during a nervous meeting sounded him out about acting as regent with his father's agreement. Alexander did not actually commit to this scheme – but neither did he report it. Soon afterwards Panin was banished to his Moscow estate and Ribas, who was gravely ill, died. Others quickly stepped into the breach but nobody would act without the backing of Alexander.

Paul had already embarked on what was described by Prince Czartoryski as 'a reign of terror'. He was suspicious of everyone and everything. Everyone lived in fear, not knowing when they went to bed whether a knock on the door would reveal a policeman with a wagon to take them to Siberia. 'Paul was too fantastic and capricious,' Prince Czartoryski wrote in his memoirs. 'No one could ever rely on him.'[10]

Alexander and Constantine were terrified of their father. The least hint of anger would reduce them to trembling. Paul overburdened them with minor duties which carried no power, so they were left with no time for anything else.

By early 1800 the governor-general of St Petersburg, Count Peter von Pahlen, whose wife was head of Empress Maria's household, thought that enough was enough. He had been dismissed twice from his post (and reappointed twice) and now decided that Paul must be removed.

In around December 1800, Pahlen finally persuaded Alexander to agree to either rule Russia himself or be regent on the abdication of his father. Alexander agreed, providing that Pahlen promise that Paul's life would be spared.

Pahlen made a promise to Alexander that he knew was impossible to keep and then set about approaching others, including Empress Catherine's former lover Platon Zubov and his brothers Nikolai and Valerian. They recruited other associates. The unscrupulous Platon Zubov (whom Paul had first confirmed in his posts and then summarily dismissed) returned from his retirement in Courland with a vengeance. Altogether there were sixty-eight people involved, all from the highest levels of society.

Pahlen, known as the 'Professor of Cunning', hinted to Paul that his wife and elder sons were plotting against him. He then told Alexander that his father was planning 'to destroy him'.[11] He now had two hundred officers in the conspiracy, including many of Paul's adjutants.

Early in February 1801, Paul moved his family into the Michaelovsky Castle even though the walls were not yet dry. Maria, Alexander, Constantine and the latter's wives had their own suites of rooms. The younger children lived above Paul, while underneath him lived Anna Gagarin and the emperor's gentleman of the bedchamber, Count Ivan Kutaisov. Pahlen was in charge of security.

Count Alexei Arakcheev, co-commandant of St Petersburg and quartermaster-general, had been dismissed after covering up a theft. By another piece of cunning, Pahlen took over as president of the foreign collegium and postmaster after Count Feodor Rostopchin was conveniently banished to his estates. As postmaster, Pahlen had the power to open letters (even diplomatic correspondence), copy them, break codes and then reseal them, but he increasingly found himself in danger of betrayal. On several occasions when he had on his person incriminating documents the emperor asked to see what he was carrying. Luckily, he was able to fob him off with an excuse each time.

Then, on 7 March, Pahlen discovered that somebody had given a list of the conspirators to the emperor and that his own name was on it. When challenged, he told Paul that he was in on the plot, that he had a grip on it and knew exactly what was happening. There was nothing to fear. He then said that Maria, Alexander and Constantine were the leaders. Paul immediately began planning with Pahlen to launch a counter-coup to arrest them all.

Pahlen's next move was to reveal Paul's plans to Alexander. The conspirators had decided to act on 15 March (the Ides of March) but, with Paul now suspicious, Alexander proposed they move the date forward to 11 March when the Semenovsky Guards, his own regiment, would be on duty.

Yet Paul clearly knew more than he had told Pahlen. On 9 March, he secretly sent letters to Arakcheev and Rostopchin ordering them to return immediately to the capital to lead the counter-coup. Pahlen opened the post and took the letters to Paul, suggesting that they must be forgeries as he had not been informed about them. Paul assured him they were genuine. The following day the emperor accused Maria, Alexander and Constantine of treason. He placed his sons under house arrest and ordered them to retake the oath of allegiance in the palace chapel.

That evening, 10 March, Paul went upstairs to play with his younger children. After he had gone, someone asked three-year-old Michael 'what game he was playing'. 'Burying father,' he replied. He was quickly silenced.[12]

That night the Semenovsky Guards were on duty outside the palace. Inside, the Horse Guards, commanded by Colonel Nicholas Sablukov (who was not part of the conspiracy), had been dismissed by Paul after Pahlen told him they were Jacobins. Only two unarmed valets now guarded him. On Pahlen's advice, Paul also locked the door to Empress Maria's rooms.

After going downstairs to visit Anna Gagarin's apartment, Paul retired to bed.

Shortly after midnight, Pahlen led a group of men to surround the Michaelovsky Castle and prevent any chance of escape. When Arakcheev arrived in St Petersburg, he was denied entry through the city gates on Pahlen's orders and despatched back to his estate.

Meanwhile, Platon Zubov and General Count Leo Bennigsen took their squad round the back of the castle and through a postern gate.

From there Paul's adjutant Peter Argamakov guided them across the moat and towards the emperor's apartments. Only twelve men made it all the way, as some of the party became lost in the dark. At the emperor's antechamber they unsheathed their swords, but Paul's valet refused to open the door as it was after midnight. Argamakov protested that it was six in the morning and he would be in trouble with the emperor if he did not submit his report. The door was opened.

As the men burst in, Paul was awakened by the cry from his valet. He tried to escape but, on his own orders, the door leading to the empress's room was locked and he failed to reach the trapdoor under his desk which led to an escape tunnel.

Bennigsen and Zubov found the emperor's bed empty but still warm, so they knew he could not be far away. Peering around with their candles, they could find nothing. Then, by the sudden light of the moon, Bennigsen spotted Paul's bare feet showing beneath the bottom of a screen.

The armed men retrieved Paul, still wearing his nightclothes. Bennigsen informed him in French that Alexander was now emperor and had ordered his arrest, adding that he must abdicate. He also told the unfortunate man that his life was not in danger but he could not offer any protection if he resisted. As Paul protested, Zubov repeated his comrade's words in Russian.

Another group of officers, led by the Georgian Prince Iashvili, then burst into the bedroom and rushed toward the emperor, knocking him down together with the screen and the lamp.

The new men threw themselves at Paul, who struggled in the tumult. The decisive blow was given by Nikolai Zubov, who hit the emperor with a massive gold snuffbox which crushed his cheek and knocked his eye in. As Paul fell down, he may have hit his head on the corner of the desk.

Three men then fell upon him – Iashvili, Lieutenant Ivan Tatarinov and Captain Yakov Skariatin (according to one contemporary source, three officers Paul had previously beaten with a cane).[13] Someone took the emperor's sash, which was hanging over his bed, and managed to put it round his neck. With Nikolai's Zubov's French valet sitting on Paul's feet, they began to tighten it as Paul begged for mercy. Soon he lay still.

They dragged his body along by the sash, kicking it all the while, until Bennigsen reappeared. After ensuring that Paul was dead, he dumped his body on the bed.

Count Nikolai Zubov went to Alexander's room and announced that it was all finished. At first Alexander did not take in the meaning of those words, until he suddenly realised that Zubov had addressed him as Your Majesty. The new emperor was distraught, knowing that people would say he had murdered his father, whose life Pahlen had promised would be spared. He was filled with guilt and remorse.

Empress Maria was woken and told her husband had suffered a stroke. She insisted he had been murdered. Taking the example of Catherine I and Catherine II, she maintained that as she had already been crowned, she was now the reigning empress.

Constantine, when woken, refused to believe the news. He found Emperor Alexander sobbing, along with his wife Empress Elizabeth.

The troops refused to take the oath of allegiance to Alexander without seeing Paul's body, so Bennigsen let them in.

Meanwhile, Pahlen hurried Alexander to the Winter Palace. With him went Constantine, Pahlen and Zubov. Alexander asked Elizabeth to persuade his mother to join him but Maria refused to leave without seeing her husband's body. The guards refused to let her in.

Only when the body had been cleaned did Bennigsen allow her entry.

Four-year-old Grand Duke Nicholas remembered being woken by the mistress of the robes Countess Charlotte Lieven. 'The Semenovsky Guards were on duty and I was taken to Mother.' After Maria had seen the body and calmed down, she took all her children to the Winter Palace. Nicholas recalled Alexander sobbing as he threw himself in front of their mother and denied any involvement in the murder. 'I was glad when I was allowed to play with my wooden horses again,' Nicholas recalled.[14]

His own accession would be nearly as dramatic.

On 17 March, Paul's open coffin was placed on a catafalque in a hall of the Michaelovsky Castle. He had been dressed in military uniform and top boots with spurs, but the broad brim of his hat was pulled down to conceal his left eye and the marks on his temple. Mourners were not allowed to approach too close, so that the marks of strangulation would not be apparent.

On 23 March the funeral procession left the Michaelovsky Castle and proceeded down the Nevsky Prospekt and across the Neva to the SS Peter and Paul Fortress. Emperor Alexander I followed on foot, with his brother Constantine and his wife behind him. They were followed by ladies-in-waiting and maids-of-honour. Everyone wore deep mourning.

Inside the SS Peter & Paul Cathedral 'the catafalque, resembling an antique temple, was raised on fifteen steps'. The bier bore Paul's monogram and 'the canopy was surmounted by a large gilt imperial crown'. Two urns were placed at the balustrade's corners. At the foot of one was the Maltese Cross.[15] Later that day Paul was buried in the cathedral.

Every year until 1917, Russia's rulers attended a mass for Paul on the anniversary of his murder.[16]

8

'Tomorrow morning I shall be either Emperor or dead'

Nicholas I, Charles's 3x Great-grandfather

Paul and Maria's third son, Grand Duke Nicholas Pavlovich, was not expected to be emperor but a series of dramatic events brought him to the throne.

Nicholas was born at Tsarskoe Selo on 25 June 1796 and unlike his older brothers, who were whisked away by their grandmother Catherine the Great, he was raised by his parents. When he was just over four months old his father became emperor and appointed him a colonel in the Imperial Horse Guards. His first formal appearance at court came on 2 February 1798 at a ceremony celebrating the birth of his brother Michael.

Nicholas and Michael saw their mother Empress Maria for only a few minutes each day, hedged in by the demands of court etiquette. Their father played with the boys when time permitted and called them his 'little sheep'.[1]

Nicholas was raised by nannies and governesses but even they were from a military background. His Scottish nurse Jane Lyon had received ill-treatment at the hands of the Poles while in captivity in 1794 and never tired of recounting her experiences. Her stories may have influenced Nicholas's attitude to Poland in later life.

Then in March 1801 Nicholas's life changed when his father was murdered.

His eldest brother, now Emperor Alexander I, entrusted the overseeing of Nicholas and Michael's education to their mother the Dowager

Empress Maria. General Count Matvei Lamsdorff, who had been appointed their governor by Paul, was kept in his post.

Nicholas received a spartan education with 'cold rooms, frugal meals and frequent punishments'[2] and was forced to sleep on a military camp bed, a habit he maintained throughout his life. He learnt to ride, was fluent in German, English and French and 'studied the classics, economics, law and political science', although he did not enjoy academic studies. He wanted to become an army officer. Nicholas later recalled the feeling of terror instilled by Lamsdorff: 'Fear, and efforts to escape punishments, occupied my mind more than anything else.'[3]

Napoleon Bonaparte crowned himself emperor of France in 1804 and proceeded to conquer Europe. Russia joined a coalition against the French in 1805. Nicholas was not old enough to take part in the war, nor was he old enough 'to grasp the bitterness ... of defeat in 1807 and peace with France'.[4]

Maria, having been deprived of her two eldest sons, was determined that the younger children would be brought up in her own way. With few other close relatives, they formed an unusually united family with common interests. They could all play a musical instrument (Nicholas played the flute) and word games were popular. On rainy evenings there were poetry readings, charades and amateur theatricals. Nicholas, Michael and their elder sister Anna formed a club called the Triopathy, wearing special rings engraved with their motto, 'Firmness and Hope.' Empress Maria was given one as an honorary member.

Nicholas and Michael used tables and chairs to build fortresses and sometimes constructed fortifications out of earth in the palace grounds. Their games always ended in fights and tears.

In 1810, when Nicholas was fourteen, he and Michael were told to dress in 'civilian clothes and focus on their studies'.[5] Yet Nicholas would never be at home in society. Maria complained that at parties he and Michael refused to dance and stood in the corner looking bored. Nicholas preferred the parade ground.

The fragile peace with France did not last.

In 1812, Napoleon invaded Russia, which Nicholas saw as a new opportunity for glory for the Russian empire. Emperor Alexander departed for the army but, in another bitter blow, sixteen-year-old Nicholas was forbidden to go too. 'Holy Russia does not lack for defenders,' his mother told him. As the army drove Napoleon out of Russia and marched on Paris, Nicholas found consolation in his military studies.[6]

In February 1814 Nicholas and Michael were finally allowed to go to France, supervised by Lamsdorff. To Nicholas's disgust, he reached Paris when peace had already been signed so did not see any action.

On the way back to Russia the brothers visited various European courts. In Berlin, eighteen-year-old Nicholas was impressed by Prussian militarism. He was also enthralled by Princess Charlotte, the daughter of King Frederick William III, who was described by a contemporary as 'pretty, sentimental and a flirt'.[7] His mother and brother Alexander had already picked her out as a suitable bride.

Soon after Nicholas returned to Russia, Napoleon escaped from his exile on the island of Elba and raised a new army. In May 1815 Nicholas and Michael returned briefly to Europe but the following month Napoleon was defeated at Waterloo. Nicholas again passed through Berlin where he courted Princess Charlotte. On the Pfaueninsel – the Peacock Island – he proposed.

Before they could marry, Nicholas had to travel. Between May and September 1816 he toured the Russian provinces. He then spent four months in England, where he was received by the Prince Regent at Brighton Pavilion, met the Duke of Wellington and was a great hit with the ladies of London society.

On 9 June 1817, Princess Charlotte of Prussia arrived at the Russian border. Nicholas, wearing the green uniform of the Semenovsky Guards, was waiting with a mounted escort to greet her. The Russians were delighted by her grace and merriment.

Nicholas and Charlotte were betrothed in October and she was received into the Orthodox Church as Grand Duchess Alexandra Feodorovna.

On 1 July 1817, her nineteenth birthday, she and Nicholas were married in the Winter Palace. Catherine the Great had bequeathed the jewels to be worn by all Romanov brides. There was a diamond necklace, a triple row bracelet, an agraffe which fixed the bride's heavy mantle in place and a pair of enormous drop earrings like cherries, which were so heavy they were attached to gold hoops and hung over the ears. To these Empress Maria Feodorovna added a diadem with a beautiful pink diamond in the centre. The jewels were 'so heavy', the frail bride recalled, 'that I thought I'd die'.[8]

Alexandra (whom Nicholas called Mouffy and his mother called Alexandrine) spent her time learning Russian and the customs of her new country. She never completely mastered the language, as French was widely spoken at court and the imperial family often spoke German.

Meanwhile Nicholas continued in his role as head of the Corps of Engineers and commander of a Guards brigade. The twenty-one-year-old grand duke was devoted to duty and severe with himself and others. 'To tell the truth, absolutely no one liked him,' wrote the memoirist F. F. Vigel.[9] Yet when he and Mouffy were alone in their apartments, he was a tender and loving husband.

Nicholas and Alexandra set up home in the Anichkov Palace at the junction of the Nevsky Prospekt and the Fontanka Canal. In 1818 there was great rejoicing when Alexandra gave birth to the couple's first child. Grand Duke Alexander (Sasha) was born in the Kremlin on 17 April, 'as all the bells of Moscow were ringing to celebrate the Easter festival'.[10] This birthplace was not accidental. The Dowager Empress Maria had decided that the baby should be born there to stress the growing importance of Nicholas and his family.

A daughter, Maria, was born in 1819, but the following year Alexandra's pregnancy ended in the birth of a stillborn girl. To help her recover from a deep depression, Nicholas took her to Berlin, where they remained until the summer of 1821.[11] Olga was born in 1822.

They travelled to Berlin again in July 1824. At this point the emperor was afraid that the couple were thinking of leaving Russia for good, and in March 1825 he summoned them home. He gave Alexandra the Alexandria estate at Peterhof, which they called 'our favourite little corner of the earth'.[12] Another daughter, Alexandra, was born on 24 June 1825.

Nicholas and Alexandra's first eight years of married life passed happily, although her health was frail.

By this time, it was apparent that neither Emperor Alexander nor Grand Duke Constantine would have a legitimate heir. There was every possibility that Nicholas, or his son, would one day reign.

Although Alexander I and Elizabeth had a daughter, Maria, in 1799, she died the following year; a subsequent daughter called Elizabeth was born in 1806 and died in 1808. Both would have been ineligible to succeed according to Emperor Paul's law of succession, which required the emperor to have a male heir. Alexander also had two illegitimate daughters by his mistress Maria Naryshkin, although neither lived beyond adolescence.

On the accession of Alexander I, Constantine therefore became heir presumptive to the throne. In 1801, his wife Grand Duchess Anna Feodorovna, fed up with his brutal treatment, went to visit her family in Coburg and refused to return. There were no children from the marriage, although Constantine had an illegitimate son named Paul, born in 1808.

At a small family dinner in 1819, Emperor Alexander told Nicholas that he intended to abdicate at some future point.

Constantine's marriage was annulled on 20 March 1820 and in May he contracted a morganatic marriage with the Polish Countess Joanna Grudzinska. Two years later Constantine told Alexander that he had decided to renounce his rights to the Russian throne. In 1823 Alexander I signed a manifesto, drafted secretly by the Archbishop of Moscow, which ratified this decision and appointed as his successor his next brother, Grand Duke Nicholas. The manifesto was then deposited in the cathedral at Moscow, the Senate, the Council of State and the Synod, all of whose members were unaware of the contents of the sealed envelopes entrusted to them. This manifesto was never made public, nor was Nicholas *officially* informed. 'The emperor hinted about it to us, but we did not expand any more and we made every effort to avoid [the subject,]' wrote Nicholas.[13]

The problem was that when Emperor Paul issued his 1797 law of succession he also made it illegal for any reigning emperor to alter it. Only Constantine could designate his successor, and he would need to do it publicly. He did not do so.

In the autumn of 1825, Emperor Alexander took his wife south to Taganrog on the advice of doctors. Empress Elizabeth was suffering from tuberculosis. While there the emperor was persuaded to make an inspection tour of the southern provinces, but in the mild Crimean climate, with its cold nights, he became increasingly ill.

He returned to Taganrog and took to his bed with a fever.

In the early hours of 27 November, the military governor-general of St Petersburg, Count Miloradovich, arrived at the Winter Palace where a mass was being said for the emperor's recovery. He brought the news that on 19 November, more than a week earlier, Alexander I had died.[14]

Nicholas still had no idea that Constantine had *formally* renounced his rights to the throne. His first act was therefore to swear allegiance to Emperor Constantine I and order everyone else to follow suit. Nicholas knew he was unpopular with the Guards regiments, who had played a pivotal role in earlier succession crises. When informed by his mother about the letter of 1823 ratifying Constantine's renunciation, he panicked and denied all knowledge of it.

Meanwhile, in Warsaw where he was *de facto* viceroy, Constantine had learned of his brother's death two days earlier and insisted that Nicholas was now emperor. As Constantine refused to accept that he himself was emperor, he also refused to come to St Petersburg, formally abdicate and declare Nicholas his successor.

For two weeks there was an interregnum while Nicholas and Constantine batted the crown back and forth in letters carried between them by Grand Duke Michael. As their sister Anna, now the Princess of Orange, wrote to Constantine: 'It will perhaps be a unique example to see two brothers fighting over who will *not* have the crown!'[15]

The deadlock was broken on 12 December when Colonel Frederiks arrived from Taganrog. He brought letters indicating that a dangerous conspiracy had been discovered among young officers who were members of secret societies founded during the Napoleonic Wars, devoted to overthrowing the autocracy. An uprising involving officers from some of the greatest families in the empire was imminent.

At midnight on 13 December, Nicholas hastily issued his accession manifesto. 'Tomorrow morning I shall be either emperor or dead,' he said.

Nicholas's accession day was Monday 14 December 1825. According to Russian superstition, Monday was an unlucky day of the week. The new emperor was aware that there might be a revolt that day, but he did not want the taking of the oaths of allegiance to be preceded by arrests.

The atmosphere in St Petersburg was tense. From the early hours groups of soldiers in the streets were calling for Constantine, and by early afternoon rebels had congregated in Senate Square near the statue of Peter the Great. They declared allegiance to Constantine and demanded a constitution. The revolt was led by officers at the head of some 3,000 men, who were alarmed that Grand Duke Constantine had seemingly been overlooked. The men refused to take the oath of allegiance to Nicholas and the governor of St Petersburg was killed when he tried to explain that Constantine had renounced the throne.

Nicholas had already arranged for his family to be moved to Tsarskoe Selo. They refused to leave and remained in the Winter Palace, where the children had already been taken from the Anichkov Palace.

At around midday, Nicholas rode out into Senate Square with loyal troops and announced an amnesty. It was to no avail. Grand Duke Michael was almost shot when he demanded the rebels' surrender.

Soon after 3.00 p.m., as darkness fell, Nicholas gave in to the pleas of his generals and ordered the artillery to open fire. Fifty-six people were killed.

The uprising, later known as the Decembrist revolt, was successfully put down. Nicholas punished 289 young men for their part in the conspiracy, interrogating many of them himself. Five men were hanged, which caused a shock in society as there had been no executions in Russia for over fifty years. Many more were imprisoned, sentenced to hard labour or sent off on the long trek to Siberia.

Although Nicholas regarded the affair as closed, the Romanov family from then on lived with an unsettling foreboding of new rebellions.[16]

On 25 July 1826, Emperor Nicholas I made his official entry into Moscow with his brother Michael and his eight-year-old heir, Alexander (Sasha), who acquitted himself admirably in the great review on 30 July.

The coronation took place in the Uspensky Sobor on 3 September. As was customary, Nicholas crowned himself. Maria Feodorovna was delighted when Constantine arrived to assist his brother, as he had done previously for Alexander. 'The coronation went very well and was extremely solemn,' the dowager empress wrote to her daughter Anna in the Netherlands. 'Constantine was sublime and earned the veneration of everybody for his fine noble conduct…'[17]

The violent start to his reign convinced Nicholas that he needed to enforce discipline and exercise vigilance. He regularly toured the provinces, where he dispensed frequent punishments and bestowed rewards. In 1826 he ordered Michael Speransky to head a committee drawing up a detailed survey of the empire. It was a land of strange contrasts. To the north-west was St Petersburg, and to the east lay the frozen wastes of Siberia, stretching up towards the Arctic. The gulf between rich and poor was tremendous.

Nicholas I looked like a man born to rule. He was tall and imposing, with a severe expression. He was also firm. 'The Emperor Nicholas ... desires to be obeyed, where others desire to be loved,' wrote the Marquis de Custine in 1839. He still kept to his old habit of sleeping on a military camp bed, which travelled everywhere with him. On his visit to Windsor Castle and Buckingham Palace in 1844, Queen Victoria's staff were astonished when his valets requested straw from the stables so that they could stuff his mattress.[18]

'During the first two decades of his reign, Nicholas's power was undiluted at home, respected abroad, and he was served by advisors he trusted.'[19] His reign was marked by territorial expansion, repression of dissent, economic stagnation, poor administrative policies and a corrupt bureaucracy.

Nicholas was hardworking, believing that he had to attend to everything himself, from the style of new uniforms to the design of churches in even remote parts of Russia. He ruled directly through His Majesty's Own Chancellery. In 1826 he created the notorious Third Section, headed by Alexander Benckendorff, charged with hunting down subversives and rooting out corruption in every corner of the empire. Letters were opened and read to keep abreast of any possible conspiracies and, later in the reign, even members of the imperial family were not exempt from this surveillance, although it was done without the emperor's knowledge.

Uniforms predominated. Officers from the elite Guards regiments appeared in the streets perfectly turned out, complete with epaulettes and weapons. Even the lowliest private soldier was forbidden to go out without such accoutrements. Cossacks galloped along the streets wielding '8-foot-long lances, pistols and sabres' while the Chevalier Guards and the Horse Guards wore their distinctive silver helmets 'surmounted by a shining double eagle'. The emperor loved nothing more than to hold a review of his troops on the Field of Mars, or in front of the Winter Palace, where crowds gathered to watch the stirring sight of immaculate rows of men lined up 'with pennants fluttering and lances shining in the sun'.[20] Even in the bitterest winter weather, the emperor refused to wear a cloak.

In May 1829, Nicholas travelled to Warsaw to be crowned King of Poland in what his brother Michael called 'a smaller version of the Moscow ceremony'.[21] At the Congress of Vienna in 1815 Poland had been established as a kingdom in personal union with Russia, comprising most of the former Grand Duchy of Warsaw and with Warsaw as its capital. Alexander I had granted Poland a liberal constitution and was named as king with his brother Constantine as viceroy. Although Poland 'preserved its own customs and laws',[22] it remained a Catholic country within an Orthodox empire. With nationalism high on the European agenda, Poland resented the link with Russia.

Sensing hostility in Poland, Constantine opposed the coronation. He thought the ceremony should be postponed 'until the re-opening of the promised Polish Diet could be announced'.[23]

The emperor's private life was happy. Christmas and the winter season, with its round of entertainments and balls, was usually spent in the aptly named Winter Palace. During carnival week (*Maslenitsa*), the emperor by custom attended the masquerade ball at which any decently dressed person, from whatever class of society, was welcome and he could be approached by masked young ladies. One young milliner, strolling on the arm of Nicholas, was heard to say, 'Oh, but how handsome you are!' to which came the emperor's reply, 'Ah, but if you could have seen me as I once was!'[24] In the last days of *Maslenitsa* the emperor and his court joined the traditional promenade in carriages, until the church bells tolled to signal the beginning of the Great Easter Fast and Nicholas and his family moved to the Anichkov Palace.

On the Thursday before Easter, Nicholas shepherded his children through the Palm Market in St Petersburg where toys, coloured paper flowers and brightly coloured eggs were sold.

Easter was the principal feast day in Russia. At midnight the imperial court gathered in the chapel for the Easter vigil. Afterwards all the things forbidden during Lent were served. On Easter Sunday the emperor and empress distributed coloured eggs of porcelain, malachite and jasper to the household and servants, giving everyone the traditional three kisses. Emperor Nicholas had to kiss not only the members of his large household but every visitor who called as well as any sentries he passed.

Following the cholera epidemic of 1831, the imperial family usually spent spring at the Alexander Palace at Tsarskoe Selo, built by Catherine the Great for Nicholas's brother Alexander. They returned from August until late autumn. Official receptions and festivities were held at the nearby Great Palace (from 1910 known as the Catherine Palace).

In the years following Nicholas's accession Empress Alexandra gave birth to Constantine in 1827, Nicholas in 1831 and Michael in 1832. At the Alexander Palace a slide was installed in one of the large halls, and on the Children's Island (specially set aside for their use) was a cottage where Maria, Olga and Alexandra learnt to cook. The children grew vegetables in the kitchen garden and the boys played in the toy fort near the White Tower – all very reminiscent of Queen Victoria's family at Osborne. In the park they played with their dogs, horses, donkeys and ponies. They had games of hide-and-seek or charades and visited the Chinese Theatre. The emperor was keen to project an image of a happy family life, but the children were also carefully educated to equip them for their future responsibilities.

Although his own tastes were modest, Nicholas surrounded his family with unbelievable luxury. On every fête day and at the birth of every child, for instance, he gave the empress a parure of magnificent jewels. Nevertheless, his court was renowned for its parade-ground atmosphere and at the Arsenal at Tsarskoe Selo he kept the large collection of arms which he had acquired since his youth. It eventually held more than five thousand rare items.

The family's happiest times were spent at Peterhof in the summer, well away from court life, where evenings were spent playing games, acting and making music. In the wooded Alexandria Park, lying east of the main Peterhof estate, Adam Menelaws built The Cottage, a pretty yellow-and-white neo-Gothic home with verandas, gables and balconies. The Alexandria motif – a wreath of white roses pierced with a sword, Nicholas and Alexandra's special emblem – appeared everywhere. Pretty wrought-iron porches stretched across the outside of the main bedroom, drawing room and small study. Glass doors opened onto the romantic wild park, and the Naval Study at the top of the house led out to a veranda with marvellous views over the Baltic. On one of the covered balconies the children learned fencing and played when it was raining outside. The rooms were small, giving the place an intimate and homely feel, but it was large enough for the sovereigns, their seven children and just two servants. By 1841 the family had outgrown it so extra rooms were added and outbuildings converted.

Lady Londonderry met the sovereigns in 1837. She described the empress as 'a tall, graceful figure, her face not very handsome, but her little head beautifully set and her expression pleasing and features regular, her hands and arms beautifully shaped and an air of imperial dignity and grace I never saw before'. The emperor she thought was 'not like his brother Alexander. He has neither the softness, the gentleness, nor the winning smile; he is taller and larger, a perfect colossus combining grace and beauty. His face is very handsome ... His countenance is severe, his eye like an eagle's and his smile like the sun breaking through a thundercloud; and on the whole, I think everyone must admit he is a singular and magnificent-looking being...'[25]

On 24 October 1828, the family were saddened by the death of the Dowager Empress Maria Feodorovna. She had never really recovered from the deaths of her husband Paul and son Alexander. Her detailed will left capital for the many charitable institutions she had founded, while Pavlovsk went to her youngest son, Grand Duke Michael.

Emperor Nicholas, meanwhile, was preparing for war.

Nicholas had already gone to war with Persia in 1826, adding the khanates of Erivan and Nakhichevan to his empire and securing the right to build a fleet on the Caspian Sea.

Then the Greeks rose against their Turkish overlords. Nicholas, who regarded the Sultan of Turkey as the legitimate ruler of the Balkans, was reluctant to encourage the Greeks in their bid for autonomy. The sultan rejected an offer of mediation by Russia, Britain and France and began an offensive in Greece, where the Christians were massacred. In October 1827 the allies defeated the Egyptian fleet (which had come to the aid of Turkey) at Navarino, and the following year the Greek republic was founded by insurgents.

In 1828, Nicholas declared war on Turkey. It proved a more costly (and horrific) venture than he had imagined, but in 1829 the sultan sued for peace. Under the Treaty of Adrianople, Turkey had to recognise Russia's territorial gains in the Caucasus and Georgia as well as the autonomy of Greece. Autonomy was also granted to Moldavia and Wallachia under Russian protection.

In 1830, a conference was held in London during which Russia, Britain and France agreed that Greece should be an independent monarchical state and that they would be its protecting powers. This would affect Nicholas's descendants in a way he could never have imagined.

In November 1830 a Warsaw brewery was set on fire. This was 'the signal to begin a revolt against Poland's Russian rulers'. The Poles were demanding 'observance of the 1815 constitution, a general amnesty, inclusion of a part of eastern Ukraine [former Polish territory], ... Lithuania and Belorussia into the Polish kingdom, and Nicholas's consent to the Polish occupation of Austrian Galicia'.[26] The emperor was severe with the Poles. In 1832 he abolished their parliament and army, imposing a greater degree of direct rule from St Petersburg as the process of Russification began. Universities were closed and older schoolchildren were forced to learn Russian. Belorussia and Ukraine received similar treatment.

All these problems caused Nicholas's regime in Russia to become more reactionary, dedicated to the suppression of new ideas. The emperor had no wish for his country to become part of western Europe. The slogan 'Orthodoxy, autocracy, nationality' was circulated among the schools by Sergei Uvarov, the minister for education. Nicholas dropped all Alexander I's plans for reform.

By the nineteenth century St Petersburg had become one of Europe's most dazzling cities. 'Nothing is more beautiful than this city of gold, on a horizon of silver, where the sky retains the paleness of dawn,' Théophile Gautier mused.[27] Grand buildings in various colours lined the wide boulevards and over sixty bridges linked the canals. The enormous semi-circular General Staff Building, with its two triumphal arches adorned with trophies, had been constructed along two sides of Winter Palace Square. In the square itself a 98-foot granite column commemorated the victory of Alexander I's army over Napoleon. Nicholas I sponsored the creation of public parks. Fashionable people promenaded every day along St Petersburg's main thoroughfare the Nevsky Prospekt, or along one of the River Neva's quays. The emperor and his family favoured the English Quay, where they strolled daily among their people. Two burly flunkies dressed in purple coats accompanied Empress Alexandra everywhere, carrying her purchases and opening doors.

Nicholas opened the first Russian railway line, from Tsarskoe Selo to St Petersburg, in 1835, with a short extension to Pavlovsk. A line from Moscow to St Petersburg was begun in 1842. It is said that arguments over the various proposed routes ended when Nicholas picked up a ruler and drew a straight line between the cities.

In December 1837, fire ravaged the Winter Palace. Nicholas was at the theatre when he received the message. He hurried to the scene and directed the firefighting, giving instructions that letters to him from his wife must be saved at all costs. Alexandra packed up her rooms, helped by ladies-in-waiting, until the heat became too much and Nicholas ordered her out. Much of the furniture and interior decoration was destroyed but many of the treasures were taken outside and left in the snow. It took three days to extinguish the flames. Thirty guardsmen were killed and the palace was left as a smoke-blackened shell.

Nicholas moved to the Anichkov Palace and ordered the immediate rebuilding to begin. It was to be finished in a year, he said. This almost impossible schedule was achieved, but the cost in lives among the 6,000 workers was immense.

The new Winter Palace of Nicholas I was said to have 1,050 rooms, 117 staircases and 1,786 windows. Behind 40-foot-high wooden doors inlaid with gold, the state rooms – St George's Hall, the White Hall, the Malachite Room and the Small Throne Room – were decorated with gold, silver, onyx, malachite, lapis lazuli and marble. Huge chandeliers were suspended from the ceilings and the light from thousands of candles was reflected in the mirrors and the parquet floors. The Nicholas Hall was 180 feet long, its gilded walls set off by two rows of colonnades. The rooms were filled with priceless paintings, *objets d'art*, gold and silver plate and richly carved furniture with gold inlay which luckily had been saved from the fire. It became the perfect setting for the Russian court, which by the end of the nineteenth century was the most magnificent in Europe. 'There was something still barbaric in its splendour,' wrote Prince Christopher of Greece. 'Its ceremonies were based on those of the old Byzantine Empire', more eastern than European.[28]

The New Hermitage was built as a museum where, admission free, the public could view Roman and Greek sculptures, rare artifacts and masterpieces painted by the best artists, collected since the days of Catherine the Great.

Nicholas also wanted a new Grand Palace in the Kremlin. The only way this could be done was to incorporate the Faceted Palace, parts of the Terem and several churches into the new building. A ceremonial staircase and a domed hall would connect the old to the new. The old Golden Palace 'was buried underneath St George's Hall', the new St Andrew's Hall (which served as the throne room) rose above the reserve palace, while a hall named for the Order of St Vladimir hid the boyars' court. The Grand Kremlin Palace was opened at Easter 1849, but many visitors considered it an eyesore. The Earl of Mayo thought it looked 'more like a Manchester cotton factory than the Imperial residence of the sacred Kremlin'. Nicholas, however, was delighted, and for the first time since 1797 a Russian ruler and his family spent Easter in Moscow.[29]

At Nicholas and Alexandra's silver wedding celebrations in 1842, Grand Duchesses Olga and Alexandra rode with their mother in medieval costume to attend the lavish tournament outside the Alexander Palace. '… a merry-go-round was arranged, with sixteen cavaliers and ladies, in medieval costumes, with sixteenth-century arms and armour. A cortège, accompanied by music and with heralds, took a ride along the avenues of the park on brightly decorated horses and lined [up] near the Alexander Palace for a tournament.' The scene was recorded in a painting by Horace Vernet, *Merry-Go-Round at Tsarskoe Selo*.[30]

The problem of suitable marriages for their daughters had already begun to exercise the sovereigns. Marriage with the Catholic monarchies of Spain, Austria and France proved difficult for religious reasons and suitable bachelor protestant princes were often hard to find, especially given the splendour to which the Russian grand duchesses were accustomed.

On 2 July 1839 Maria had married Maximilian de Beauharnais, 3rd Duke of Leuchtenberg, a grandson of both King Maximilian I of Bavaria and Empress Josephine of France. It was a love match. Maria did not want to live outside Russia, so the emperor built the Maryinsky Palace in St Petersburg for them, where their seven children grew up.

Alexandra married Prince Frederick William of Hesse-Cassel, the only son of Prince William of Hesse and Princess Charlotte of Denmark, on 28 January 1844 but shortly after the wedding Alexandra fell ill. Sources vary as to whether it was tuberculosis or measles but her condition gradually worsened. As she was in the early stages of pregnancy there was no chance of her leaving Russia to set up their new home in Copenhagen.

On 29 July, when seven months pregnant, Alexandra gave birth to a boy called William who lived for only a few hours. She died soon afterwards. Her parents and husband were devastated. 'This dear Angel was so excellent, so pure, her patience and resignation so exemplary and her end so sublime and edifying that we can hope that it goes well with her up above,' the broken-hearted emperor wrote to his sister Anna in the Netherlands. Nicholas had the rooms redecorated and placed a small chapel where her bed had stood, with an icon of St Alexandra. 'It was awful to look at Papa,' Grand Duchess Olga wrote in her memoirs, 'he has suddenly become an old man.'[31]

The lovely Olga married Prince Carl of Württemberg in 1846 and became queen on his accession in 1864, but there were no children from the marriage.

On 2 June 1844, Emperor Nicholas arrived at Buckingham Palace having travelled to Woolwich incognito as Count Orlov and stayed overnight at the Russian embassy.

A heavily pregnant Queen Victoria greeted him at the door of the Grand Hall. Nicholas was dressed in the red uniform of the Chevalier Guards with high boots and the Garter Star on his breast. He chivalrously kissed the queen's hand and she embraced him. Although he was already forty-eight, Victoria thought his appearance striking: 'Handsome, very tall and with a very good figure.' They sat talking and had lunch before the emperor left with Prince Albert to call on the Duke of Wellington and members of the royal family.

At dinner that night Victoria sat between the visiting King of Saxony and Emperor Nicholas, who was now in civilian evening dress. She noticed a slight defect in one eye, which gave him a rather terrifying stare. 'There is a strange expression in the emperor's eyes, one might almost say wild, which is not prepossessing,' she recorded. 'But his manners are excellent, dignified and simple. However, he gives me the impression of not being a happy man, and not being quite at his ease. He seldom smiles, and when he does, it is hardly an amiable expression. Altogether, to me, he is not fascinating and Albert agrees…'[32]

Nicholas made no secret of the fact that the purpose of his visit was political. Face-to-face meetings, he thought, were essential. During his stay the emperor had discussions with Prince Albert, Prime Minister Sir Robert Peel, the Duke of Wellington and the foreign secretary Lord Aberdeen.

He hoped Britain and Russia might become allies as they had a common rival in France, but his main concern was Turkey – the 'Sick Man of Europe' – and what would happen when the Ottoman empire crumbled. Nicholas had a high regard for England but was uneasy about the close relationship that was being forged with France, especially between the queen and King Louis Philippe. France's current good relations with Egypt and the Ottoman empire would affect his own plans for the expansion of Russian territory at the expense of Turkey.

It is alleged in Lord Malmesbury's memoirs that a secret memorandum was drawn up between the emperor, Wellington, Peel and Aberdeen, although it was never signed. Whether this is true or not, Turkey was certainly at the forefront of Nicholas's mind.

The problem was that he was unable to comprehend the parliamentary system, its debates and the constrictions under which English diplomats had to work. Most important of all, he did not understand the way English statesmen negotiated and, as an autocrat, he did not understand that the ministers were answerable to parliament. He took the statements of Peel and Aberdeen as statements of policy, and any unsigned memorandum would doubtless have been viewed as an agreement on the Eastern Question.[33]

This was to have consequences in the years to come.

In 1848, Hungary declared independence from the Habsburg empire and deposed the dynasty.

The new Austrian emperor, Franz Joseph, was desperate for Nicholas's aid. He was forced to agree that Russian troops under Russian generals would be 'free to act independently in Hungary' and in June 1849 Russian troops began marching in. Nicholas's intervention tipped the balance of troop numbers in favour of Austria and Russia. It took barely two months for the rebellion to be crushed and by the autumn it was all over. Yet as Nicholas ordered celebrations in St Petersburg, his officers concealed from him the 'shortcomings in the military establishment'.[34] These would become apparent when war broke out in the Crimea a few years later.

Nicholas and Alexandra had visited the Crimea in 1837, when they made plans for the development of Yalta. The beauty of the area around Oreanda delighted them. That estate, south-west of Yalta, was purchased by Alexander I in 1825. Nicholas gave it to his wife and decided to build a palace to harmonise with the beauty of the landscape. The result was the Neoclassical White Palace, built on the edge of a cliff above the Black Sea on the designs of Andrei Stackenschneider and completed in 1852. Nicholas visited the palace just once before the Crimean War broke out in 1853.

The emperor had been demanding the right to protect the Orthodox citizens of the sultan's empire since 1850. The Catholics (backed by France) and the Greeks (backed by Russia) were quarrelling over who should control the Holy Places which lay within the borders of the Ottoman empire. Sultan Abdul Mejid had previously respected the rights of the Orthodox Church, but in November 1852 Turkey granted the Catholics the right to hold the key to the Church of the Nativity, giving them free access to the building. The French were aggressively promoting their rights, determined to be seen as a Great Power again after years of suppression following the fall of Napoleon.

Nicholas, furious that Turkey had submitted to French pressure and believing that after his official visit to London in 1844 he had the British government's support, outlined his plans for Turkey to the British Minister Sir George Hamilton Seymour early in 1853. He stressed that Turkey was a very 'sick man' and it was imperative that Britain and Russia reach agreement before the Ottoman empire collapsed. Maybe Britain and Russia should carve up the Ottomans' European possessions between them. He would not, he insisted, allow the English to establish themselves in Constantinople but would have no objection if they occupied Egypt or Crete.

Seymour was alarmed at Nicholas's statement that Russia might have to temporarily occupy Constantinople, the link between Europe and Asia which was Britain's lifeline to India. He was also suspicious of proposals that Wallachia, Moldavia, Serbia and Bulgaria should be placed under Russian protection as independent princely states to save the Orthodox Christians there. The French were equally suspicious of Russian plans to increase their territory. Seymour immediately contacted the Foreign Office, who declined to enter into any kind of secret agreement with the emperor.

Nicholas was furious. In February he sent Prince Alexander Menshikov to Constantinople to force the sultan to restore Russia's rights to the Holy Places and demand the nullification of the ruling in favour of the Catholics. Britain attempted to mediate and arranged with the European powers a reasonable compromise, the Vienna note, the terms of which Nicholas accepted. The sultan rejected the proposals and asked for amendments.

The emperor refused to appease Turkey and resorted to military means. His troops occupied Turkey's Danubian principalities of Moldavia and Wallachia to ostensibly protect the Orthodox subjects there. Turkish nationalism was stirred and, with diplomatic means having failed, on 23 October the Ottoman empire declared war on Russia.

In November the Turkish fleet was destroyed at the battle of Sinope. Britain and France, fearing a collapse of the Ottoman empire (and in Britain's case, a Russian threat to shipping routes to India), sent their fleets to the Black Sea to protect the Ottoman transports.

Nicholas ignored their ultimatum to withdraw from the Danubian principalities and early in February he recalled his ministers from Paris and London. On 27 March 1854, fearful of Russian penetration into the Mediterranean, France declared war on Russia; England followed suit the next day.

To keep Austria out of the war, Nicholas agreed to their demand to withdraw from the principalities. An expeditionary force was then sent by the allies to the Crimea in the hope of capturing the naval base at Sevastopol, which would end Russian domination of the Black Sea.

As was feared after the intervention in Hungary in 1848, the Crimean War emphasised the Russian army's backwardness. Only a fraction of Russia's manpower could be sent to the Crimea because of the lack of a proper railway network in such a vast country. 'It took longer for supplies to reach the Crimea by land from Moscow than by sea from Paris and London.' Incompetence, disorganisation and corruption were rife.[35] Only 4 per cent of the infantry had rifles and there was only one musket for every two men. At the battles of Balaklava and Inkerman the Russians failed to drive the allies into the sea and, as winter began to bite, losses on both sides from disease and exposure to the bitter cold were appalling.

On 31 January 1855, Nicholas caught a cold at the wedding reception for Count Kleinmichel's daughter but ignored advice from his doctors and carried on as usual. On 13 February he reviewed the troops in temperatures of -23°C, but two days later he handed over some duties to his eldest son, Sasha.

The doctors insisted that there was nothing seriously wrong with the emperor, but his condition worsened and turned to pneumonia. On 17 February, a priest was summoned. Nicholas was told he had only hours to live.

Lying on his customary camp bed in the Winter Palace, he ordered the Guards to be assembled, ready to take the oath to his son as Alexander II. He had not forgotten the chaos of his own accession day.

As the long night wore on, he blessed each member of his family and asked for messages to be sent to his sons Nicholas and Michael, who were with the army in Sevastopol, where the main Russian naval base had been under siege for months. He felt ashamed that he had failed the army and asked for their forgiveness.

Nicholas died on 18 February 1855 with his devoted wife Mouffy by his side. In his dying moments he urged Sasha to 'serve Russia'.[36] To dispel any rumours of rivalry, Grand Duke Constantine Nicolaievich was the first to pledge loyalty to his elder brother Alexander II.

Emperor Nicholas had forbidden the doctors to issue bulletins about his health, so the sudden news of his death came as a shock and led to the rumour that he had committed suicide. Others said he had died of a broken heart caused by news of heavy defeats during the autumn, along with the carnage on all sides at Balaklava (although the Russians claimed it as a victory), or that he had been poisoned by a doctor with a German name. The official cause of death was pulmonic apoplexy.

'What an event! The man who destroyed peace in the whole of Europe is dead! Dead without seeing the end of the struggle which he, and he alone, began,' wrote Queen Sophie of the Netherlands to Lady Malet on 2 March (NS). The news had arrived in a dispatch to Dowager Queen Anna of the Netherlands, who thought it was a letter from her brother Nicholas but 'it was already the *nephew* announcing his father's death'.[37]

After Nicholas's death, Mouffy, now the dowager empress, remained at Tsarskoe Selo, seeing her family as much as she could. She also spent long periods in Nice, at that time under Italian rule. During her stay in 1857 she sponsored the building of a Russian Orthodox Church on the rue de Longchamp, which was completed in 1859. Dowager Empress Alexandra Feodorovna died in the Alexander Palace on 1 November 1860.

Nicholas I was Russia's last absolute monarch. It would be up to his son Alexander II to end the war, modernise his empire and raise Russia to the status of a major European power again.

Yet, as we shall see, it was Nicholas's second son, Grand Duke Constantine Nicolaievich, who forged a link with the navy that would carry on down through the generations to the House of Windsor today.

9

'I want shipwrights and sailors, not clerks'

Grand Duke Constantine Nicolaievich, Charles's 2x Great-grandfather

Nicholas I's second son was born in St Petersburg in 1827. 'Alexandrine [Mouffy] gave birth, very easily, to a baby boy this morning at 3.30,' Dowager Empress Maria Feodorovna told her daughter Anna, the Princess of Orange, on 9 September. 'He is strong, healthy and well nourished … The dear child was given the name of Constantine…' He was the first of the emperor's children to be born 'in the purple' (born to a reigning monarch) and was said to be proud of this fact. 'Master Constantine is a big, fat, handsome fellow, so quick and heavy that I cannot hold him,' Nicholas told Anna nine months later. 'He seems really to belong to the family as the only thing he hears with pleasure is the drum.'[1]

The following year, Constantine was described by his grandmother as the noisiest of all Nicholas's children. 'He has a loud voice and is always laughing, jumping, singing and talking in his own way.'[2] He had an English nanny, so spoke Russian and English when he was small but later learnt German and French as well.

The Princess of Orange, Constantine's aunt, sent him some uniforms from different troops of the Dutch army but his father had destined him to be Grand Admiral of the Russian navy, head of the naval department. Emperor Nicholas had a special fondness for Peter the Great's association with this service, which he felt had been neglected in recent years.

Constantine became boisterous as he grew, and the emperor saw the need for male discipline. The boy was naughty and often 'behaved like a stubborn bully, unrestrained and uncouth',[3] so in 1832, when Constantine was five, the emperor appointed a tutor.

Feodor Litke was a naval scientist and geographer of German descent 'who had recently completed a voyage to the northern Pacific'.[4] As assistants Litke had, among others, A. F. von Grimm, a German historian who also taught languages; a priest named Bashanov who gave religious instruction; and the poet Vassili Zhukovsky, head tutor to Constantine's brother Tsarevich Alexander. Constantine was educated with the son of his mother's friend Baroness Krüdener, and his education included carpentry and other practical elements in shipbuilding. In the large games room at the Winter Palace there was a scale model of a ship so big that Constantine and his brothers could climb up the mast. Here was a chance for the young grand duke to learn the art of seamanship on dry land.

He had a deep interest in history and once gave his sister Olga a wonderful guided tour of the Kremlin, where he got up to all sorts of mischief, trying on Peter the Great's boots and sitting on the throne. Litke had to stop him putting on the historic Crown of Monomakh, formerly used to crown Russia's rulers. His interest in history and music was shared with his sister Alexandra, to whom he remained close. He loved to read and had a talent for art.

After three hours of actual study each day, the remainder of his time was spent in gymnastic exercises, fencing, weapons instruction, walks and play. He kept a diary from the age of eight and took part in military drills with the *Corps des Cadets* in the ballroom of the Winter Palace with his younger brothers, Nicholas and Michael. In 1835 he was described rather unkindly by his father as 'small and ugly but very unusual',[5] quite unlike the other tall, handsome males in the family. Nevertheless, he was given a good education just in case any accident should befall his elder brother.

Constantine's naval education began in 1835 when he was given a small English yacht anchored near the Winter Palace. He ate, slept and had his lessons on board. In summer he sailed from Peterhof to Kronstadt, or to the shores of nearby Finland. The following summer a frigate was named after him and, escorted by Litke, he sailed to Reval (now Tallinn), Helsingfors (now Helsinki) and the Hanko Peninsula on the Baltic in a five-vessel squadron. The voyage took three weeks, encountering storms on the way.

At the age of ten he became a naval cadet, taking his place in the running of the ship, standing watch at night in all weathers. In 1837 and 1841 he sailed to Holland, where his aunt Anna was now queen.

His education continued, however, and there was a trip to Peter the Great's log hut in Zaandam.

In 1844 he took his final examinations. There were a huge number of written tests in languages, natural history, arithmetic and geography, naval science and shipbuilding. Most frightening of all was the cross-questioning held in front of his family and members of the court, with his father as chief examiner. Constantine 'acquitted himself with flying colours'.[6]

By the age of nineteen he had commanded his first ship, the *Ulysses*, in which he sailed around the Baltic, Turkey (where he met the sultan), France, Spain and England. In 1845 he became chairman of the Imperial Geographical Society. Although he had above-average administrative skills, he was allowed no further scope during his father's reign.

Later, Emperor Nicholas gave him a dacha called the Admiral's House, converted from the old Gothic guardhouse in the Alexandria Park at Peterhof. He chose as his badge an anchor within a circle of roses.

The grand duke had become close to his aunt Grand Duchess Elena Pavlovna, wife of the emperor's younger brother Grand Duke Michael. Constantine frequented her salon, where she expanded his knowledge of literature, music and science and encouraged his political idealism. Like Elena, Constantine became an active supporter of Pan-Slavism, unity of the Slavic peoples. She also introduced him to his future wife.

In 1846, Constantine accompanied his sister Olga to Germany. In Altenburg he met Elena's sixteen-year-old cousin Princess Alexandra of Saxe-Altenburg and was immediately captivated. 'I don't know what is happening to me,' he wrote. 'It's as if I am a completely new person. Just one thought moves me, just one image fills my eyes: forever and only she, my angel, my universe. I really do think I'm in love. But what can it mean? I've only known her just a few hours and already I'm up to my ears in passion!'[7] In his diary he drew the morning star, which would be his symbol for her in his diaries and letters for many years.

Princess Alexandra of Saxe-Altenburg was born on 8 July 1830, the youngest surviving daughter of Joseph, Duke of Saxe-Altenburg and his wife Amalie, a princess of Württemberg. Alexandra was spoilt by her father and, apart from music and the arts, was not particularly well educated. She was tall and slim, with luxuriant dark hair which curled into ringlets down her back, and eyes of a striking deep blue. Elegant but headstrong, people were instantly attracted to her.

Emperor Nicholas had already noticed Princess Alexandra (who was also related to the empress) and was suitably impressed. He allowed Constantine to propose on condition that they wait two years to marry, when the bride would be eighteen. In the meantime, she was sent to St Petersburg to learn Russian and prepare for her conversion to Orthodoxy.

Princess Alexandra made her state entry into St Petersburg on 30 September 1847, accompanied by her parents. She was present when twenty-year-old Constantine swore the oath of allegiance to his father in the Winter Palace chapel on his coming of age and afterwards at a public ceremony in St George's Hall before various dignitaries and representatives from the army. The following February she became a member of the Orthodox Church. A *ukaz* issued by the emperor proclaimed her change of name to 'the truly believing Grand Duchess Alexandra Josifovna'. The next day she and Constantine were formally betrothed.

The marriage took place in the Winter Palace on 30 August 1848. The couple spent their wedding night in the room where Catherine the Great died. On his marriage, Constantine was promoted to rear admiral, head of the Naval Cadet Corps and commander of the Life Guards' Finnish Regiment.

Alexandra soon became Emperor Nicholas's favourite daughter-in-law. The marriage began happily, and she grew to love the extravagance and magnificence of the Russian court. Her lack of tact and lapses of judgement were regarded rather as one would look upon a spoilt child. To the imperial family she was 'Sanny', while to Constantine she was his beloved *zhinka*, 'little lady'.[8]

Their marriage began harmoniously, a situation which unfortunately was not to last. Constantine and his wife were totally different characters. He was 'boisterous, liberal, widely read and politically moderate'. Sanny was 'conservative, shy and deeply religious'.[9]

As a wedding present the grand duke received the Marble Palace on the Neva Quay in St Petersburg, which was named after the thirty-two colours of marble used in its construction. Catherine the Great had given it to Gregory Orlov, then it passed back to the imperial family. Emperor Nicholas granted Constantine the palace for life, to be passed on to his heirs. Its interiors were renovated and altered and it soon became the scene of an active literary and music salon, where 'academics and representatives of the art world met'.[10] The grand duke's favourite spot was the library, three rooms containing gold monogrammed books. At the Marble Palace Constantine was autocratic and a despot, terrifying new servants by fixing them with a withering glance and screaming out their name. He (and many of the old servants) saw this as a joke, a rite of initiation. The victims, however, often fled in terror, never to return.

As a country home the couple had the large and magnificent palace of Strelna, surrounded by parkland on the Gulf of Finland.

In 1849, on the death of his uncle Grand Duke Michael, Constantine inherited Pavlovsk, although he and Sanny preferred to live in one of the dachas rather than the large palace. He compiled a very detailed record of the building's history to mark the palace's centenary in 1877. It became the definitive volume.

Pavlovsk became a fashionable place to spend the summer. All planned construction work had to be submitted for approval to the grand duke and he also vetted the lists of people wishing to rent dachas, crossing out the names of those he did not like. The grand duke and duchess continued the tradition of holding concerts in the hall built by Grand Duke Michael in 1838. The pleasure gardens surrounding it were named *Vokzal*, after the Vauxhall Gardens in London. Constantine and Sanny attended, always sitting in a side box rather than the central imperial box. Constantine, who was chairman of the Imperial Musical Society, played the cello (he was an excellent player) while Sanny accompanied him on the piano. She composed several pieces, among them a duet for the piano dedicated to her eldest son and a cantata memorialising her parents. Johann Strauss the younger was the conductor for several seasons. He composed the 'Alexandra Waltz' in Sanny's honour, and after a particularly happy holiday at their estate on the Gulf of Finland he composed a quadrille, 'The Terrace of Strelna'. The coming of the railway made the estate more accessible and the word *Vokzal* soon entered the Russian language as the word for station. Cynics said the railway was only built 'to connect the capital to the cabaret'.[11]

In 1849, a Hungarian rebellion against the Habsburgs broke out and Emperor Nicholas sent troops to aid the Austrian emperor Franz Joseph. Constantine participated in the campaign, fighting in the battles of Waitzen and Debrecen. At the former, forty of his men were killed and his forces took only two or three of the eight guns he had marked out as easy to capture. He was also badly injured by a cannon ball, which he kept and later used as a paperweight. Although he earned the Cross of St George for bravery, the grand duke never felt he had earned it. After the rebellion was crushed, he appealed directly to Franz Joseph for clemency for the Hungarians.

When Constantine returned to Russia he was to become a father.

In 1850 a son, Nicholas, was born, followed by Olga in 1851, Vera (1854), Constantine (1858) and Dmitri (1860). Unusually for those times, Grand Duke Constantine became closely involved in every detail of childbirth and infant care, writing to his elder brother to inform him that Sanny was progressing well after the birth of their second son. 'Little Kostya is also doing well, and lies in bed with his mother the whole day. Our Mama is invaluable, she is with us every day, and is pleased to stay for a long time. Yesterday she had dinner with me.'[12]

Although Constantine was intelligent, he had an uncontrollable temper. Small and undistinguished looking (by Romanov standards) with a forked beard, he wore glasses (or sometimes a monocle) which he suspended from a broad black ribbon. He never forgot that he was 'born in the purple' and seemed unwilling to subordinate himself to his elder brother, maintaining that Alexander had been born while their father was only a grand duke while he was born when their father was emperor. This had worried Emperor Nicholas, especially after the incident when as a young frigate captain Constantine arrested his brother when he visited his ship. The tsarevich remained a prisoner for several days until the emperor arrived to rescue him.

The death of Nicholas I in February 1855 brought Constantine's brother to the throne as Alexander II in the middle of the Crimean War.

'Perhaps the new Emperor, whose disposition is more weak, would wish for peace,' Queen Sophie of the Netherlands wrote to her friend Lady Malet, 'but he has opposite to himself the fanatic Russian party whose head is his brother Constantine, and to promote *his* chances he will give way to that party.' Constantine, as head of the navy, 'had sent resources to the Black Sea Fleet' and appealed to high society for donations so that the naval hospitals in the Crimea would be better organised and equipped.[13]

The new emperor did indeed wish for peace.

By the Treaty of Paris, signed in March 1856, Russia was forced to dismantle her Black Sea naval bases. The emperor's representative wanted the Black Sea 'closed to ships of all nations'. This had been urged by Constantine, who 'saw the possible danger of a strong Turkish fleet to the undefended southern shore of Russia'. In this, he was supported by the emperor.[14] The Black Sea was declared neutral territory open to all nations, with neither Russia nor Turkey stationing warships there. The Danubian principalities of Wallachia and Moldavia became independent from Russia as Romania. The Ottoman empire was proclaimed a European power, while Montenegro and Serbia soon became autonomous states.

Many people were unhappy about the peace, by which Russia lost her status as the strongest European power. Constantine was angry. The court began to blame him and was united in its resentment of the grand duke, who was seen as a bad influence on Alexander II.

Between 1857 and 1861 Constantine undertook several diplomatic missions on behalf of the emperor, journeying to Greece, Italy, Malta, Naples, Sardinia and France.

In May 1857, he met Queen Victoria and Prince Albert at Osborne House. This was an attempt to restore relations after the Crimean War. The grand duke had previously visited Osborne in 1847 and was now surprised at the changes he found, both on the estate and in the increased number of children in Victoria's family. (She had given birth to four since his previous visit.)

Constantine seemed happy to talk about the recent war, telling the queen that both of his *aides-de-camp* had been in the Crimea and that one was wounded. Rather less tactfully he then proceeded to give the details. He also discussed the size and calibre of the Russian guns, the navy and defences. Less welcome were his attempts to bargain with the British government in a bid to reverse the clause in the peace treaty which forbade a Russian fleet in the Black Sea. In a slightly surreal moment, Victoria, Albert and Constantine cruised on the royal yacht, flying the Russian standard and with Russian officers who had fought in the recent war.[15]

The Royal Navy was the best in the world. The grand duke returned from his visits to France and England full of ideas for resurrecting the Russian navy, only to find that no funds existed and the flow of materials to the shipyards had been interrupted.

Constantine was now Grand Admiral. He had a seat on the commission appointed to enquire into graft and embezzlement in the army, supervised the work of the committee revising the laws of censorship and was involved in the reformation of naval and military colleges.

Following the war, the Black Sea Fleet was non-existent and the Baltic Fleet had only 200 sailing ships, all poorly maintained. First of all, he had to thin out the administrative posts at the Admiralty and other naval establishments. 'I want shipwrights and sailors and not crowds of clerks,' he said angrily. He set about cutting the red tape of bureaucracy and getting down to the business of reform. 'Our first duty is to work hard and not expect any brilliant results,' he wrote, 'work not for our day but for the future...'[16]

After Constantine succeeded in carrying out major reforms in the navy, Grand Duchess Elena saw that he was just the man to play a leading role in another major project. At that time over 75 per cent of the population belonged to the peasantry, who lived in small, isolated villages and worked the land for six months of the year. When the snow lay thick on the ground, they huddled, starving, inside their log huts. According to the 1858 census, 37.7 per cent of Russians were serfs, half of whom were tied to individual landlords. With the help of Constantine's aide Alexander Golovnin, Elena recruited the grand duke to the cause of peasant emancipation.

Constantine promised to endorse the reform but stressed that, as the brother of the emperor, he would 'not step beyond his prescribed duty: blind obedience and discipline'. The grand duke and Elena continued to bring promising men to the emperor's notice, although Constantine protested that he was a sailor above all else and often said that he 'was sick of paperwork'.[17]

In 1857, Alexander appointed a secret committee under the chairmanship of Prince Alexei Orlov to look into the question of emancipation. Constantine was asked to become a member. The emperor hoped his brother's 'energy and temper would at least enliven the sessions'.[18] In February 1858, satisfied with the outcome, the emperor appointed a main committee for the peasant emancipation issue.

The reactionaries stopped at nothing to impede the progress of reform and after a year Constantine was so frustrated that he lost heart. By June the opposition was accusing him of usurping the emperor's authority. To let passions cool, in October 1858 Emperor Alexander sent him abroad until the following June. He set off on a cruise in foreign waters, ostensibly for reasons of health. His desire to be involved in state business had evaporated; all he wanted was his work at the Admiralty. There was no quarrel with his brother, as some people maintained, but his absence threw an additional burden on the emperor.

In 1859 the emperor persuaded Constantine to resume his work on emancipation. He was in constant communication with Grand Duchess Elena, seeing her at least twice a week, although all the hard work he was putting in often made him extremely tired. 'She told me at length about the intrigues of the retrograde opposition, [collectively] signed petitions, [Alexei] Orlov's memorandum against me and Lanskoy [Sergei Lanskoy, Minister of Interior], and about the difficulties it all creates for Sasha [the emperor],' he recorded in his diary on 22 October 1859. Constantine was reluctant to support Lanskoy, whom Elena thought was the only one to defend the peasants' interests. 'He does not want to step in for fear that others will speak badly of him to the emperor,' she wrote.[19]

In late 1860 Constantine became chairman of the main committee. This upset Sanny, who knew the anti-reformers hated her husband and feared he would attract the rage of the opposition. Nevertheless, he obtained the emperor's authorisation to meet with the reformers and hear their arguments.

The final session of the main committee took place on 26 January 1861. The emperor publicly thanked Constantine for speeding up the process.

On 19 February, after a special mass at the Winter Palace, the emperor signed the manifesto liberating the serfs. 'From this day forth a new history, a new era, has begun,' Constantine recorded in his diary. 'They had predicted revolution and other nonsense for today, but the people were as quiet and calm as ever.'[20]

When the emancipation became law Alexander was hailed as the 'Tsar Liberator' but there were dangerous undercurrents in the rejoicing. The peasants thought they were being made a gift – riots broke out when they realised they had received only half the land they had previously cultivated, and that they would also have to pay taxes and make redemption payments. The alliance between the dynasty and the nobility, on which the Romanovs had based their power, was destroyed.

It is clear that Constantine and Elena Pavlovna were prominent forces in the drive for emancipation. Although the final act favoured the landlords more than the reformers had originally hoped, some landowners never forgave Constantine for his support and sought to undermine him.

Spiritualism was all the rage in Russia and one of the chief enthusiasts was the mystical Sanny. She often claimed to have received visions, and said she had seen a white spectre twice before Nicholas I's death.

Emperor Alexander decided to try and contact his father, so Sanny arranged some séances. Constantine, although 'a well-known sceptic', attended along with the emperor, empress, dowager empress (Mouffy) and two ladies-in-waiting, one of whom recorded what happened.

The first séance was conducted by the medium David Home in the Great Hall at Peterhof. As the table levitated, Mouffy 'felt a hand touch the ruffles of her dress, grab her hand, and take her wedding ring off. Then that hand grabbed, shook, and pinched everyone present ... It took a bell out of the sovereign's hands ... This elicited cries of fear, terror and surprise.'

Altogether three seances were arranged at which Emperor Nicholas and his daughter Alexandra (Constantine's sister who died in childbirth in 1844) appeared. They responded to questions by 'knocking the letters of the alphabet' but the answers were 'inapposite and empty', recorded the lady-in-waiting Anna Tyutcheva.

Yet something strange happened. A clock in the Winter Palace which had three monkeys playing musical instruments had remained unwound for a long time. In the middle of the night the terrified Tyutcheva was woken by the sound of the instruments playing.[21]

In late 1861 Alexander II appointed Constantine as his viceroy in Poland, which at this time was partitioned between the occupying powers of Austria, Prussia and Russia (the latter part of which included the capital, Warsaw, as a nominally separate kingdom of the Russian empire).

Sanny, who was heavily pregnant, had longed for this appointment. She refused to let her husband go alone to a country seething with unrest and under martial law, where the streets of Warsaw were filled with blood. Many in Russia began to wonder if Constantine wanted to set himself up as king. It was widely believed that Sanny would not object to this. 'With all her will she wishes to be queen,' remarked the grand marshal of her court.[22]

In February 1862, Constantine and his family moved to Warsaw. His official residence was Warsaw Castle but as often as possible he preferred to be at the Lazienki estate, where he entertained lavishly. The Polish people, however, wanted nothing less than independence and the grand duke was seen as a symbol of the hated Russian oppressor. Two days after his arrival, he went to the opera. 'At the end of the second act I wanted to leave the theatre,' he recorded in his diary. 'I went into the Square and a man came out of the crowd and approached me. He pulled a pistol from his breast and fired. I ran back into the theatre – otherwise I'd have been dead now.'[23]

The assailant was a tailor's apprentice and nationalist terrorist called Yaroshinsky. He fired at point-blank range, but the bullet glanced off Constantine's shoulder blade and lodged in the chain of his monocle. Yaroshinsky had planned the attack for the previous day but was put off by the presence of the heavily pregnant grand duchess in the carriage. Constantine was treated at home in the palace, and as soon as he had recovered he publicly appealed for an end to the violence. From that time, he and his wife were always given a Cossack escort. Yaroshinsky was tried and hanged.

Alexander recalled Constantine to St Petersburg but he refused to leave.

In July 1862, Sanny gave birth to their youngest son. As a compliment to Poland they called him Vacslav. This caused problems because the Russians at the court in Warsaw refused to use this Polish name, preferring the Russian form, Viacheslav.

His christening was marked by a week-long carnival. Among those who came from St Petersburg was Constantine's nephew, the emperor's second son Grand Duke Alexander Alexandrovich, a 6-foot giant with a heavy build who completely lacked grace. His clumsy, awkward behaviour annoyed Constantine. 'See what a pig they have sent us from St Petersburg,' Constantine yelled as his nephew knocked over a decanter of red wine during a formal dinner. Alexander said nothing – but he would remember the remark years later and take his revenge.[24]

The viceroy appointed Marquis Wielopolsky as head of administration in the hopes of securing a peaceful solution. Constantine had some sympathy for the Poles. He ended martial law, reinstated Polish as the official language, reopened the Medical Academy, began a programme of liberalisation with Poles occupying administrative positions, and freed the peasants from all compulsory service to landowners. His attempts to introduce reforms were a failure, however. The Poles wanted nothing less than complete autonomy.

His rule was brought to a violent end after he called for a conscription levy, which would see hundreds of young men called up when they were known to belong to secret revolutionary circles. The plan was betrayed, leading the potential recruits to flee into the forest and attack Russian garrisons. Thus began the carnage of the Polish Mutiny, which raged for fifteen months.

The viceroy's family were by then living in a state of siege. Husband and wife barely saw each other and Constantine was exhausted by the effort of trying to maintain order. Queen Sophie of the Netherlands described him during that year as doing 'half the mischief, with his harsh, cruel way, his despotic manners…'[25]

In August 1863, the emperor recalled him to St Petersburg, where he concentrated on naval reform, especially on the need for a Black Sea Fleet. The following year the grand duke was appointed president of the Council of State in recognition of his service to Russia. He continued to support the emperor in his programme of constitutional reform.

Family problems now surfaced. From childhood Constantine's younger daughter, Grand Duchess Vera, had suffered from 'a nervous condition' (possibly epilepsy or St Vitus's Dance) which was little understood at the time.[26] She was now so traumatised by the violence in Warsaw that she became wild and difficult to manage. The doctors wanted to put her into an asylum but Constantine's childless sister Olga, now Queen of Württemberg, agreed to take in the nine-year-old and give her a home. Queen Olga loved Vera like a daughter and legally adopted her in 1870.

Gossip then indicated that Sanny was too close to some of her husband's adjutants. Some said that, 'being a powerful, passionate and highly sensual woman', she made no attempt to conceal her 'romantic intrigues'; others said that the couple's long, happy marriage had aroused envy and that the slander against Sanny was an effort to discredit Constantine.[27]

In 1868 he sent her to Lake Geneva for an extended stay. She arrived at the Hotel Monnet accompanied by Viacheslav and an entourage comprising her marshal of the court, two ladies-in-waiting, a physician, pianist, masseuse, hairdresser, keeper of the jewels and of the purse, two footmen, a woman of the wardrobe, four maids and an NCO for the young grand duke. In addition, there were the valets and maids for the ladies and gentlemen of the suite, plus a grand piano because Sanny refused to play on any other. As the wife of the Russian Grand Admiral, she refused to sail on any commercial vessel, demanding a military ship for her journeys around the various ports. When the Russian government refused, she appealed to Napoleon III, who put a military vessel at her disposal. In Genoa she was greeted by the whole fleet and a special pier had to be built for her to go ashore as she refused to board the small launch. According to the memoirs of Alexander Mossolov, she was something of a *grande dame* 'who regarded St Petersburg and most of its aristocrats as too modern and morally corrupt'.[28]

Cracks began to appear in the marriage. Constantine 'could no longer stand his wife's bigotry, her ecstatic mysticism, spiritualism and many imaginary diseases'.[29] He threw himself into his work, spending days at Kronstadt or on obligations that took him away from Russia, also finding consolation in music. He also began to have affairs.

A daughter named Maria or Marianne Condorusso (Condourioti or Contourini) was said to have been born in St Petersburg around 1870; the mother was not named. Maria was later sent to Greece where she became a lady-in-waiting to her half-sister, Constantine's elder daughter Grand Duchess Olga, who had married King George of the Hellenes in 1867. In around 1887, Maria married Count Dmitri Cosmatos di Lorenti. She left numerous descendants.[30]

He also took a regular mistress. Anna Kuznetsova was a student at the St Petersburg Conservatoire. Born in 1847, she was the illegitimate daughter of the actor Vasili Karatyguine and the ballerina Tatiana Kuznetsov and was twenty years younger than Constantine. She was said to have 'good looks which were not matched by her dance technique either, but she was effective in mime roles'.[31] The grand duke began pursuing her around 1868 and she resisted his advances for several years.

Constantine and Anna's first child, Sergei, was born around 1873 but sadly died before his first birthday. A daughter, Marina, was born in December 1875, followed by Anna in March 1878. Two sons completed the family – Ismail, born in a dacha at Pavlovsk in April 1879, and Lev, born at Oreanda in the Crimea in April 1883. Surviving letters from Constantine to Marina and Anna 'show utmost love and tenderness'.[32]

The grand duke had inherited the Neoclassical White Palace at Oreanda on the death of his mother in 1860. He loved the dramatic setting and is said to have planted a metal cross on the summit of his favourite mountain climb. In the summer he moved his second family into a villa nearby.

According to Jacques Ferrand, on 24 December 1880 Alexander II accepted his brother's request to grant hereditary nobility, the name Kniazev and the use of the patronymic Constantinovich to the grand duke's natural children. The emperor ordered a u*kaz* to be prepared but it was never issued because of his death.

In St Petersburg, Constantine bought a house for his second family at 18 English Prospekt (which later became the home of another famous ballerina, Mathilde Kschessinska). Sanny remained at Strelna.

Society was used to the grand dukes taking mistresses (especially actresses or ballerinas, who were regarded as little more than courtesans) but none flaunted the association as openly as Constantine. The situation gained Sanny much sympathy and she concentrated on charitable works and her children. Using her own fortune, she founded a children's hospital at Strelna in the grounds of the estate, as well as an agricultural and horticultural school that was free to qualified students. She also founded the St Petersburg Orphanage Council. Her reforms assisted hundreds of destitute children desperately in need of care.

The humiliation of her husband's affair must have been intense for such a proud woman, but Sanny always believed Constantine would come back to her. Nevertheless, when Ismail and Lev died from scarlet fever in 1885 Sanny sent a telegram of condolence to Constantine. In response he referred to her cruelly as his 'government issue wife up north'.[33]

As far back as 1861, Constantine had condemned his brother Alexander's extramarital affairs in his diary. Now Alexander refused his request for a divorce. However, he did nothing further to discourage his brother's open liaison. Alexander was by now starting a second family of his own with his 'wife before God', Princess Catherine Dolgoruky, by whom he had three surviving children and who would marry him soon after the death of his wife, Empress Marie Alexandrovna, in 1880.

Constantine and Sanny's children were offended by their father's affair and took their mother's side.

A scandal now broke upon the grand duke's family.

In 1874, as Sanny was preparing to leave for Vera's wedding to Duke Eugen of Württemberg in Germany, she discovered that three valuable diamonds were missing from the frame of her wedding icon.

An investigation began, led by city governor Feodor Trepov. Count Peter Shouvalov, head of the Third Department (the secret police), who ruled Russia as informal prime minister from 1866 (and who openly hated Grand Duke Constantine), also took part. The thief proved to be Sanny's eldest and favourite son, Nicholas. He had become involved with a twenty-six-year-old American adventuress called Hattie Blackford (who later changed her name to Fanny Lear), described by a contemporary as the most beautiful woman he ever saw.[34]

The couple met at a ball in 1872 and soon embarked on a torrid affair, which even survived a surprise encounter with Grand Duke Constantine after Nicholas sneaked her into his own bed at the Marble Palace, as well as Nicholas's posting to central Asia with his regiment. Nicholas lavished expensive gifts on Hattie. They travelled in Europe (always shadowed by the emperor's secret police), and he bought her an apartment in St Petersburg. Alexander II demanded discretion and the pair fled to Vienna, planning to marry. Constantine learned of this plan and hurried to Austria. The emperor, he told his son, was sympathetic, felt sorry for the couple and was giving them a second chance. 'But he orders that you are to return to Russia and remain there for several months, quietly, no attention, no scandal. There's been too much talk already.'[35] In the autumn of 1873 the couple returned to St Petersburg, where they were anything but discreet.

During the winter of 1874, Nicholas, Hattie and a cornet from the imperial army carried several bottles of champagne up to his mother's deserted rooms in the Marble Palace. During the evening (which in at least one version ended in a drunken orgy on his mother's bed), Nicholas broke off several large diamonds from the jewelled crown adorning the wedding icon given to his mother by Nicholas I.

When the theft was discovered, the servants were questioned without result. On hearing of it, Constantine told his brother the emperor. In the ensuing investigation, Grand Duke Nicholas's adjutant was arrested and under torture confessed that he had been ordered to pawn the diamonds. A search of Nicholas's rooms then revealed a pawnbroker's receipt.

Trepov visited Constantine on 24 April. He 'reported that the diamonds from the icon were found in a pawnshop!!!! And that they were pawned by my son's adjutant,' the incredulous grand duke wrote in his diary.[36]

Nicholas showed no remorse when confronted. It appeared that he had given his mistress a promissory note for 100,000 roubles and this was the only way he could pay her.

Hattie was arrested, then ordered to return the promissory note and leave Russia immediately. Alexander II had Nicholas declared insane, stripped of his rank of colonel and sent under strict surveillance to Oreanda. 'No matter how painful and hard, I can be the father of a sick and mad son,' Constantine wrote, 'but being the father of a criminal, publicly stunned by the blow, would make my future impossible.'[37] Many predicted Constantine's imminent fall. Instead, his enemy the reactionary Count Peter Shouvalov was sacked.

Meanwhile, at Oreanda Nicholas met Alexandra Demidov-Abaza, who became his mistress and followed him as he was moved from place to place. In 1876 Nicholas was removed to Orenburg in central Russia.

Sanny would never see her son again. His downfall led to her being stricter with her other sons, Constantine, Dmitri and Viacheslav. The younger Constantine was a talented poet and playwright, writing under the pseudonym of 'K.R.'. In 1884 he married Princess Elizabeth of Saxe-Altenburg (Mavra), a marriage pressed on him by his mother and which gave Sanny and Constantine nine grandchildren. Dmitri's passions were charity work and horses; he remained unmarried. Viacheslav (Slava) liked to draw ceremonies, especially funeral processions.

One evening in 1879, Sanny saw a ghostly white lady in a gallery at Pavlovsk. Terrified, she considered it a bad omen as the spectre always appeared to members of royal houses foretelling disaster. Her fears were realised when Slava was taken ill soon afterwards. He died on 15 February.

There had already been several attempts on the emperor's life. In early 1880, a terrorist disguised as a workman smuggled sticks of dynamite into the Winter Palace basement. Above the basement was the guardroom which, in turn, lay under the emperor's private dining room. On 5 February it was to be used for a family dinner. Before leaving the palace that evening, the terrorist lit a slow-burning fuse timed to explode while the imperial family were in the dining room two floors above.

Luckily, Empress Marie Alexandrovna's brother, the guest of honour, was late because his train was delayed. As the family walked towards the dining room half an hour behind schedule there was a loud explosion. Dust filled the air, the huge chandelier crashed down onto the table, the windows were shattered and the crumbling walls began falling in. Through a hole in the floor the wrecked guardroom could be seen, revealing many men were dead or injured.

Badly shaken, the imperial family realised that if the train had been on time they would all have been killed. 'We are reliving the Terror,' Constantine wrote, 'but with this difference: the Parisians during the revolution saw their enemies face to face. We neither see them nor do we know them.'[38]

Constantine, usually a frequent visitor to the Winter Palace, was away from St Petersburg when the bomb went off. 'There is always something to take [him] away from the palace whenever something happens,' wrote Mme Bogdanovich. A rumour began spreading through the court that Constantine was behind the terrorism.[39]

As president of the Council of State, Constantine was a prime mover in Alexander II's plans to prepare for a limited national assembly. Minister of the Interior Count Michael Loris-Melikov had presented the emperor with a draft manifesto for reform of the Council of State, paving the way for full enfranchisement in the future. The manifesto was brought to the Winter Palace for the emperor's signature.

The following day, Sunday 1 March 1881, Alexander II was due to review the troops at the riding school. He ignored entreaties not to go because of terrorist threats against his life; Sanny asked him to attend because her son Dmitri was to appear that day for the first time as imperial adjutant of his Guards sapper cavalry regiment, and Alexander did not want to disappoint the boy. Before leaving the palace, the emperor signed the manifesto. It was to be made public the following day.

As the emperor's carriage rattled along the Catherine Canal on his way back to the Winter Palace, a terrorist threw a bomb. It landed under the back axle, wounding some of the Cossack escort and killing a baker's boy in the crowd. Shaken but unhurt, Alexander alighted from his carriage but, instead of using another vehicle to speed back to the palace, insisted on seeing his would-be assassin and enquiring after the casualties.

As he stood there talking, a young man standing unnoticed by the canal railing calmly hurled another missile at Alexander's feet, mortally wounding him.

He was rushed back to the Winter Palace where he died later that afternoon. Constantine's hopes of constitutional reform died with him.

1. Russia's rulers from Tsar Michael to Empress Anna Ivanovna. (Author's collection)

2. Russia's rulers from Empress Elizabeth to Alexander III. (Author's collection)

3. The Cathedral of the Assumption, the Cathedral of the Epiphany and the Cathedral of the Ipatiev Monastery, Kostroma. It was here in 1613 that Michael Romanov was offered the crown. (Author's collection)

4. The exterior of the Romanov Boyars' House in Moscow. (Author's collection)

5. The dining room of the Romanov Boyars' House in Moscow, traditionally the birthplace of Tsar Michael. The building was restored during the reign of Alexander II and afterwards. It is now a museum. (Photo: G. Alexandrovna, Creative Commons)

6. The old regalia of the Russian empire. The Crown of Monomakh is at the extreme right at the front. Next to it is the replica made in 1682 for Peter I. (Photo: Coryne Hall)

7. The silver double throne of Ivan V and Peter I. The regent Sophia sat behind them whispering instructions through a curtain. (Photo: Coryne Hall)

Above: 8. The Kremlin from the bridge, around 1900. (Author's collection)

Right: 9. The Great Kremlin Palace, the Red Staircase and the Palace of Facets. (Photo: Coryne Hall)

Below right: 10. The gatehouse at Kolomenskoye, the summer palace of Tsar Alexei which was dismantled by Catherine the Great. (Photo: Coryne Hall)

11. Peter the Great, depicted in the simple clothes he would have worn in his incognito travels in Europe. He introduced western ideas into Russia and founded St Petersburg, Russia's 'Window on the West'. (Rijksmuseum)

12. Peterhof, built by Peter the Great to rival Versailles. (Photo: Coryne Hall)

13. Peter the Great's daughter Anna Petrovna. Although her sister Elizabeth became empress, it is from Anna, wife of Charles Frederick of Holstein-Gottorp, that King Charles descends. (National Museum in Warsaw)

Above left: 14. Catherine the Great, by Ivan Argunov. Born a minor German princess, she seized power from her husband Peter III after a coup. (National Museum in Warsaw)

Above right: 15. The interior of the SS Peter & Paul Cathedral, burial place of the Romanovs since Peter the Great. Behind the railings are the tombs of Catherine the Great and her murdered husband Peter III. (Photo: Coryne Hall)

16. The Uspensky Sobor in the Kremlin. All Russia's rulers from Ivan IV (the Terrible) to Nicholas II were crowned here. (Photo: Coryne Hall)

17. Emperor Paul. (National Museum in Warsaw)

18. Paul's wife Empress Maria Feodorovna. (Rijksmuseum)

19. Gatchina. Emperor Paul transformed the gigantic palace into a military parade ground and barracks. (Photo: Coryne Hall)

20. The Michaelovsky Castle, St Petersburg. Despite Emperor Paul's security precautions, he was murdered in his bedroom during a palace coup in 1801. (Author's collection)

Above left: 21. Emperor Nicholas I, whose watchwords were Orthodoxy, autocracy and nationality. (Private collection)

Above right: 22. Nicholas's wife Alexandra Feodorovna with their children Alexander (later Alexander II) and Maria, by George Dawe. In 1994 Elizabeth II and the Duke of Edinburgh had lunch in Maria's former palace. (Private collection)

23. The Cottage, Peterhof, in 1991. The favourite home of Nicholas I and Empress Alexandra Feodorovna, King Charles's 3x great-grandparents. (Photo: Coryne Hall)

24. St Alexander's Hall in the Great Kremlin Palace, built by Emperor Nicholas I and still used today. (Photo: Coryne Hall, 2001)

Above left: 25. King Charles's great-great-grandfather Grand Duke Constantine Nicolaievich, the Grand Admiral who transmitted his love of the navy to his descendants. (Private collection)

Above right: 26. King Charles's great-great-grandmother Grand Duchess Alexandra Josifovna (Sanny) with her daughter Olga, who in 1867 became Queen of the Hellenes. (Private collection)

27. Pavlovsk. Built by Emperor Paul, whose statue stands in the courtyard, it was the beloved childhood home of Queen Olga. (Photo: Coryne Hall)

Left: 28. The Greek royal family, 1885. Standing left to right: Marie, Nicholas, George, Crown Prince Constantine, Alexandra, King George. Sitting: Queen Olga holding Andrew. (Private collection)

Below: 29. Tatoi, north of Athens, pictured in 2002. Modelled on The Cottage at Peterhof, it was the only place in Greece where Russian-born Queen Olga did not feel homesick. (Photo: Ove Mogensen)

Above: 30. Queen Olga of the Hellenes, 1908. She never lost her love for Russia and the Russian navy. (Ian Shapiro collection)

Right: 31. Princess Alice of Greece, Prince Nicholas of Greece, his wife Grand Duchess Elena Vladimirovna and Prince Andrew of Greece. Nicholas and Elena were the grandparents of the Duke of Kent, Princess Alexandra and Prince Michael, who therefore also have Romanov blood. (Eurohistory Photo Archive)

32. Prince Andrew of Greece showing his sense of fun by riding a child's tricycle. (Eurohistory Photo Archive)

33. The silver wedding of Prince Andrew and Princess Alice of Greece, 1938. Front: Margarita, Philip, Alice, Andrew and Theodora. Back: Cécile & Sophie. (Eurohistory Photo Archive)

34. The tomb of Prince Andrew of Greece in the royal cemetery at Tatoi, 2002. (Photo: Ove Mogensen)

Right: 35. Prince Philip of Greece in national costume. (Eurohistory Photo Archive)

Below: 36. King Michael of Romania and Prince Philip of Greece riding on the shores of the Black Sea, 1928. (Eurohistory Photo Archive)

Bottom: 37. The wedding of Princess Elizabeth and Lt Philip Mountbatten, 20 November 1947. (Dutch National Archives, CC0)

Above: 38. The Russian and British royal families on the Isle of Wight, 1909. Although Nicholas II and George V were cousins, George had no Romanov blood. Back, left to right: Prince Edward (later Edward VIII), Queen Alexandra, Princess Mary, Princess Victoria, Grand Duchess Olga and Grand Duchess Tatiana. Seated, left to right: the Princess of Wales (later Queen Mary), Nicholas II, Edward VII. Empress Alexandra, the Prince of Wales (later George V), Grand Duchess Marie. Front: Tsarevich Alexei and Grand Duchess Anastasia. (Eurohistory Photo Archive)

Left: 39. The tomb of Nicholas II, Empress Alexandra, three of their children and four retainers in the SS Peter & Paul Cathedral, photographed three days after their burial in July 1998. (Photo: Coryne Hall)

Alexander II's eldest son, Tsarevich Nicholas, had died in 1865, so the new emperor was his second son, Alexander, who reigned as Alexander III. He had no love for Grand Duke Constantine or his scandalous living arrangements. Nor had he forgotten the insult and humiliation inflicted on him by Constantine after his clumsiness at dinner in Warsaw in 1862. He now had his revenge.

Constantine was a liberal and a progressive reformer; Alexander III was a conservative reactionary. He dismissed Constantine as chairman of the Council of Ministers, a post he had held for sixteen years; he also stripped him of his role as Grand Admiral after thirty years in the position, replacing him with his own younger brother Alexei. Having made it clear that Constantine would no longer be welcome at court, he also refused to pardon his son Nicholas, who was sent to Tashkent to live out the remainder of his life. This hostility did not go unnoticed.

In 1886, Alexander III decreed that in future only sons and grandsons of an emperor in the direct male line would be permitted to use the grand ducal title. Constantine, whose grandchildren would now be only princes or princesses with the style of highness, saw this as a personal attack.

Left with no proper role, the grand duke threw himself into his affair with Kuznetsova, spending more time with his second family.

On 6 May 1883 the tutor to the grand duke's children, Constantine Golenko, renewed the request to Alexander III to grant *hereditary* nobility, the name Kniazev and the use of the patronymic Constantinovich to Constantine's natural children. The political disagreements between the new emperor and his uncle now came into play. A u*kaz* was promulgated on 17 May but it only granted *personal* nobility to the surviving children along with the granting of the name Kniazev and the use of the patronymic Constantinovich. On 19 December 1891 a second *ukaz* granted the name Kniazev and *personal* nobility to Anna Kuznetsova.[40]

While Sanny remained at the Marble Palace or Strelna, Constantine increasingly spent winters abroad, then went to the Crimea or Pavlovsk in spring and autumn with Anna and their daughters. He socialised with musicians, academics, theologians and philosophers. He visited his daughter Queen Olga and her family in Greece, witnessed archaeological digs and attended sessions of the parliament in Paris.

On 7 August 1881, fire swept through the palace at Oreanda. The few servants there were unable to control the inferno; when the flames died, the roof was gone and only the blackened walls remained.

It was never rebuilt. Later, rumours said that 'Constantine had been conspiring to take the throne and that the palace had been burnt to destroy the evidence'.[41]

Constantine now used the little one-storey wooden former lodge of the palace. In 1885, he commissioned a semi-circular colonnade, built from columns and marble from the original palace, to be perched on the hillside above the ruins. He also commissioned the Church of the Protecting Veil of the Mother of God, built with salvaged stone.

In June 1889, Constantine and Sanny's granddaughter Princess Alexandra of Greece (elder daughter of Queen Olga and King George) came to Russia to marry the emperor's brother Grand Duke Paul. During the wedding celebrations Constantine suffered a slight stroke.

In August he suffered another, more severe stroke which left his legs and right arm paralysed. He was confined to a bath chair, unable to speak and only able to communicate through notes or grunts, reliant on his servants' assistance to move around. His violent temper now came to the fore and, as Prince Christopher of Greece was told, 'even my grandmother could not always pacify him'.[42]

Constantine and Sanny had lived separate lives for almost twenty years, but despite his flagrant unfaithfulness she now cared for him. She moved him into a new suite of rooms at Pavlovsk where he would be easier to control.

Anna Kuznetsova and her children were permitted to remain in their home in Pavlovsk and the two women even reached some sort of understanding, exchanging cordial messages and gifts of fruit and flowers to mark important dates. Yet Sanny now had her revenge, ensuring that Constantine was never able to see Anna again. The staff were informed that anybody who helped the grand duke to meet Kuznetsova would be summarily dismissed.

Prince Christopher of Greece recalled a family story he was told: 'It was his custom to call on her during his morning drives. Grandmother did not approve of these visits, which were duly reported by the old coachman who had been in the family for years, but her remonstrances were ignored.' Sanny therefore instructed the doctor and the ADC who accompanied the grand duke that he was not to be taken in the direction of Anna's house. During his next drive Constantine suddenly noticed that they were taking a different route. 'He shouted loudly, but the coachman took no notice. The doctor and the ADC were apparently absorbed in studying the landscape.' He shouted louder, hammering on the carriage door and pointing across the park to the house. 'Yes indeed, Your Imperial Highness, the leaves are turning brown very early this year,' was the bland reply, as the carriage continued on its way. He finally gave up – but this was not the end of the matter. When they arrived back at Pavlovsk earlier than usual Sanny walked up to the carriage with a welcoming smile and a look of triumph in her eyes. As soon as she came close enough, he seized her by the hair and gave her a sound beating with his stick.[43]

He still enjoyed whatever pleasures were available to him. His great-nephew Grand Duke Cyril recalled attending skating parties at Pavlovsk, with Constantine (always smelling of cigars) watching from his sledge.

Yet he remained bitter and disappointed that, having achieved much, he could never do as much as he had wished.

Constantine died at Pavlovsk on 13 January 1892. When he was dying, Sanny asked all the servants to come and say goodbye while the grand duke tried to show his displeasure at this idea. She insisted to them that this was redress for the ills she had suffered.

There is a story that Sanny, whose anger was not directed towards Anna Kuznetsova, summoned her to Pavlovsk and allowed her to pray at Constantine's bedside. However, 'descendants of the Kniazev daughters maintain that the bedside vigil was a clandestine one, achieved only with the aid of an ADC sympathetic to Constantine'.[44]

Sanny continued to live in splendour and entirely in the past. When electricity was eventually installed at Pavlovsk in about 1910, the bulbs replaced wax candles.

She remained regal and impressive even in old age. Prince Christopher recalled her at the unveiling of a statue, dressed in 'cloth of gold, cut in the traditional way with a tight-fitting bodice and a train that was yards long'.[45] Her white hair was always beautifully arranged, her close-fitting dresses set off her erect, slim figure. A stickler for etiquette, she never forgot her rank for a minute.

Just before his death in 1894, Alexander III purchased Oreanda from Sanny, intending to have the palace rebuilt. These plans stopped on his death.

Sanny came out of retirement for the 1894 wedding of Nicholas II and Princess Alix of Hesse, and in 1896 she attended the coronation in Moscow. 'All eyes were upon her,' wrote an eyewitness, 'as she stood in the front row of the grand duchesses in her court dress of solid cloth of silver, with a magnificent diamond tiara and a parure of sapphires three inches in diameter.'[46]

In the early 1900s she suffered a stroke, after which she was confined to a wheelchair. From 1903 she was completely blind and lived in the service building in the Marble Palace, attended by her devoted staff.

Grand Duchess Alexandra Josifovna died in the Marble Palace on 23 June 1911, a few days short of her eighty-first birthday. She had been present at three coronations and was a witness of many great events. Her death marked the end of an era.

Constantine's body was exhumed and buried beside Sanny's in the new grand ducal vault of the SS Peter & Paul Cathedral on 30 June 1911.

During Constantine's life all sorts of accusations were levelled against him, including 'embezzlement … being self-interested, and speculating on concessions and government contracts'. In 1881, 'the rumour that Constantine was implicated in his brother's [Alexander II] murder spread through the courts of Europe'.[47] Yet under his leadership the Ministry of Marine flourished into the most incorrupt ministry in the empire. He was a well-educated, advanced government official whose love of history enabled him to spot many of the problems that would eventually face Nicholas II.

Grand Duke Constantine passed his love of the navy to his daughter Queen Olga of the Hellenes, and through her to his great-grandson Prince Philip of Greece.

10

'I fell in love with the man, not with the king'

Queen Olga of the Hellenes, Charles's Great-grandmother

Grand Duchess Olga Constantinovna, the elder daughter of Grand Duke Constantine and Grand Duchess Alexandra Josifovna (Sanny), was born at Pavlovsk on 22 August 1851. Among her godparents was her grandfather Emperor Nicholas I.

The family moved between Pavlovsk, the Marble Palace and a dacha at Strelna as the seasons changed. Olga and her elder brother Nicholas were joined by younger siblings Vera, Constantine and Dmitri but Olga remained her father's favourite. He called her *Muguet* (lily-of-the-valley). She was unaffected by this favouritism and according to her mother was 'tender, joyful, simple and obedient'.[1]

With the accession of Alexander II in 1855, Grand Duke Constantine became Grand Admiral of the Russian Fleet. Olga developed a deep love of the navy that lasted all her life. She was educated by a governess, Madame Rossiet, but when questioned in the classroom was inclined to burst into tears and often ran from the room.

On 7 November 1861, ten-year-old Olga accompanied her parents to Windsor Castle for a two-day stay with Queen Victoria. The queen thought Olga was 'a great darling, with a lovely face' but was intrigued by her hair, which was cut short so that it would grow stronger. She enquired how long Olga's hair had been like this. 'Since I was a child, Your Majesty,' the little girl replied, as the adults burst into laughter.[2]

Nevertheless, Victoria was impressed and marked her out as a possible bride for Prince Alfred.

In February 1862 Olga's father became Viceroy of Poland and the family moved to Warsaw. Although the castle was their official residence, the children preferred the Lazienki estate to which they moved in spring. Olga and Vera were allowed to ride in the park with friends, including Countess Marie von Keller (later Countess Kleinmichel), whose father was Minister of the Interior. Fifteen-year-old Marie remembered Olga as 'a delightful child, gifted with incomparable grace and kindness'.[3]

In July, Olga's brother Viacheslav was born. A week of festivities followed, including gala performances at the court theatre and a ball which, to her delight, the young grand duchess was allowed to attend.

After the attempt on her father's life Olga became anxious, despite the Cossack escort which accompanied her parents when they went out. After barely two years the Polish mutiny ended the grand duke's tenure of office and the family returned to St Petersburg.

When Vera left to live in Germany, Olga became closer to Nicholas, with whom she shared lessons on French literature given by Monsieur Ricard, the French master of the naval and commercial schools. Olga also learnt German, French and English. Their playmates included their cousins Grand Dukes Sergei and Paul, the younger sons of Alexander II.

As she entered her teens, fair-haired, blue-eyed Olga was blessed with good looks and a kind heart. She was already attracting attention. Crown Prince Frederik of Denmark, eldest son of King Christian IX, had hopes of marrying her. Then, early in 1867, Frederik's twenty-one-year-old brother King George I of the Hellenes arrived in Russia in search of a bride.

The Greek monarchy was relatively new. The country had been freed from Turkish occupation in 1829 and, backed by Greece's guaranteeing powers Great Britain, France and Russia, proceeded to choose a monarch. Their choice fell on Prince Otto of Bavaria, seventeen-year-old son of King Ludwig I, who ruled until he was swept from the throne by revolution in 1862. The country then needed to find a new king. This was not an easy task given the turbulent state of Greek politics.

Greece's guaranteeing powers looked around and in 1863 agreed on seventeen-year-old Prince William of Denmark, whose sister Alexandra had recently married the Prince of Wales. The Greeks assented, hoping that a choice backed by Britain would restore to them the Ionian Islands, a British protectorate since 1815.

The lively, mischievous Prince William, realising that this would mean an end to the dreaded examinations at the naval academy, readily agreed. His own account of how he learnt he was to be king was typically humorous. Nobody told him, he claimed; at the naval academy he read the announcement in the newspaper in which his lunch of sardine sandwiches was wrapped.

Thanks to some astute negotiations, he would receive £12,000 a year (double the proposed income), plus 'an additional £10,000 from the revenues of the Ionian Islands' and a pension if the Greeks deposed him. He would not be obliged to convert to Orthodoxy, although his son and heir should be Orthodox. He remained in the line of succession to the Danish throne but would come *after* his younger brother Prince Waldemar. The Greek royal family would therefore be princes of Greece *and* Denmark, which would become important in the future, but it was stipulated that the monarchies 'should never be united under one sovereign'.[4]

He was proclaimed king in a formal ceremony in Copenhagen on 30 March 1863. William took the name King George I of the Hellenes, indicating that he was monarch of *all* the people of Hellenic ethnic identity, whether they lived in Greece or not. He became a king *before* his own father, who became King Christian IX of Denmark that November.

The new king arrived in Greece in October to find himself in one of Europe's poorest, most ill-organised, unstable countries. Athens was an untidy group of houses, the roads were tracks, bandits roamed the mountains and the government had almost ground to a halt.

The royal palace was barely habitable. Wind whistled down the long corridors into lofty salons where porcelain stoves did little to alleviate the cold and there was only one bathroom, with a mere trickle of dirty water. The king had to fashion butlers, aides-de-camp, footmen and grooms out of unpolished palace functionaries. However, he quickly learnt the language and began travelling the countryside to meet his people. Even so, George always kept a bag packed in case he was deposed.

The king's next duty was to marry and ensure the succession, preferably with someone of the Orthodox faith. In 1866 his sister

Dagmar had married Tsarevich Alexander (later Alexander III) and taken the Russian name of Marie Feodorovna, so in the spring of 1867 George travelled to St Petersburg, where he met all the eligible Russian grand duchesses.

One in particular caught his eye. Grand Duchess Olga Constantinovna was fifteen and still in the schoolroom but George saw the plump, pretty young girl peeping over the banisters at Pavlovsk. He had seen her briefly during his journey to Athens in 1863. Marie Feodorovna schemed hard to help her brother achieve this marriage, against the wishes of Grand Duke Constantine.

The wedding was timed to take place after Olga's sixteenth birthday. Sanny brushed off protests about her daughter's extreme youth, declaring that 'Olga would not stay sixteen all her life'.[5] Nevertheless, King George once found his fiancée in a playhouse with her toys.

On 17 June, Olga arrived in Denmark with her family on board the steamship *Olaf* to join the reunion of the Danish royal family. At Bernsdorff Palace she met George's parents, King Christian and Queen Louise, his brothers Frederik (who had once aspired to her hand) and Waldemar, and sisters Alexandra (the Princess of Wales), Marie Feodorovna (to whom Olga became especially close) and Thyra, who was still unmarried. The Danish court chamberlain described the young grand duchess as 'a sweet, blond little ball with pouty lips, lovely full light blonde hair and a good eye'.[6]

Olga settled in well with George and his family. His parents were so pleased to have them there together that her return to Russia was delayed.

The official betrothal ceremony, in Russia as important as a wedding and equally binding, took place in the Marble Palace in October. In accordance with tradition Olga cut a lock of her hair and presented it to George, receiving in return bread and salt (signifying that they would never be hungry) and a silver ring. Olga said later, 'I fell in love with the man and not with the king.'[7]

The wedding day, 15/27 October, began with five cannon shots from the SS Peter & Paul Fortress, marking the beginning of five days of festivities. Alexander II raised the sixteen-year-old bride to the rank of admiral, the only lady ever to be so appointed.

That evening, shortly before eight o'clock, Olga was driven to the Winter Palace through streets decorated with the illuminated initials G & O. Her gilded carriage was drawn by six horses and she wore the traditional wedding attire of a Russian grand duchess – a cloth of silver gown and an ermine-lined crimson mantle with an ermine-lined cape over it. Her hair fell to her shoulders in three ringlets on each side and on her neck and head sparkled the magnificent Romanov diamonds bequeathed by Catherine the Great. Olga was the youngest bride ever to wear them.

At the Winter Palace chapel Olga and George, who wore a Greek general's uniform, were met by the emperor and the metropolitan. The bridegroom was supported by his brother Frederik. Among the distinguished guests was Olga's old nurse, dressed in the festive clothing of a Russian peasant.

When the ceremony had concluded, a salute of 101 guns was fired from the fortress. The wedding party then proceeded to the Alexander Hall of the palace, where a Lutheran marriage service was conducted.

After supper and a ball in St George's Hall, Olga and George retired to a special bridal suite where Tsarevich Alexander greeted them with the traditional bread and salt.[8]

After a few days' honeymoon at nearby Ropsha they travelled to Warsaw, before moving on to Vienna where Emperor Franz Joseph organised celebrations at the Hofburg in their honour. The court chamberlain was impressed by the new queen's determination to make a good impression on the ladies of the Greek community. Olga arranged for ten chairs to be set out and on the seat of each placed the name of the lady who would occupy it. She then stood before each chair with a notebook, writing down the words of greeting she would give and what she would say to each guest.[9]

They continued their journey to Trieste, Venice and Brindisi, from where they boarded the frigate *Hellas*, which took them to Corfu.

Britain had surrendered the Ionian Islands to Greece in 1864. The royal family therefore had two homes on Corfu. There was the imposing three-storey stone palace which had been the formal residence of the British High Commissioner, and the villa Mon Repos, completed in 1826. The latter was set among 'olive, lemon and orange trees, cypresses and magnolias' and looked out over the town 'towards the Venetian citadel'.[10]

After a few days in this idyllic setting they crossed the Aegean Sea to Piraeus. There they were greeted by George's uncle Prince Hans of Glücksborg, who had been acting as regent in his absence.

Olga entered Athens on 24 November wearing a dress of the Greek national colours, blue and white. The crowds were captivated by their lovely young queen and cheered themselves hoarse. 'The people showed the pleasure they felt at the king's return, and the delight with which they welcomed an Orthodox queen,' reported *The Times*.

Unbeknown to them, in her luggage was a trunk full of dolls. After a thanksgiving service in the cathedral, they drove to the palace.

Olga's new home was an enormous building set on a hill. The rooms were lit by oil lamps and even by the 1880s there was still only one bathroom. The queen's suite consisted of seven rooms on the garden side with a balcony and a long, narrow gallery containing bronze busts of members of the Romanov dynasty. She had a deep religious faith and all her rooms were hung with icons, giving the appearance of a religious sanctuary. She converted a guest room on the top floor into an Orthodox chapel so that she and her children could worship. Sometimes a Russian choir came 'to sing Russian church music'.[11]

Olga had left home and family for a country whose language she did not speak and, despite her enthusiastic reception, she was shy and homesick. Greece's cultural splendours made no impact, for which Olga was scolded in frequent letters from her mother. Countess Coucheleff, her mother's elderly Russian lady-in-waiting, had accompanied Olga to Greece to instruct the Greek ladies on their court duties, and Olga had also brought her Russian maid Maria Baulina and her governess, so she could continue her education.

One day the young queen was due to give an audience. The ladies had assembled but Olga could not be found. She was eventually discovered under a staircase, sobbing bitterly and clutching her favourite stuffed bear. It took much coaxing to persuade Olga, her eyes red and swollen, to hold the reception.

Yet over the years she fulfilled her dynastic duty admirably. Less than a year after the wedding she gave birth to Crown Prince Constantine, a name with great significance in Greece whose people dreamed of the proclamation of a Greek empire in Constantinople. The heir was followed by George (1869), Alexandra (1870), Nicholas (1872), Marie (1876), Olga (1880), Andrew (1882) and Christopher (born at Pavlovsk in 1888). Olga also quickly mastered Greek and Danish. 'We spoke Greek to each other, but English with our parents,' Princess Marie recalled. 'My father and mother talked to each other in German, because when he first went to Russia he was not very fluent in French. My mother at first spoke her own mother's language, German, better than she did English'.[12] Seven languages were spoken among the family and the household resembled a Tower of Babel.

The king and queen worked as a team. Aged just eighteen, Olga acted as regent when the king went abroad to convalesce from malaria.

The illness sometimes recurred, so George began taking an annual holiday alone in Aix. Olga remained in Greece as regent, sensible enough to ignore rumours of her husband's affairs, knowing that her marriage remained strong.

Although the queen disliked large balls and receptions, she organised the social aspects of the court and instituted a form of the Greek national costume as court dress for her ladies-in-waiting. According to Olga's secretary and friend Iulia Karolou, the queen always wore simple practical dresses in white sailcloth made from local materials. The cloth was woven for her by women prisoners, thereby supporting local production.[13] Extremely short-sighted from youth, she used her lorgnettes elegantly as an accessory.

King George liked to stroll informally through Athens but he also had to preside over balls, banquets and receptions. Even these were democratic. Prince Christopher recalled the story of a foreigner hiring a carriage to drive him to the palace. 'Do you mind going rather early?' the coachman enquired. 'Because I'm going to the Court Ball myself and shall have to go home and change.'[14]

In 1871 George bought Tatoi, an estate of 50,000 acres at the foot of Mount Parnes about 15 miles north of Athens, where he built a small two-storey summer home. Olga wanted something bigger, so in 1886 construction began on a larger villa modelled on The Cottage at Peterhof. The family spent as much time as possible there.

At Tatoi, King George ran a home farm entrusted to Danish agents. There was a Danish-style dairy and they kept pigs and cows, as well as poultry to supply eggs. George also produced his own wine. Yet he was never a sportsman and refused to allow anyone to shoot the deer roaming the forest. This reminder of home was where Olga liked to celebrate her birthday. She built a small Orthodox church in the pine forest at the back of the palace, where the family worshipped on Sundays and fête days. To the children Tatoi meant freedom. To Queen Olga 'it was the only place on earth where she did not feel homesick'.[15]

George and Olga usually spent spring and summer on Corfu. Two of their children, George and Alexandra, were born on the island.

Every April the royal family toured the provinces, travelling over the mountains to remote villages where they received a warm welcome from the country people. As there were few roads in Greece these journeys were made by horse-drawn carriage, or by train if possible, using the king's yacht to visit the islands. On one occasion some local dignitaries were invited to lunch. To Olga's horror, the prefect began to eat with his knife. Terrified he would cut himself, she told him to be careful but was reassured that he was used to eating in that way. At a second lunch he cut right through his lip. 'I told you so,' said the queen. 'But you see your knives are so sharp!' he protested.[16]

Olga believed it was her duty to help others. A new hospital was built with the assistance of a wealthy benefactor, and she also collected money to build a women's prison and a reformatory school for young boys (they had previously all been confined together in the same prison). These buildings were completed in 1892 with a gift of money received for the queen's silver wedding anniversary. She gave 3,000 drachmas to finance a nurses' training school and built the Evangelismos, a modern hospital financed by the Orthodox Church at the queen's request. It opened in 1884 and was described by the British diplomat Sir Horace Rumbold as 'a hospital worthy of any great Western capital'. Olga encouraged donations towards its upkeep and visited regularly, sending food to poor families until their breadwinner recovered from illness.[17]

She built the huge Russian Hospital, constructed at Piraeus on land bought with her own money, furnished and maintained out of her personal funds, to care for Russian sailors who arrived in Greece. The queen took a great interest in the welfare of these sailors, sending delicacies to the hospital and summoning relatives to see those who were dying. Many died in her arms. She always had a supply of Russian soil available to be sprinkled on the coffins of those who died in Greece and she established a Russian cemetery where they could be buried.

Olga's love of the Russian navy never dimmed, and she seldom missed an opportunity to visit warships arriving at Piraeus. In the royal palace she had a Navy Room, which she showed to visiting Russians with great pride. Displayed there were gifts from individual sailors and ships' crews, photographs and paintings, models of ships and menus from ships' dinners she had attended. Often she would give tea parties for the Russian sailors, which immensely amused her family although they worried that this attachment sometimes went too far.

On her summer visits to Peterhof Olga arrived with a stack of beautiful Greek embroideries in her luggage, which she then proceeded to try and sell in aid of her many charities. In 1880 she took her elder children to Russia for the first time. Shortly after the queen's return she had the sadness of losing her seven-month-old daughter, Olga, after only a few days' illness. She was the first royal to be buried near the little church at Tatoi.

Queen Olga kept in touch with her brother Nicholas after his banishment and in 1883 was named as one of the godparents of Artemi, the elder son born to him by Nadezhda Dreyer, whom he married morganatically in Tashkent.[18] She visited him at the end of 1904 in Balaklava, where he was confined while another place of residence was found for him. In a letter to Marie Feodorovna, Olga despaired that, when it came to women, he had 'completely lost all moral sense of what he can do, and what is demanded of him'.[19]

The Greek royal family went to Denmark every second year to join the reunions at Bernstorff or Fredensborg. Olga was very fond of her sisters-in-law Marie Feodorovna and Alexandra. There were also frequent visits of her own family and foreign relatives to Greece. Olga became close to her nephew Prince George, younger son of the Prince of Wales, whom she called Tootsum even though he was only thirteen years her junior. The pair had a 'special bond' and George always loved to spend time with her when he visited Greece.[20]

The one charge made against Olga by the Greeks, and also by the Danish royal family (who were worried about the possibility of divided loyalties), was that Olga remained too Russian. In later years this excessive love for Russia caused comment, often offensive, in the Greek press. The people resented her pride in being Russian and her family rather turned against that country and became strongly pro-Greek. Of the queen's children, only Christopher evinced a strong interest in Russia, possibly because he was the only one born there.

Given this attachment, Olga was naturally delighted that three of her children married Russians. Her cousin and former playmate Grand Duke Paul had been a regular visitor to Greece for several years because the winter climate was beneficial for his weak chest. In 1889 (only a year after the birth of Olga's last child), Paul married George and Olga's elder daughter Alexandra at a grand ceremony in St Petersburg. Olga returned to Russia for the birth of their first child, Grand Duchess Marie Pavlovna, in April 1890, which made the queen a grandmother at the age of thirty-eight. That July brought the birth of an heir, George, to her son Crown Prince Constantine and his wife Princess Sophie of Prussia. Over the next few years they had five more children.

In 1900, Olga's younger daughter Marie married Grand Duke George Michaelovich of Russia, another of the queen's first cousins. At the bride's request the wedding took place at the fortress church on Corfu instead of St Petersburg. Although she took the name of Grand Duchess Marie Georgievna, she was more commonly known as Grand Duchess George of Russia. The couple had two daughters, Nina and Xenia, and Marie returned to Greece whenever she could.

Another link with Russia was forged in 1902, with the wedding of Olga's third son Prince Nicholas to his second cousin Grand Duchess Elena Vladimirovna. They had three daughters, Olga, Elizabeth and Marina.

Queen Olga enjoyed her ever-growing band of grandchildren.

In September 1891, George and Olga were in Denmark when a telegram arrived from Grand Duke Paul saying that their twenty-one-year-old daughter Alexandra was 'dangerously ill' from complications in childbirth. They immediately left for Russia.

Alexandra and Paul had been staying at his brother Sergei's country estate of Ilinskoe outside Moscow. On 5 September, Alexandra, now some eight months pregnant, remained in her room feeling unwell. Early the following morning she suffered seizures of eclampsia. Paul gave permission for the doctors to induce the birth by artificial stimulation and a son was born at 7.00 a.m. on 6 September. As the seizures became violent, Alexandra slipped into a coma. In the anxiety for the mother, the newborn Grand Duke Dmitri Pavlovich was completely forgotten. He was later found bundled on a chair in a heap of blankets. Small and feeble, it was thought unlikely he would survive.

Alexandra's seizures continued until the evening of 11 September, when a sudden decline occurred. She died at 3.00 a.m. on 12 September. King George and Queen Olga arrived an hour later.[21]

Everyone was devastated. Olga told Prince George of Wales that it was impossible to describe what they all went through. 'I only wonder how it did not kill us…'[22]

Alexandra's coffin was lifted shoulder-high by the peasants of Ilinskoe and carried the 8 miles to Odintsovo station as Alexander III, Marie Feodorovna, Tsarevich Nicholas and the Greek royal children hurried from Denmark.

In Moscow the coffin lay in state in a special hall of the Nicholas station. The entire imperial family attended a requiem mass before it was placed in a special train carriage with white silk-lined walls and gold hangings. A priest recited prayers throughout the journey. All along the track peasants knelt in prayer as the funeral train passed. On 18 September Grand Duchess Alexandra was laid to rest in the Cathedral of SS Peter & Paul in St Petersburg.

Queen Olga's deep faith sustained her during this difficult time. 'I can't realise yet that I will never see the sweet child again in this world!' she told Prince George of Wales.[23]

In the autumn of 1894 Queen Olga and her mother hurried to the Crimea, where concern was rising over the health of Emperor Alexander III. He had been diagnosed with nephritis, for which there was no cure and little in the way of treatment. George and Olga had offered him the use of Mon Repos but the doctors advised a few days rest at Livadia first, to see if this would help.

By mid-October there were five doctors at Livadia and the journey to Corfu was cancelled. When the empress could take a break from nursing her husband, she was found on a bench by the sea pouring out her heart to Olga. As King George and other relatives arrived, Tsarevich Nicholas summoned his fiancée, Princess Alix of Hesse, from Darmstadt.

Alexander III died on 20 October/1 November. 'The sun of the Russian Land has set down!' Queen Olga wrote to her brother Grand Duke Constantine.[24] In her eyes, his death was a tragedy for the whole empire.

George and Olga remained in Russia for the funeral ceremonies, as well as the marriage of the new sovereign, Nicholas II, to Princess Alix, who had been received into the Orthodox Church as Alexandra Feodorovna.

In May 1896, Queen Olga returned to Moscow for the coronation of Nicholas II and Alexandra Feodorovna. Although it was unusual for a foreign monarch to attend the crowning of another sovereign, an exception had been made for Olga as she was born a Russian grand duchess.

Later that year Greece hosted the first modern Olympic Games, which George and Olga opened in Athens before a crowd of 10,000 people. Greece's triumph was short-lived.

In February 1897, the people of Crete rebelled against their Turkish overlords and demanded union with Greece. King George sent troops to help his people, who were demanding that Crete be freed from the Turks. The Great Powers would not permit the Ottoman empire to be dismembered. They sent an international force to Crete and ordered the Greeks to withdraw their troops. Greece refused. Encouraged by their countrymen, the Greeks in Turkish-ruled Macedonia (on the Greek–Turkish border) then rebelled. In April the Sultan of Turkey declared war.

Queen Olga visited the barracks at Piraeus to help distribute bedding and food to the refugees who flooded in from Crete and then put the women to work making army uniforms. She went to lectures on nursing with her daughter-in-law Crown Princess Sophie and attended the final examinations of the Red Cross nurses.

It soon became apparent that Greece had insufficient nurses to cope with the casualties. The Princess of Wales sent nurses and medical supplies from London, while Olga and Sophie nursed both Greek and Turkish soldiers. One young man had an infected leg and the queen ordered it to be amputated to save his life. He reacted so badly that Olga sat and patiently calmed him down. Later she had a house built for him at Tatoi and appointed him church bellringer. She also bought him a knitting machine so that he could work to support himself.

By the middle of May, Athens lay open to the Turks and the Great Powers forced Turkey to grant an armistice. Queen Victoria ordered a ship to stand by in case the Greek royal family had to be evacuated. As mediation continued, Olga left hastily for Russia to plead the Greek cause with her nephew Nicholas II.

Nicholas responded by sending an urgent message to the sultan requesting an immediate ceasefire, which the potentate granted for humanitarian reasons. Although Greece had to withdraw its troops and struggle to raise a £4 million indemnity, the threat of a Turkish occupation of Athens was averted.

As typhoid spread through the Greek army, Olga and Sophie continued to tour the military hospitals. Olga prayed at the bedside of a dying man as the priest arrived to administer the sacrament, and in another hospital she left some money to enable a man suffering from rheumatism to have medicinal baths. At one military hospital the queen was so disgusted at the dirty conditions that she ordered 200 patients be sent to Athens, even taking some with her on the royal yacht. In December 1897, Olga and Sophie were awarded the Royal Red Cross by Queen Victoria.

In 1898, after another outbreak of violence, Turkey was ordered to withdraw its troops. Later that year George and Olga's second son, Prince George, became High Commissioner of Crete, under sovereignty of the sultan.[25]

In the wake of the defeats, the people turned against the royal family. As anti-monarchist feeling rose, German-born Crown Princess

Sophie, whose brother Kaiser William II had sided openly with the Turks, was blamed.

With feelings running high, Olga never ceased to worry about the safety of her husband and children. In 1898, six shots were fired at the king as he was driving in a carriage with Princess Marie. Luckily neither was hurt and the incident rallied support for the monarchy.

In 1901, Olga offered to pay for a New Testament in modern colloquial Greek so that the people could understand the Gospels. The task of translation was undertaken by the queen's private secretary, Ioulia Karolou, and approved by the Metropolitan of Athens.

The politicians made the most of rumours that the queen wanted to introduce the Bible in *Russian* to the Greek churches. 'The most fearful lies were told, that their religion was to be changed, that the Gospels were to be read in church in Russian and so on,' a despairing Queen Olga told Dowager Empress Marie Feodorovna. 'Every day it became more obvious that it was politics, and the opposition made use of the Gospels to regain power. Nothing is sacred to those people ... and they were not in the least embarrassed to slander me in front of the people.'[26] There were even calls for the queen and Ioulia Karolou to be excommunicated.

Riots broke out in Athens that November, but despite the unrest and the risk of being jeered at or attacked Olga continued her daily drives with a lady-in-waiting to visit the Russian Hospital. The hostile crowds always maintained a respectful silence as she passed.

The queen founded a magazine, *Helping Hand*, available to rich and poor, which contained religious and uplifting moral stories. There were also children's books and booklets with sayings from the Bible, which Olga translated from Russian or German.

She never ceased to think of others. 'You have probably received Doctor Baron Kosinsky's petition ... to find a government-supported place for his daughter at the Kiev Institute,' she wrote to her niece Grand Duchess Xenia. 'If at all possible, I would like to entreat you to fulfil his request, as he is a very nice man who carries out his duties not just conscientiously, but with complete dedication...'[27]

In 1904, Queen Olga was present at the christening of Tsarevich Alexei, the long-awaited heir, at Peterhof. Escorted by Grand Duke Michael, with her 9-foot train carried by an inexperienced page, Olga entered the chapel behind the dowager empress. Unfortunately, the wrap the page was carrying caught twice on door handles and the lace split. Expecting severe consequences, the poor young man nervously answered a summons for Queen Olga's page. Entering the room where the imperial family were gathered, he was amazed when Olga led him to Alexei's crib so that he could see the heir. As the kindly queen led him from the room, she expressed the hope of seeing him again soon.[28] It was a sympathetic gesture towards an obviously anxious young man.

It is doubtful that Olga was ever told that Alexei suffered from haemophilia.

In 1907, Olga's son George married Princess Marie Bonaparte, the only daughter of Prince Roland Bonaparte (grandson of Napoleon's brother Lucien) and Marie-Félix Blanc, whose fabulously wealthy father founded the Monte Carlo Casino. After a civil marriage in Paris, the religious ceremony took place with great pomp in Athens on 12 December. When they left the church Marie looked radiant. George was less happy. He had formed a close friendship with his uncle Prince Waldemar of Denmark, who even accompanied them on honeymoon. Nevertheless, they had two children, Peter in 1908 (the first Greek prince to be born in Paris) and Eugenie in 1910.

The Greeks were anxious to avenge their 1897 defeat by Turkey. In the summer of 1912 Greece, Bulgaria, Serbia and Montenegro formed a Balkan League with the aim of dividing Turkish-owned Macedonia between them. In October they declared war on the Ottoman empire. All the Greek princes were reinstated in the army, commanded by Crown Prince Constantine. As the allies defeated every Turkish army in Europe, Olga organised the hospitals, nursed the wounded, raised funds and distributed relief.

Constantine's army marched from victory to victory. His success was crowned by the liberation of the Macedonian capital, Salonika, after four hundred years of Turkish rule. Two days later, King George made a ceremonial entry into the city and celebrated the victory with a *Te Deum* in the cathedral.

In November, Olga arrived from Athens with a group of doctors and nurses. She immediately began visiting the hospitals, giving what comfort she could, frequently using her own money to help needy families. Despite the fact that the short-sighted queen was having treatment for her eyes, she soon had female prisoners making blankets for Greek soldiers and was planning to open a new maternity hospital in the town.

Yet the worst blow was still to come.

By March 1913, King George had reigned for almost fifty years. Tired and careworn, he was planning to abdicate. Fate had other ideas.

On 5/18 March, King George and his ADC took a walk through the streets of Salonika. They had just passed a rather squalid café when a raggedly dressed man standing outside pulled out a revolver and shot the king in the back. He died instantly from a bullet in his heart.

Late that night, Prince Nicholas and a group of generals carried his body, clad in his khaki uniform, on a stretcher from the hospital to the palace. In the darkness people knelt in their doorways holding lighted candles as the solemn procession passed.

The sixty-one-year-old queen was in Athens when her sons Andrew and George gently informed her that the king had been seriously injured. She knelt and prayed for him to live, but she gradually learned the truth. According to Ioulia Karolou she was shaken to the core and could only say that it was God's will. She travelled to Salonika and prayed for an hour over his body. Constantine immediately returned to Athens to take the oath as king.

King George's body was carried to Athens on the royal yacht. Huge crowds gathered for the funeral, after which he was buried at Tatoi as he had wished. Olga visited his grave nearly every day.

A letter from Queen Olga to the Greek people was published in the newspapers on 22 March expressing how touched she was by the people's sorrow and their compassion towards her. Yet it was months before she could bring herself to write to her nephew in Britain, now King George V, to acknowledge his expression of sympathy.

Olga decided to return to live in Russia. With her went her devoted lady-in-waiting Sofia Baltazzi[29] and Maria Baulina, the maid who had accompanied her to Greece so long ago.

She erected a cross at the spot in Salonika where her husband died, but her plans for a memorial chapel were overtaken by events.

On 28 June 1914, news arrived of the assassination of Archduke Franz Ferdinand of Austria-Hungary in Sarajevo. Olga was in London but she returned hurriedly to Russia as the situation in Europe deteriorated.

Since the death of Olga's father Grand Duke Constantine Nicolaievich in 1892, the Marble Palace and Pavlovsk were the homes of her brother Grand Duke Constantine Constantinovich (the poet known as K.R.), his wife Grand Duchess Elizabeth Mavrikievna (Mavra) and their large family. They were only too pleased to welcome her.

By August, Europe was at war. Russia, France and Britain (the Allies) were fighting on the same side against the Central Powers of Germany and Austria. Greece and Denmark were neutral.

In the first days of jubilation on the outbreak of war, Nicholas II changed the name of St Petersburg to the more Slavic-sounding Petrograd. Queen Olga started a military hospital near Pavlovsk and established the Marble Palace hospital train with the other ladies from the palace. She then went to nurse at the hospital at the Life Guards Barracks of the Combined Cossack regiment near Pavlovsk, spending every day at the hospital talking to the soldiers, applying dressings and returning home late at night. After snatching a couple of hours' sleep, she returned to the hospital to nurse the new intake of soldiers. 'All of them were in a bad condition, all were on stretchers, frozen to the bone and tired of all the shaking during their trip. I returned home at 4.00 p.m., slept less than five hours and feel ok. I am in a fog,' she wrote.[30]

Her son recalled that she 'performed the duties of an ordinary nurse, returning to the palace only for meals. In this labour of love and charity, my mother found her true vocation, and she gave herself up to it with all her heart and soul, either by assisting the doctors or by cheering up the sick and wounded with the sweetness of her presence. Nothing would give her greater pleasure than when, after dressing some poor fellow's wounds, the doctor declared himself satisfied with her work.'[31]

On 27 September, Constantine and Mavra's fourth son, twenty-one-year-old Prince Oleg, was seriously wounded during a cavalry charge. He died in hospital at Vilnius two days later. His parents arrived twenty minutes before his death.

Olga travelled to Moscow with other members of the family to attend her nephew's funeral at the family's nearby estate of Ostashevo. Afterwards she remained behind with the distraught parents to discuss plans to build a church on the riverbank to house Oleg's remains.

Grand Duke Constantine's health deteriorated after his son's death. He died in 1915. 'I never thought he would depart first,' Olga wrote to Ioulia Karolou. Once again, she attributed the loss to God's will.[32]

Olga's nerves were strained to the limit by the war. One night in 1915, the queen was so alarmed by strikes and disturbances in the capital that she arrived at Grand Duke Paul's home at Tsarskoe Selo saying that the revolution had begun. Reassured by Paul, she continued to the Alexander Palace, where Empress Alexandra comforted her further despite the lateness of the hour. Alexandra concluded that Olga was working too hard in the hospital and was overtired.

As well as events in Russia, Olga was worried about Greece, where King Constantine was struggling to keep the country neutral despite intense Allied pressure. News of a serious fire at Tatoi, along with the problems being experienced by the king, upset Olga. An invitation from Dowager Empress Marie Feodorovna to stay with her at the Maryinsky Palace in Kiev, where she was currently living, provided a welcome respite.

Then things began to explode in Russia.

In December 1916, Gregory Rasputin, the 'evil genius' of Empress Alexandra, was murdered by a group of right-wing monarchists determined to save the prestige of the Romanov dynasty. Alexandra's blind faith in Rasputin's counsels, covering everything from the distribution of food to the appointment of ministers and conduct of the war, was ruining Russia. Neither Nicholas or Alexandra would dismiss him, as every time Tsarevich Alexei suffered an attack of haemophilia this so-called holy man seemed able to stop the flow of blood by praying at his bedside. It appeared that the only way out was murder. Among those involved were Prince Felix Youssoupov and Olga's twenty-five-year-old grandson Grand Duke Dmitri Pavlovich, whose mother Alexandra had died after his birth.[33]

For Dmitri's part in the affair Nicholas II ordered him banished to the Persian front, despite his weak health. Olga and her relations feared for him in the harsh conditions there, worried that he would almost certainly die. Numerous relatives signed a petition asking for clemency for the young grand duke. Queen Olga's name was at the top of the list.

Nicholas rejected their plea, saying that nobody has the right to murder and that he knew many members of the family who had signed the letter also had a guilty conscience.

Dmitri left for Persia – but the sentence of banishment undoubtedly saved his life.

In the bitter winter of February 1917, columns of workers marched through Petrograd's streets protesting against the government and the war. As the situation went from bad to worse Olga's courage never faltered. When riots broke out and the revolution spread, she was still living at Pavlovsk alongside her nephew Prince Ioann Constantinovich, his wife Princess Helen and their young children Vsevolod and Catherine. Mavra remained at the Marble Palace.

On 2/15 March, Olga and Helen visited the empress at Tsarskoe Selo. Olga was one of the few members of the family who still had sympathy for Alexandra, alone with her sick children in the Alexander Palace while the tsar was at a military headquarters 500 miles away. Moved by Alexandra's anxiety for her husband, who had been trying to return to Tsarskoe Selo, Olga tried to find out where Nicholas was.

Then came news of Nicholas II's abdication and the formation of a provisional government. Nicholas returned to the Alexander Palace, where members of the imperial family were placed under house arrest. Olga continued to send them messages and gifts. On Easter Sunday she left an Easter egg with the officer on duty, requesting it be given to the empress. Nicholas appreciated his aunt's thoughtfulness, sending a message on Olga's name day to wish her 'the very best from the bottom of my heart'.[34]

The revolutionary red flag now flew over the Winter Palace and all cars were requisitioned. Olga's widowed sister-in-law Mavra sent her some spare horses. Then Pavlovsk was searched. '[In] the middle of the night eighty soldiers with officers came here,' Olga told Marie Feodorovna. '... I slept soundly, also Mme Baltazzi and Sister Catherine ... but the soldiers would come into my bedroom ... I sprang out of bed and stood in my nightdress before the soldiers ... The door was already open and the corridor full of soldiers with guns and bayonets. [The valet] asked the soldiers not to go into me ... They were kind enough to go their way but went around the whole house from bottom to top and remained from one o'clock in the night until five o'clock in the morning.'[35] Princess Helen had some valuables stolen because the maid had not locked them away and the whole palace was illuminated by searchlights.

Queen Olga travelled to Petrograd in a packed first-class carriage full of troops to visit her niece Grand Duchess Xenia and tell her the news. She was desperate to get a letter to the dowager empress, and she finally left the missive with Xenia, soon bound for the Crimea, to be delivered when and how it could.

At the end of July, Xenia's daughter Princess Irina Youssoupov returned to the Crimea from Petrograd with a letter from Queen Olga. 'I pray that this terrible time should pass, that we shall see better times in our beloved Motherland and that some happy experiences should blot the disgrace of recent days from our minds,' Olga wrote to Xenia from Pavlovsk. 'All kinds of vile acts are being committed in the name of liberty, national self-determination and justice and they are being substantiated by using pompous, meaningless words. Comrade Xenia, I hope that you have become self-determined and that you stand on a firm platform without any annexation and reparations for the good of the people and international love of your enemies and the world proletariat,' she finished, tongue in cheek.[36]

For a few weeks during the summer the family at Pavlovsk were joined by Mavra and her younger children George and Vera. News that King Constantine had left for Switzerland to avoid the possibility of bloodshed in Greece upset Olga considerably.

What should have been a happier event for Olga occurred that autumn, when on 19 September her eldest granddaughter, Grand Duchess Marie Pavlovna, married Prince Sergei Putiatin at Pavlovsk. Marie had married Prince William of Sweden in 1908 but the couple divorced and in 1914 she returned to Russia, leaving her son Prince Lennart with his father.

Olga blessed the bride with an icon but the wedding was overshadowed by anxiety and sadness. Marie's father, Grand Duke Paul, was under house arrest despite pleas to the provisional government to allow him to attend the wedding. There were also fears for the future of Pavlovsk, which, not counting as an imperial residence, was in danger of expropriation. Shortly afterwards Prince Ioann was advised to leave. He took Helen and their children to Petrograd. Although Olga spent her days at the hospital, when she returned to the palace at night she was now alone with the servants.

In October the Bolsheviks seized power under their leader, Lenin, and the situation deteriorated further. 'Such terrible horrors are happening in Petrograd,' Olga recorded. 'There was an intense battle behind Tsarskoe Selo. Brothers fought against brothers ... Lord have mercy. This is what we have been reduced to. Here, in Pavlovsk, we could hear the strongest fire; my windows trembled...'[37]

As Pavlovsk came under control of the Bolsheviks, one night a group of armed sailors arrived to search the palace for weapons. Quickly alerted by the servants, Olga came to meet the hostile band, saying she had always loved the Russian navy, had met many of the sailors when she visited the ships at Piraeus and wanted to see if any of her acquaintances were among the group. The sailors, disarmed by the queen's warm words, left quietly without doing any damage.

Shortly afterwards the sympathetic commissar of the palace called on Olga. 'I had to confess to Her Majesty that ... my work [of saving Pavlovsk] would be easier if, in the eyes of the people, there were no more links with the Imperial family,' he wrote.[38] On 15 November, Olga reluctantly left Pavlovsk and went to live in the Marble Palace with Mavra.

In Petrograd, Olga was shocked at the conditions she found. The wine cellars, beginning with those of the Winter Palace, had been broken into with the result that drunken mobs roamed the city. It became dangerous to walk anywhere because of the shooting in the streets, with bullets ricocheting everywhere. Olga called it 'the triumph of madness'.[39]

All property had been nationalised. Olga and Mavra had very little money, food was scarce and they were living off the funds Olga's brother Grand Duke Dmitri Constantinovich received for selling some possessions. 'It is difficult to get potatoes, bread and everything else are [*sic*] scarce; we have all lost weight,'[40] she wrote. They had to steal their own belongings and sell them to buy food.

In March 1918, all male members of the family were ordered to register before being exiled to remote regions of Russia. Olga's nephews Princes Ioann, Constantine and Igor Constantinovich were sent with other members of the family to the Urals. Her brother Dmitri Constantinovich, son-in-law George Michaelovich and his brother Nicholas were sent to Vologda. Grand Duke Paul, who was in poor health, remained under house arrest at Tsarskoe Selo.

It was almost impossible to receive news from Greece.

In June 1917, King Constantine had handed royal power to his second son, Alexander, and gone into exile. The following summer Queen Olga heard that he was dangerously ill. For many months she had refused to leave Russia, but now she finally decided to join the rest of the family in Switzerland.

The arrangements were made by the Danish Minister Harald Scavenius, who, as Olga was a Danish princess by marriage, considered himself responsible for her safety. After some difficulty he managed to obtain a visa, although the authorities refused to recognise the title 'Queen of the Hellenes'. They compromised with the name of Mme Olga Hellenes. He also arranged for her jewels to be taken to Denmark.

Olga left Russia with Sofia Baltazzi, Maria Baulina and a secretary from the Danish Legation in a private carriage attached to the end of a train carrying repatriated German prisoners of war. During the night the train was stopped and the local soviet tried to uncouple the queen's carriage. Only the quick action of the secretary, roused from sleep by the disturbance, saved her from being captured. He managed to have the carriage hooked into the middle of the train and they reached the frontier safely.

After changing at Berlin, she travelled to Lucerne in Switzerland. In July 1918 she was reunited with her sons Constantine, Nicholas and Christopher in Zurich, where the former king was recovering from an attack of Spanish flu which nearly killed him. The reunion was bittersweet.

Olga was now only 'the ghost of her old self' according to Christopher. She had been exiled from Russia *and* Greece. 'It is *such* happiness to be reunited with my chicks again after so long – but the going away from my old home was terribly hard,' she told King George V.[41] She was now approaching seventy and months of worry about the family, combined with a diet of stale bread soaked in oil, had worn her to skin and bone. Although Olga was forced to economise, she continued to help others as much as she could.

By the summer of 1918, disturbing rumours were circulating about the fate of Olga's relatives in Russia. It soon transpired that many had been murdered, including Nicholas II and his family, as well as Princes Ioann, Constantine and Igor, her nephews. Her brother Dmitri was imprisoned in Petrograd with Grand Dukes George and Nicholas Michaelovich and Paul. '... only the Lord can save them!!' Olga wrote despairingly to Ioulia Karolou. She appealed to King George V to 'do what you can' for them all. A few months later they were shot in the SS Peter & Paul Fortress.[42]

Queen Olga went into deep mourning. 'Now I am the last one remaining in our family,' she wrote dejectedly. '[I have] no brother, no home ... but I need to endure, endure and endure.'[43] News from Russia and worry about affairs in Greece further affected the queen's health. She was sustained by her deep Christian faith.

In 1919, she and Christopher applied for a visa to come to England. On 28 June, a Foreign Office official wrote to the *chargé d'affaires* in Berne denying the request.[44]

In 1920, Olga's attention was drawn back to Greece, where Constantine's second son, Alexander, was left as a puppet king after the royal family were exiled in 1917.

On 17 November 1919 he had secretly married Aspasia Manos, the daughter of one of King Constantine's equerries. The news caused a major scandal. Not only was it unpopular, but neither King Constantine nor the archbishop had given their consent. Mademoiselle Manos (as she continued to be known) had to leave Greece. The prime minister, Eleutherios Venizelos, allowed Aspasia to return in mid-1920. It was agreed that the marriage would be recognised as legal but she would be known as Madame Manos.

On 2 October 1920, King Alexander was out walking at Tatoi when his dog was attacked by one of the vineyard keeper's pet monkeys. While the king was trying to separate the animals, the other monkey bit him severely on the leg. By the evening, blood poisoning had set in and he had a high fever. In his delirium Alexander began calling for his mother.

In Switzerland, King Constantine and Queen Sophie were desperately worried as telegram after telegram brought more alarming news. Sophie begged permission from the Greek government to go and nurse him. It was bluntly refused.

In desperation she sent a frantic plea to Queen Olga, believing that the Greek government would not object to the queen dowager's presence. In this she was correct.

Olga set off at once but she was delayed by rough seas and arrived too late. On 25 October, after three agonising weeks, King Alexander died. The queen was the only representative of the family present when he was buried near his grandfather at Tatoi.

Queen Olga now took control, comforting the pregnant Aspasia, summoning the General Staff and rallying monarchist support. In the November elections, Venizelos's government was defeated in a landslide victory and the way was open for the return of King Constantine.

Olga, who had never lost the love of the Greek people, was asked by George Rallis, the new prime minister, if she would become regent. 'The crowd blessed my mother saying she was their Good Angel, and by her return had brought back liberty and peace to them,' her daughter Marie (Grand Duchess George) wrote. 'They were continually asking "When is our King coming back?"'[45]

King Constantine and Queen Sophie returned in December after winning an overwhelming majority in a plebiscite. Queen Olga was there to greet them when they arrived by train in Athens. Jubilant crowds almost crushed Olga and Constantine as they made their way to the open carriages which would take them to the cathedral for a

Te Deum. People threw flowers all along the route as the church bells rang. More crowds greeted them when they appeared on the palace balcony. It was a triumphant homecoming.

In Britain, Olga's sister-in-law the widowed Queen Alexandra had been agitating for Olga to be allowed to visit. King George V was also in favour – but the Foreign Secretary was anxious not to encourage visits from the Greek royal family. 'In ordinary circumstances I should have been delighted to do anything in my power to carry out Her Majesty's wishes,' Lord Curzon wrote in June 1921, but he was worried that in the present climate the visit 'would be viewed with a good deal of not unnatural suspicion, and might even lead public opinion to think that Queen Olga came here charged with a mission or message from her son'. The king's private secretary then asked Lord Curzon for a letter which could be shown to Queen Alexandra explaining why Curzon 'considered it inadvisable and impolitic' at the present time. 'The king asks that his name may not be mentioned,' he added.[46]

By September Olga was in Paris for a family wedding and Queen Alexandra tried again. This time the Foreign Office was more conciliatory. As Regent of Greece, Olga had 'proceeded to act "in the name of her son King Constantine"', an official wrote. He conceded that despite objections abroad to the king's return, 'she is a perfectly harmless old lady, and the only disadvantage of her coming here will be that her visit may be exploited in Athens as a Constantinist triumph. As, however, she has been allowed to go to Paris, I see no reason why she should not be allowed to come here.'[47]

Olga arrived at Sandringham in October accompanied by her daughter Marie[48] and Sofia Baltazzi. It was the first time she had seen Alexandra since 1914. The visit had to be kept strictly private; there was no press coverage and Olga was not photographed.

The Allies did not hide their disapproval of King Constantine's return. Greece was still committed to a war in Asia Minor (the Asian part of Turkey) begun by Venizelos while he was still in power, for which the almost bankrupt country was ill equipped. After a humiliating defeat, by the end of September 1922 there were loud demands for Constantine's abdication.

Seventy-one-year-old Queen Olga was in Paris, having more treatment for her failing eyesight, when news came that the king had abdicated and was going into exile. Then she heard that Andrew had been arrested and was to be tried on trumped-up charges of disobeying orders and deserting his post during the war. His situation was critical. Olga immediately sent desperate appeals to George V, Alfonso XIII of Spain and President Poincaré of France, begging them to secure her son's release. She then went to the Russian church to pray. As she emerged, Christopher and Marie drove up and told her that Andrew was safe. 'You can imagine my suffering, when my child was going to be sacrificed as a scapegoat,' she wrote to Ioulia Karolou. 'If the King of England hadn't intervened, they would have slaughtered him!'[49]

As we shall see in the next chapter, her belief that George V was responsible was erroneous. The truth was far more complicated.

On 11 January 1923, King Constantine died in Palermo after suffering a brain haemorrhage. Queen Sophie was refused permission to inter him at Tatoi so he was buried in the crypt of the Russian Church in Florence. Queen Olga now stayed in London with her daughter Marie, at Sandringham with Queen Alexandra, or with King George and Queen Mary at Windsor.

Still proud to consider herself a Russian grand duchess, Olga was outraged when Grand Duke Cyril Vladimirovich declared himself 'guardian of the throne' and then emperor. 'I can hardly bring myself to write down the extreme indignation I feel at [Cyril's] actions – it is obvious that in his own mind all this passes for "patriotism" – what a terrible thing!' she wrote to Grand Duchess Xenia.[50]

In 1924, Prince Christopher bought the Villa Anastasia in Rome as he thought Italy would remind his mother of Greece. Ioulia Karolou arranged for the shipment of the queen's possessions from her private apartments in Athens and Tatoi. Olga had lost all her fortune in the Russian revolution and lived on a small pension paid by the Greek government. However, with her usual generosity, she paid pensions to so many former loyal retainers that she only had about £20 a month for herself.

The villa became a happy home, with constant visits from children and grandchildren. By now Olga was nearly blind, having to pass her hand over her granddaughters' faces to distinguish one from the other, or take them to the window where the light was better. Once at Windsor she mistook a statue of Lady Godiva for an equestrian monument to Queen Victoria, to the great amusement of George V.

Queen Olga died in the Villa Anastasia on 18 June 1926 after a short illness. Prince Christopher later wrote that he saw a golden glow fill her room that night.

The Greek government offered to pay for her funeral and hold it in Athens. The exiled royal family declined. She was buried in Florence alongside King Constantine. In 1932, Queen Sophie was laid to rest beside them.

The restoration of the monarchy in 1935 provided an opportunity to repatriate their remains. The coffins were drawn through Athens on gun carriages to the cathedral along streets crowded with people. Inside, Princes Andrew, Nicholas and Christopher and their nephew Crown Prince Paul stood as a guard of honour at the four corners of the catafalque as the coffins lay in state. Queen Olga now lies near King George in front of the little church at Tatoi.

Olga, who had always hoped to return to Greece, achieved her wish in death.

11

In and out of Exile

Prince Andrew of Greece and Denmark, Charles's Grandfather

King George and Queen Olga's seventh child was born prematurely at Tatoi on 2 February 1882. Called Andrea by his Greek family, he is more often known as Prince Andrew of Greece.

He joined Constantine, George, Alexandra, Nicholas and Marie in the royal palace, where family life was happy. Although the children were taught that rank entailed responsibilities, they were known by their Christian names, even in the streets of Athens. Andrew was the most Greek of the children and spoke the language more fluently than the others. He always spoke Greek with his parents.

In 1886, at the age of four, Andrew paid his first visit to Russia when Queen Olga took him to Peterhof with sixteen-year-old Alexandra and ten-year-old Marie. They stayed at The Cottage and played with their cousins Nicholas, George, Xenia, Michael and Olga, the children of Emperor Alexander III and Empress Marie Feodorovna who were of a similar age.

Andrew and his siblings loved playing practical jokes, especially on unsuspecting relatives. Princess Marie of Edinburgh (the future Queen of Romania) thought the boys were 'decidedly rowdy'. They 'stripped the sides from four-wheeled carts and raced them downhill', teased the old head gardener and 'fought mock battles with home-made swords'.[1] They roller-skated through the three huge palace ballrooms, played hide-and-seek and leapfrog in the state apartments and in later years, sometimes led by the king, cycled along the corridors or through the ballrooms on wet afternoons. At Tatoi they baited the wild stags until the beasts became so enraged that the youngsters were forced to flee. King George, a great practical joker, encouraged their natural wildness, although they dreaded the inevitable summons to his study when things went too far.

Every Christmas a tree from Tatoi was brought to the palace and placed in the Room of Heroes. Each child had their own table laden with presents, while a larger one held the gifts for the king and queen. At six o'clock on Christmas Eve everyone assembled in the Throne Room, where the lights were turned out, waiting for King George to ring a small bell. At this signal, the doors were thrown open and, in the blazing light from the Christmas tree, the children ran forward excitedly to open their presents. Dinner at eight o'clock was followed by a service in the chapel.

There were frequent visits to King George's relatives in Denmark, where light-hearted amusements, games and practical jokes filled the family's days. Andrew's uncle Emperor Alexander III was 'just like a schoolboy up to all kinds of pranks'.[2] He led the children into muddy ponds to search for tadpoles and on rainy days encouraged them to roller-skate around Fredensborg Palace's marble-floored Cupola Hall. The only formal meal was dinner, served in that hall at 6.30 p.m. Andrew and the other children liked to creep out onto the gallery which ran round the top of the hall to smell the roast pheasant and gaze at the assembled European royalty dining below.

Another brother, Christopher, joined the royal nursery in 1888 but when Andrew was nine he had his first taste of sadness. His sister Alexandra, who had married Grand Duke Paul of Russia in 1889, died in childbirth in 1891. The family travelled to Russia for her funeral.

King George insisted on his sons rising early for a cold bath (usually in a tub) and beginning lessons with their tutors at 6.30 a.m., with breaks for breakfast and lunch. There were three foreign tutors, including a French master and an English teacher, but King George insisted the children speak Greek to each other in the schoolroom.

Andrew was destined for the army. At the age of fourteen, having recovered from typhoid caught from the palace drains, he was enrolled in the miliary academy in Athens where the boys were drilled by German instructors. Andrew became friendly with Theodore Pangalos, whom he would meet again under different circumstances later.

From the age of seventeen Andrew's military education was entrusted to a private tutor, Major Panayotis Danglis, a hard taskmaster who gave him 'a strict training in artillery work, military history, technology, geography and fortifications'.[3] Even on holiday on Corfu in 1900, Andrew was mercilessly drilled by Danglis while his brothers were enjoying picnics or excursions.

All his studying paid off. After a rigorous examination by his father, brothers, the prime minister, war minister and teachers of the military academy, in 1902, twenty-year-old Andrew was commissioned as a subaltern in the cavalry.

On the death of Queen Victoria in 1901, King Edward VII succeeded to the British throne. His wife, Queen Alexandra, was King George's sister, so Crown Prince Constantine, his wife Sophie and brothers George and Andrew were invited to their uncle's coronation in June 1902.

Andrew was 'tall, quick, intelligent and handsome',[4] with a good sense of fun. He had also inherited his mother's short-sightedness and often wore spectacles. At Buckingham Palace he met seventeen-year-old Princess Alice of Battenburg.

Princess Alice was born at Windsor Castle on 25 February 1885. Her mother, Princess Victoria, was the eldest daughter of Princess Alice of Hesse (the second daughter of Queen Victoria); her father, Prince Louis of Battenberg, came from a morganatic branch of the Hesse family and had become a naturalised British subject in 1868 when he joined the Royal Navy. Besides Alice, they had another daughter, Louise, and two sons, George and Louis (known as Dickie).

Young Alice was a great beauty with golden hair and brown eyes, but she remained profoundly deaf. Her no-nonsense mother soon ensured that the princess could lipread in three languages. (Greek was later added to the list.) A relative recalled that in Alice's presence 'you had to be very careful what you said'.[5]

Alice and Andrew immediately fell in love. 'He was exactly like a Greek God,' Alice told her grandson Prince Charles many years later.[6]

The king's coronation was postponed, as he had to have an emergency operation for appendicitis. Alice returned to Darmstadt early in July determined on marriage. Although it was a genuine love match, Princess Victoria thought her daughter was too young. She was also worried about Andrew's lack of independent means. A penniless Greek prince was not what she had in mind for her lovely daughter.

When the coronation finally took place on 9 August, Andrew and Alice were again invited and in London they had more time to get to know one another. Victoria and Louis were by now in no doubt that Andrew would become their son-in-law, so there was no surprise when he asked for Alice's hand.

By 13 August 1902, when Alice returned to Darmstadt, the couple were unofficially engaged.

Andrew then left for military service. He would be away from Alice for several months.

On 8 May 1903, Andrew arrived at Sopwell near St Albans, the house Prince Louis had rented for the summer. Two days later, after approval by King Edward, Alice and Andrew's engagement was officially announced in Britain and Greece.

The Times reported: 'Lamia (Greece), May 9, 8.00pm. The King [George] has just announced the betrothal of His Majesty's son Prince Andrew, who is now in England, to Princess Alice of Battenberg, the accomplished grand-niece of King Edward and Queen Alexandra. British Philhellenes will, we are assured, heartily join Greece in congratulating their Majesties on this further bond of union between Albion and Helias.'

On 15 May, a *Te Deum* was held at the Greek church in Moscow Road, Bayswater in celebration of the engagement. After that, *The Times* reported, Princess Alice received ladies from the Greek community at the Hellenic Legation.

The Prince and Princess of Wales gave a celebratory dinner at Marlborough House before Andrew, who took his career very seriously, left for military service in Darmstadt. With King George's permission, he was attached to the Hessian Red Dragoons.

Alice and Andrew's wedding in Darmstadt was one of the last big royal gatherings before the First World War. On 6 October, they went through the civil marriage ceremony required by German law. This was followed the next day by a Protestant ceremony in the chapel of the Alte Schloss and an Orthodox ceremony in the new Russian chapel on the Mathildenhöhe, founded by Nicholas II and Empress Alexandra. Andrew wore his Dragoons uniform; Alice was dressed in white lace. The crowns held over the couple's heads were the wedding crowns of Catherine the Great. Although she had been coached beforehand, Alice became confused by the complicated Orthodox marriage service and answered 'no' when asked if marrying of her own free will, and 'yes' when asked if she had plighted her troth elsewhere.[7] As the bride was a British subject, King Edward wanted a fourth ceremony at the British Legation, but the couple felt that three ceremonies were quite enough.

The atmosphere in Darmstadt that day was relaxed and happy. As one guest remarked, it was 'more like a Bank Holiday on Hampstead Heath than royal ceremonial'. Among the 260 guests was Andrew's cousin Nicholas II, who gave the couple a Wolseley motor car. 'Andrea [*sic*] is delighted with the motor car and has used it several times with great success,' Empress Alexandra told the dowager empress.[8]

As the newlyweds drove off, Nicholas saw that there was a chance to catch up with them on the corner. He raced off, followed by a host of royalty and horrified private detectives, charging through the spectators lining the route just as Alice and Andrew's car was about to pass. Alice then 'received the contents of a rice bag in her face. A satin shoe followed. Adroitly, she caught it and leaning over the back of the open car proceeded to hit the tsar over the head', calling him a stupid old donkey.[9]

After a short honeymoon at the Hesse property of Heiligenberg, the couple left for Greece.

Bad weather delayed the Greek royal yacht *Amphitrite* at the entrance to the Corinth Canal, so it was not until 6 January 1904 that they arrived at Piraeus, accompanied by Andrew's sister Marie and her husband Grand Duke George Michaelovich of Russia. They were greeted by King George and Queen Olga, who accompanied them to the cathedral in a state procession for a *Te Deum*. Later, Athens was illuminated by fireworks.

Andrew and Alice spent the first winter of their married life in the royal palace. A short distance away in their own palace were Crown Prince Constantine and his wife Sophie, while Prince Nicholas and his wife Grand Duchess Elena Vladimirovna lived in the nearby Nicholas Palace. Alice did not yet understand Greek, so she and Elena began taking lessons together.

Andrew and Alice often went riding at Phaleron Bay. Andrew was an accomplished equestrian but Alice was not, and he often feared for her safety as she tried to race with him.

Summers were usually spent at one of the villas at Tatoi, or on visits to Alice's family in England, Germany and Malta.

On 18 April 1905, Alice gave birth to Princess Margarita at the royal palace. Queen Olga remained with her throughout the long labour and insisted that Andrew be present part of the time too. 'It's only right that men should see the suffering they cause their wives and which they completely escape,' she told Princess Victoria, who had arrived to support her daughter.[10] Margarita was christened on 11 May.

After a trip to Denmark (without Margarita) to visit Andrew's eighty-seven-year-old grandfather King Christian IX, they returned to Greece in September. Andrew was transferred to the 1st Cavalry Regiment at Larissa, a garrison town in Thessaly, where he trained recruits, most of them peasants who had never before left their mountain homes. Alice and Margarita joined him and they went on excursions in Andrew's car.

At the end of May 1906, Andrew left for Madrid to attend the wedding of Alice's cousin Princess Victoria Eugenie (Ena) of Battenberg and King Alfonso XIII of Spain. It was a dramatic occasion. As the king and queen returned from the cathedral a bouquet was thrown from a balcony towards their carriage. Among the flowers was a concealed bomb which exploded near the front wheels, killing the horses. As panic reigned, the king and queen were urged to get into the empty Carriage of Respect travelling behind. All around them was carnage, with dead and wounded everywhere. Ena's wedding dress was spattered with blood. When they finally reached the royal palace, both broke down in front of Andrew and other relieved relatives.

It was therefore two weeks before Andrew returned to Greece and saw his second daughter, Theodora, who had been born on 30 May at Tatoi. They remained there throughout the summer while Alice recovered from the birth.

The following year attacks against the royal family appeared in the Greek press, fired by reports alleging that the princes were to receive annuities which they had done nothing to deserve. 'To be remunerated for doing nothing is the privilege of Russian Grand Dukes,' wrote the newspaper *Chronos*.[11] The attack was undeserved. The scope of Andrew and his brothers was limited but they did what they could.

During the next few years Andrew and Alice travelled frequently. They attended Royal Ascot in June 1907 and, at King Edward VII's birthday parade on Horse Guards Parade, Andrew rode directly behind the monarch. At Heiligenberg they visited Alice's family before returning to Tatoi to settle into their new house there.

In April 1908 they were at Tsarskoe Selo for the wedding of Andrew's niece Grand Duchess Marie Pavlovna to Prince William, second son of King Gustav V of Sweden. Marie's mother was Andrew's sister Alexandra, who tragically died in 1891.

In Moscow they were present at the laying of the foundation stone of the convent being built by Alice's widowed maternal aunt Grand

Duchess Elisabeth Feodorovna (Ella). From Russia they travelled to Sweden and Denmark, returning to Greece via Constantinople. To the annoyance of the Greek press, they were not received by the sultan.

In 1909, the people of Crete, under their leader Eleutherios Venizelos, again began calling for union with Greece. The Great Powers would not agree to this, insisting that Crete should remain under Turkish sovereignty. Several disaffected junior officers formed the Military League, through which they demanded the government's resignation and the dismissal of the Greek princes from the army, justifying this by saying 'they were being relieved of responsibilities likely to injure their prestige'.[12] This was an attempt to block them from undertaking responsible work or holding high commands. To save their father from embarrassment, Andrew and his brothers immediately resigned. King Edward VII sent the Mediterranean Fleet to stand by in case the royal family needed to leave.

The Military League was eventually disbanded but in September republican agitation and the rise of Venizelos (who became prime minister in 1910) caused Andrew to cancel a visit to Berlin, afraid that the royal family might be thrown out of Greece in his absence.

Andrew was now without a job and would have to attend official events in civilian clothes. He began to question what real purpose he could serve in Greece.

Andrew, Alice, Christopher, King George and Queen Olga were at Tatoi on 6 January 1910 when they were informed by telephone that the royal palace was on fire. They immediately rushed to Athens, where they found only one handpump at work. Soon 400 men from two British warships anchored in Phaleron Bay arrived to assist and Andrew, Alice and Christopher helped to contain the fire. Fearing that the blaze had been caused by an insurrection, twenty marines arrived to protect King George but Andrew, afraid of the effect this could create, asked them to leave. The blaze had begun in the Orthodox chapel and the upper floor of the central block was completely destroyed. Rumours circulated that the palace had been set alight on the king's orders to attract sympathy.

In early May, Andrew and Alice hurried to London with Queen Alexandra, who was visiting Corfu when she learnt that King Edward's health had deteriorated. He died at Buckingham Palace on 6 May and was succeeded by his son George V. Andrew walked behind the coffin at the funeral, which was attended by a large number of royals.

On 24 June, wearing evening tails and the ribbon of a Knight Grand Cross of the Royal Victorian Order (the GCVO), Andrew was present at the confirmation of Prince Edward, the new Prince of Wales (later King Edward VIII and Duke of Windsor). Queen Mary, Alice and the other ladies were dressed in deep mourning. Andrew quipped that the public, seeing them pass in their car, would assume 'this must be a party of widows, accompanied by a conjurer'.[13]

Andrew's family increased on 22 June 1911 when Alice gave birth to Cécile at Tatoi. King George V (whose coronation was taking place that day) was asked to be a godparent.

Six-year-old Margarita and five-year-old Theodora (Dolla) were now having English and Greek lessons with their governess. Margarita and Dolla had become what Alice's mother called 'the most amusing little girls'. Dolla was always imagining that 'she had seen fairies flitting around in the grounds'. As for little Cécile, Alice's sister Louise described her as 'quite delightful' and 'always cheerful'.[14]

In 1912, the First Balkan War broke out when Greece, Bulgaria, Montenegro and Serbia, who had each won independence from the decaying Ottoman empire, declared war on Turkey. Prime Minister Venizelos reinstated all the princes into the army. Crown Prince Constantine once more became commander-in-chief, while Andrew became a lieutenant-colonel with the 3rd Cavalry Regiment and departed for Larissa with Alice.

The well-equipped and highly trained Greek army went from success to success. They achieved a great victory at Elassona at which Andrew, newly promoted to colonel on the staff of the crown prince, rode the Irish hunter which had been a present to Alice from Nicholas II. There are glimpses of Andrew, 'damp and bedraggled', seeking shelter in a church after a battle. The villagers offered 'some straw' but said he 'could sleep in the choir stalls'. He and his men roasted a pig over the fire and ate it with their bare hands. Meanwhile, inspired by the example set by her aunt Ella at her Moscow convent, Alice established hospitals in Larissa and Servia and became a nurse.[15]

In November, King George arrived in newly liberated Salonika. Andrew, Alice and the king settled into a villa formerly owned by the sultan. Nona Kerr (the lady-in-waiting and close friend of Alice's mother) arrived from England to help. She praised Andrew, saying, 'He has got such a good head on his shoulders!'[16]

At the end of December Andrew and Alice's children arrived, delighted to see their father again. As the Turks delayed signing the peace, Andrew was bored with nothing to do and inwardly suffered from nerves.

By early March, the Turks were soundly beaten. They were forced to give up all their European possessions except Constantinople.

On 5/18 March 1913, Andrew and Alice were in Athens when news arrived that sixty-eight-year-old King George had been assassinated in the streets of Salonika. After the tragic news was broken to Queen Olga, Andrew left to bring his father's body home.

King George was buried at Tatoi on 2 April as Andrew and his brothers tossed 'bunches of violets and earth into the grave'. He left money to Andrew and Christopher, the sons with the least wealth. He also left Andrew and Alice an annuity of £4,000 and Mon Repos, complete with 'all the silver, linen and glass'. This sounded grand but in fact even by the early 1920s there was 'no electricity, gas, running hot water or proper heating' in the villa.[17]

In August, Andrew and Alice left for England. Officially, one of Andrew's duties was to return his father's Garter insignia and other British orders to King George V, as was customary. Unofficially, he visited his tailor and made some other vital purchases in case another war broke out and he had to hurriedly return to Greece.

In January 1914, he was appointed commander of the Cavalry School.

On 26 June 1914, Alice gave birth to a fourth daughter at Mon Repos rather later than the expected date, causing Andrew to prolong his leave from the army several times. Named Sophie, she was a large, healthy child.

Two days later came news of the assassination of Archduke Franz Ferdinand of Austria and his wife at Sarajevo. By August the First World War had broken out.

Greece was officially neutral, although suspected of sympathy with the Central Powers of Germany and Austria-Hungary, despite approaches from the allies to join them. This decision would later cause problems. King Constantine's wife, Sophie, was a sister of Kaiser William II of Germany. As such, she was distrusted by the Greek people.

Andrew's family were scattered. His mother Queen Olga was in Russia, as was his sister Marie's husband Grand Duke George Michaelovich. Marie was in Harrogate with the couple's daughters. Nicholas and his wife Elena lived in Greece with their daughters, while George and his French-born wife Princess Marie Bonaparte were visiting Denmark. Christopher was in London.

Alice had family on both sides of the conflict. Her German-born father was forced to resign as First Sea Lord in October because of anti-German sentiment but her brother George was in the Royal Navy and her sister Louise was nursing in France. Her maternal uncle Ernest Louis, the Grand Duke of Hesse-Darmstadt, was on the side of the Central Powers. As a neutral, Alice helped his wife Eleonore obtain parcels for their prisoners and acted as a conduit to pass on family news. Alice's maternal aunt Irene was married to the kaiser's brother Prince Henry and lived in Kiel – and, of course, Alice had two maternal aunts in Russia, Empress Alexandra Feodorovna and her sister Ella.

In September 1915 Andrew was posted to Salonika, where he spent the next six months. He was joined by Alice but the children remained in Corfu. Military duties in this garrison town took up most of Andrew's time and he had a narrow escape when a bomb nearly killed him as he drilled his troops. They spent Christmas there, without the children.

In Greece things were going from bad to worse. In the hot, dry summer of 1916 a fire broke out in the pine forest at Tatoi, leaving the royal family fleeing for their lives along a small goat track amid smoke and flames. The small summer home originally built by King George was utterly destroyed and the forest was reduced to blackened stumps. Queen Olga's house, which was surrounded by evergreens, survived. Empty petrol cans were later found in the area, and arson was suspected.

In July 1916, King Constantine sent Andrew on a diplomatic mission to London and Paris to reassure the Allies as to Greece's neutrality and to assure them that the king had not entered into 'a secret pact with Germany or Bulgaria'.[18]

He stayed with Queen Alexandra at Marlborough House and had lunch with King George and Queen Mary at Buckingham Palace. There were talks with the king and Foreign Secretary Sir Edward Grey but, at the Foreign Office, Lord Hardinge of Penshurst, the permanent undersecretary of state, was less friendly. 'What can we expect when your Queen [Sophie] is the sister of the Kaiser?' he asked pointedly.[19] In Paris the government was hostile and Andrew was told that they no longer needed Greece's military co-operation. He was soon recalled to London.

Fed up with the way things were going, Andrew stayed with his parents-in-law at Kent House on the Isle of Wight, spending the night in the room of Alice's brother George with his feet poking out through the end of the iron bedstead. His sister Marie then took him to Harrogate, where she had opened some wartime hospitals.

In August, Andrew and Marie were invited to stay with the king and queen at Windsor Castle where Andrew sneaked a bottle of whisky into Marie's room. His ADC, Major Metaxas, vanished in the maze of castle corridors when he tried to return to his quarters. After spending the night sleeping on some stairs, the poor major was detained the next morning by guards who mistook him for a burglar.

When Andrew returned to Greece to rejoin his regiment, the Portuguese minister the Marquis de Soveral told him to advise his brother to join the Allies.

King Constantine's refusal brought things to a crisis point.

In October 1916, a provisional Greek government was set up in Salonika under Eleutherios Venizelos in opposition to King Constantine, who had dismissed him. As the king clung to neutrality, in November Venizelos declared war on the Central Powers and was supported by the Allies. There were now two governments in Greece – the neutral administration of King Constantine in Athens and the rival government of Venizelos in Salonika.

On 1 December, Athens was bombarded by Allied warships. As the situation worsened, Alice and Queen Sophie set up soup kitchens to help the starving children.

The Russian revolution in 1917 added to Andrew's concern, as he feared for the lives of Nicholas II and other relatives. For King Constantine, Nicholas's abdication also meant the loss of a powerful advocate, who had prevented the British and French from deposing him. Rumours circulated that the king was considering taking refuge in Switzerland.

Constantine now realised that he must accept defeat. In May 1917 he formed a new government under Alexander Zaimis and sent Andrew to the meeting of the reconstituted Military League to convey his wish 'that discipline should be maintained and superior orders obeyed'.[20]

By June, most of the royal family had taken refuge in the royal palace. The Allies were closing in, the French occupied Thessaly and Senator Jonnart, the Allied High Commissioner in Salonika, summoned the prime minister and demanded that King Constantine abdicate in favour of one of his sons. The only proviso was that it must not be Crown Prince George, who was also considered pro-German. If the king failed to comply there would be a military occupation of Greece and another bombardment of Athens. Left with no choice, Constantine handed royal power to his second son, Alexander. Neither Constantine nor George renounced their rights.

As the majority of the Greek royal family left for exile it seemed at first that Andrew and Alice would be allowed to remain, but Constantine's brothers soon found themselves labelled wicked uncles. The name stuck. Two weeks later Andrew and Alice were also asked to leave, probably because the prince was seen as a man who would be able to give the young inexperienced King Alexander a lot of support.

They headed for St Moritz in Switzerland, taking some money that Andrew had managed to save. They were accompanied by Major Metaxas, who helped Andrew sell his cars before they left Greece.

Alice went to the Isle of Wight to stay with her parents, who had recently undergone a change of name.

In the wake of the Russian revolution, George V was nervous. There were calls to abolish the British monarchy and the king was being attacked as half-German, surrounding himself with relatives with German names. In June 1917, the House of Saxe-Coburg-Gotha became the more British-sounding House of Windsor and George asked all his relatives with German titles to give these up and assume English surnames. This included the Battenbergs.

'It has been suggested that we should turn our name into English, viz: Battenhill or Mountbatten,' Prince Louis told his younger daughter Louise. 'We incline to the latter as a better sound … Of course we are at his mercy. We are only allowed to use our German title as the Sovereign has always recognised it, but he can refuse this recognition any moment. If so we are plain Mister, which would be impossible…'[21] Prince Louis and Princess Victoria now became the Marquess and Marchioness of Milford Haven. Princess Louise of Battenberg became Lady Louise Mountbatten; George (now married to Countess Nadejda Torby, daughter of Grand Duke Michael Michaelovich of Russia) became the Earl of Medina and Dickie became Lord Louis

Mountbatten. Alice, married to a prince of Greece, was unaffected by this change. She remained Princess Andrew of Greece and never became a Mountbatten.

As the First World War ended, Andrew and Alice moved between Lucerne, where most of the Greek royal family were based, and the Dolder Grand Hotel in Zurich. There was little that Andrew could do in this aimless existence, as diplomats in Greece, Switzerland and Italy were monitoring the Greek princes' movements. In 1919 he sent a petition to the Foreign Office requesting that he be allowed to go to Corfu. Venizelos apparently supported this plan but nothing happened.

In June they received a visit from Alice's father and sister, helping to pave the way for a reconciliation between Louis and some of his German relatives after the war. In July Andrew and Alice went to the Pension Villa Maria at Vulpura in the Engadine, near the border between Italy and Austria, where they were joined by Alice's mother Victoria. Nearby, at the mountaintop castle of Tarasap, were Alice's uncle Ernest Louis of Hesse and aunt Eleonore. While Andrew went for long walks in the countryside, some family reunions took place.

In Greece the government was convinced that ex-king Constantine was initiating plots against it, including an attempt on Venizelos's life. When Andrew and Christopher moved to Rome at the end of September, British diplomat Howard Kennard reported that it was believed that they were 'trying to create atmosphere in favour of the ex-king'.[22] They were warned not to engage in any activity which might lead the Italian authorities to take action.

In 1920, Christopher was finally given permission to marry Mrs Nancy Leeds, widow of a wealthy tin magnate and some fifteen years his senior. Nancy's money gave Christopher and his brothers considerable sums to spend on press coverage. As well as meetings with significant figures in politics they were said to be communicating with the former Greek prime minister Dmitri Gounaris.

Then, in the middle of all this, on 25 October 1920 King Alexander of Greece died from blood poisoning following a bite from a monkey. Venizelos then offered the throne to King Constantine's third son, Prince Paul, who refused it. Prince Christopher donated vast sums of Nancy's money to the anti-Venizelos cause. He was defeated in the elections in November and Georgios Rallis became the new prime minister, with Queen Olga as regent. Although the Allies refused to recognise Constantine as king, the government in Greece decided that he could return.

On 22 November 1920, Andrew and Christopher arrived in Corfu to an enthusiastic welcome, followed by a triumphant reception in Athens the next day when they were carried on the shoulders of the crowd. Andrew had to make a speech from the palace balcony to the vast throng below. Alice, the children and Nancy arrived a few days later.

Andrew was restored to the Greek army as a major-general of the Cavalry Brigade but, so that his influence would be negligible, he was at first denied a command.

On 19 December, after a plebiscite, King Constantine was restored to the Greek throne amid immense enthusiasm and emotional demonstrations of loyalty. Venizelos, now in self-imposed exile, was still suggesting that the king abdicate and leave Greece, together with Crown Prince George and the rest of the royal family.

In February, Crown Prince George married Princess Elisabeth of Romania in Bucharest, while the following month Alice and Andrew were present when George's sister Princess Helen married Crown Prince Carol of Romania in Athens. Neither marriage would last.

On 28 May/10 June 1921, Andrew and Alice's last child, Prince Philip, was born at Mon Repos.[23] Andrew was not present at the birth; he was away commanding the 12th Division Army Corps in the Asia Minor campaign against Turkey.

The prince was a reluctant commander, feeling that he had neither the experience nor the disposition to be a leader. King Constantine, who was commander-in-chief, needed Andrew to inspire the men, many of whom were raw recruits. The deficiencies in equipment and training soon became apparent, as did the 'divided political loyalties among the officers', some of whom marked out Andrew as a good scapegoat. A report was even sent claiming that he had died of wounds, which was planned to undermine confidence in Athens.[24]

Early in August, in recognition of his role during victory at Eski Shehr, Andrew was promoted to lieutenant general of the Second Army Corps. Although he then led a successful advance, it was a pyrrhic victory. The Greek army had been left with very little ammunition and even less food. There was no wood to light a fire to cook and the horses had no fodder. The enemy, meanwhile, had sustained few losses in either men or equipment.

The political intrigue continued. Andrew believed that the whole thing was a move by the republicans so that his men would suffer disasters for which he could then be blamed. When General Papoulas, the acting commander-in-chief, ordered Andrew to advance on Ankara he refused, realising the carnage it would entail without reinforcements. The retreat of Mustafa Kemal's army further seriously weakened the Greek lines of supply. At the battle of Sakaria the Greek army was heavily defeated but Andrew's repeated requests to be relieved of his command were refused.

At the end of September, Andrew was finally granted three months' leave. He returned to Corfu and at last saw his baby son when Alice returned from England, where her father had died.

By 1922, the Greeks had been driven back to the sea and all their earlier victories were wiped out with huge loss of life. 'Something must be done quickly to remove us from the nightmare of Asia Minor,' Andrew wrote to Ioannis Metaxas (a cousin of his ADC) in January. 'I don't know what but we must stop bluffing and face the situation as it really is.'[25]

Andrew had been working with the Supreme Army Council. On his return to Smyrna, he tried unsuccessfully to persuade General Papoulas to 'put an end to the disloyal plotting which was rife among the forces under his command'.[26]

In December he was transferred to Janina as commander of the 5th Army Corps of Epirus and the Ionian Islands. Alice joined him to organise his accommodation. They returned to Corfu for Easter but Andrew remained behind when Alice went to London for the wedding of her brother Dickie to the heiress Edwina Ashley, at which Andrew and Alice's daughters were bridesmaids.

The Turkish leader Mustafa Kemal demanded Greece's evacuation from Smyrna, which was under military occupation. Knowing that Constantine would not do this and thus expose the town's Greek population to the vengeful Turks, in August Kemal attacked the Greek army. As Andrew had feared, Smyrna was completely overwhelmed, with the loss of several thousand Greek troops and civilians when the Turks looted, burnt and occupied the city. Millions of Greeks became refugees.

Public morale in Greece hit a new low. Andrew had been on leave as all this unfolded and his absence from the front did his reputation no good. In Athens, the politicians demanded a scapegoat and blame fell on Andrew, who was unjustly said to have insisted on the advance.

A revolutionary committee was formed under Colonel Nicholas Plastiras and Colonel Stylianos Gonatas who, at the head of 'a party of defeated troops', demanded the king's abdication 'and the appointment of a new emergency government'. If this was not done, they would advance on Athens.[27]

King Constantine, who was ill and appalled by the idea of civil war, called a meeting at the palace between Andrew, Nicholas and the editor of the paper *Kathemerini*. Andrew suggested the king go abroad and then abdicate citing ill-health. Nicholas was against this idea. As demands for the king's abdication grew and British warships stood by in case the royal family needed to be evacuated, King Constantine finally yielded to pressure. On 27 September, he agreed to abdicate in favour of Crown Prince George who would reign as George II. On 30 September, Constantine and Sophie left for Palermo.

Andrew and his family remained at Corfu. The new government, which consisted of the more violent Venizelists, had given assurances of their safety but the revolutionary committee gave instructions that their letters were to be opened and they were to be carefully watched.

On 26 October, Colonel Loufas from the revolutionary committee arrived at Mon Repos to interview Andrew about the Asia Minor campaign. He conducted a preliminary examination before saying that Andrew would have to accompany him to Athens for two days as a witness at the trial of various ministers who were accused of initiating the debacle. Andrew left with him on the destroyer *Aspis*.

After two days, he had not returned home.

Prince Christopher learnt of King Constantine's abdication in Paris. He returned immediately to Greece and took out all his stocks and bonds before they were seized. Christopher was only granted an eight-day visa but he was safe from arrest as Nancy had given him a large cheque as a donation to the Red Cross. When he went to see King George, he found him almost a prisoner at Tatoi.

He then went to Mon Repos. The house was under police surveillance and Alice was extremely nervous. All she had received from Andrew was a pencilled note. He had been summoned to Athens on a false pretext, arrested and kept in solitary confinement while he awaited trial. Although he was kept in two rooms at the home of a former ADC of his brother Nicholas, nobody was allowed near him except his valet. Any letters or parcels arriving for him were immediately confiscated.

Christopher returned to Athens but was refused permission to see him, although messages were sent concealed on the cigarette papers used by Andrew's valet. Andrew appeared courageous but wrote that General Theodore Pangalos (his old classmate from the military academy, who now presided over the commission of enquiry) had asked how many children he had. 'Poor things, what a pity they will soon be orphans!' Pangalos replied.[28]

As stated previously, Queen Olga appealed to George V, Alfonso XIII of Spain and President Poincaré of France imploring them to save her son. Aware that he needed to act quickly, Venizelos speeded up the trials of the former ministers and army officers arrested in connection with the affair, despite protests by the Great Powers.

On 25 November, Pangalos was appointed Minister of War in the new government. Three days later, six ministers were shot after a summary trial in the parliament building during which they were charged with high treason. Two more were sentenced to life imprisonment.

Andrew's position was now dangerous. Relations between Britain and Greece were immediately severed and the ambassador Sir Francis Lindley departed, leaving Charles Bentinck as *chargé d'affaires*. Alice arrived in Athens to be near her husband.

The Great Powers sent emissaries, and on 28 November the forty-four-year-old Commander Gerald Talbot arrived. Talbot had been naval attaché to Athens from 1917 to 1920 and was a friend of Venizelos. He was also an officer in the British Secret Service.[29]

By the following day, with some considerable difficulty, he had obtained a promise from General Pangalos and Colonel Plastiras ('who though outside the cabinet, shares at present with General Pangalos the chief power of the country,'[30] Bentinck reported to London) that Andrew would be allowed to leave Greece.

The plan was that Andrew would be sentenced to either penal servitude or death. 'Colonel Plastiras would then exercise the right which he claimed for himself and commute the sentence to perpetual banishment,' Bentinck reported. The prince would be permitted to leave with Talbot on a British warship. Secrecy was vital, as the Greek revolutionary government 'could not be seen to be submitting to British naval pressure'. Despite Queen Olga's belief, George V's role was negligible. He 'did not initiate the operation or even express encouragement except through the constitutional channel of the

Foreign Office'. According to Hugo Vickers, 'the impetus came from Venizelos'. *He* sent Talbot to Greece, not King George V.[31]

Prince Andrew was brought to trial in parliament's Chamber of Deputies on 3 December. He was pronounced guilty of disobeying orders at the battle of Sakaria and abandoning his post in the face of the enemy.[32] In view of his inexperience in commanding such a large unit, he was banished from Greece for life. It was obvious that Andrew was the scapegoat for the politicians and generals, but his life was saved.

Alice and Andrew left Greece with Commander Talbot on HMS *Calypso*, bound for Brindisi. The next day the ship called at Corfu so that Alice could collect her family and some belongings. Fires burned in every grate as Andrew and Alice's daughters threw letters and other documents into the flames. 'It was a terrible business. Absolute chaos,' Princess Sophie recalled many years later. 'My sisters, who were seventeen and sixteen, had to get everything ready.'[33]

None of them knew if they would ever return to Greece.

Talbot had given assurances to the Greek government that Andrew would be taken directly to London but George V (who had already refused asylum to the Russian imperial family in 1917) was still worried by the thought of unrest in Britain. He and the prime minister were anxious not to have foreign princes living in the country.

Andrew and Alice had no money and no passports. From Brindisi they took a train to Rome. 'The British Ambassador lent them 14,000 lire and private arrangements were made for their entry into France.'[34]

On 8 December they arrived by train in Paris, still accompanied by Talbot, and went straight to the hotel apartment of Prince Christopher, who was currently in America. Talbot then went to London to facilitate arrangements. (He was knighted by the king while he was there.) Nervousness about Greek royals coming to London delayed their departure and they remained in Paris until parliament was prorogued.

At the end of 1922, Andrew received a letter from his brother, the ex-king Constantine. 'I regret that you considered it necessary to give me your assurance that the accusation of abandoning your position before the enemy is not true,' he wrote. 'You might have known my opinion of you by now, that I consider you an honourable, conscientious and able soldier.'[35]

They arrived almost surreptitiously in London on 17 December, and two days later Andrew had a meeting with King George. It was not reported in the Court Circular.

After a visit to Christopher and Nancy in New York, where they learned of the death of ex-king Constantine in Palermo, they returned to Paris where it had always been their intention to settle.

Andrew's finances were slender. He received 'the proceeds from the sale of a small agricultural property in Greece' and a small legacy from King Constantine. Alice's brother George Mountbatten paid her a small allowance and there was assistance from Prince Christopher. Andrew's brother Prince George also helped significantly. His wife Princess Marie (who inherited a fortune from the Blanc family, founders of the Monte Carlo Casino) offered them rooms in their townhouse near the Bois de Boulogne. Finding this too expensive, they moved to a smaller property owned by Marie at 5 rue de Mont-Valérien at Saint-Cloud. Marie's son Prince Peter of Greece said she paid all their expenses, although Andrew's daughter Sophie recalled that 'there were always problems paying the bills'.[36]

When Andrew gave an interview about his arrest, he was accused of propaganda by the American *chargé d'affaires* in Athens.

In 1924, Greece was proclaimed a republic. The royal family were deprived of their Greek nationality and rights to the throne. Their property was expropriated and they were forbidden to live in Greece. Properties which had been given to them by officials of the state would revert to their previous owners and they would not be compensated. Worried about the fate of Mon Repos, which he had inherited, in 1926 Andrew leased it to Alice's brother Dickie Mountbatten for twenty-one years. As the family were princes/princesses of Greece *and* Denmark, Andrew's cousin King Christian X of Denmark arranged for them to be issued with Danish passports.

They still had hopes of returning to Greece, but in the elections of 1926 the republicans remained in power. Alice hatched a plan that Andrew should become president of Greece but it came to nothing, despite her attempts to involve George V and others. She helped out in a Greek charity shop while Andrew devoted his time to writing an account of the catastrophe in Turkey.

They remained in Paris throughout the 1920s, with occasional trips to London for the Season in the hope of finding husbands for Margarita and Theodora.

In October 1928, Alice and Andrew celebrated their silver wedding anniversary. Soon afterwards, Alice's life descended into crisis. She had converted to the Greek Orthodox faith and became deeply religious, claiming her hands possessed healing powers and that she received messages from above about possible spouses for her daughters. By the end of 1929 Andrew was so worried that he appealed to her mother for help. Victoria Milford Haven arrived at Saint-Cloud in January 1930 and told Nona Kerr that she found Alice 'in a quite abnormal state mentally and bodily'.[37] On the advice of Andrew's sister-in-law Princess Marie, a trained psychoanalyst, Alice was admitted to a Berlin clinic.

After suffering a severe nervous breakdown, Alice was diagnosed with paranoid schizophrenia and, on her mother's instructions and with the agreement of Andrew, was forcibly placed in a sanatorium in Kreuzlingen, Switzerland. The princess protested that she was sane and repeatedly tried to leave.

Following his trial and humiliating flight, Andrew was also prone to fits of despondency and self-pity, feeling that he had no serious prospects and little chance of returning to Greece. He now closed the family home and moved between Paris (where he stayed with his brother George or at the Travellers' Club), Germany and the South of France.

He only saw Alice on infrequent occasions. In 1930 he published his account of the Asia Minor campaign, *Towards Disaster*, which she had earlier translated into English for him.

He received reports about Philip's educational progress and saw him now and then in the school holidays. Andrew had often been an absent father but he was present when all four daughters were married in 1931, although Alice was not well enough to attend. Cécile was first at the beginning of the year, marrying Grand Duke George Donatus of Hesse. In April it was the turn of Margarita, who wed Prince Gottfried of Hohenlohe-Langenburg. Then came Theodora's marriage to her second cousin Margrave Berthold of Baden, and finally at the end of the year Sophie married Prince Christophe of Hesse with ten-year-old Philip as a train bearer.

Up to now, Andrew had lived off an income of £3,500 per year from some shares but when these collapsed his funds evaporated. In 1931 the Greek authorities took possession of Mon Repos after Dickie and Edwina Mountbatten refused to hand it over to them. In 1934 Andrew's ownership of the villa was confirmed when he won a court case against the Greek state, but later that year he sold it to his nephew King George II. He then lived on an annuity he purchased with the sale proceeds, together with another £50 a month sent to him by the king.

When Venizelos made disparaging remarks about the exiled royal family in parliament, Andrew retaliated in the press.

Andrew usually spent the summer in Monte Carlo where he enjoyed the hospitality of Gilbert Beale, a well-to-do bachelor 'living off hefty profits from the sale of his family business', whose yachts were moored in the harbour at Cannes. Margot Hambling later recalled that although Andew was enjoying what might be called the good life, he was sad at not being able to return to Greece. His great-niece Queen Alexandra of Yugoslavia remembered his tall, soldierly bearing, calling him a genial uncle who was always well dressed and who, seldom angry, liked to turn everything into a joke. He was 'a connoisseur of all the good things of life', attentive and courteous.[38]

In around 1930 he met Comtesse Andrée de la Bigne, whose 'golden hair, blue eyes, fine forehead and lovely figure'[39] made her one of the most beautiful women in France. It was not her real name. She was born Andrée Rose Godard in Normandy on 19 May 1903, the daughter of a train driver. Her grandmother was Emilie Louise Delabigne, who later adopted the name of Countess Valtesse de La Bigne, a celebrated nineteenth-century courtesan who counted princes, several painters (including Edward Manet) and even Napoleon III among her conquests and soon became fabulously rich.[40]

Andrée became an actress under the name of Andrée Lafyette, starring in twelve Hollywood films between 1923 and 1934 and another two in the 1950s. In April 1923 she married the actor Max Constant. By the 1930s she had returned to Paris as a celebrated film star. The courtesan Liane de Pougy (with whom she had a lesbian flirtation) called her 'really stunning'. Andrew's former ADC Menelaos Metaxas described her as an 'adventuress, feathering her own nest'.[41]

She and Andrew were soon permanent guests on Beale's yachts. Lapping up the lifestyle (drinks were served at 11.00 a.m.) and with a real live prince as her lover, Andrée took a leaf out of her grandmother's book and began styling herself Comtesse Andrée de la Bigne.[42]

The Greek monarchy was restored in November 1935 under King George II. He was now divorced from Queen Elisabeth, and the marriage had been childless. Sir Sidney Waterlow, who was looking after British affairs in Athens, warned that the monarch's success could be jeopardised if Princes Andrew and Nicholas returned to Greece. He said they should certainly not remain long and definitely not mix themselves up in Greek affairs.

In late January 1936, Andrew's sentence of perpetual banishment was declared void. In mid-May he returned to Greece on board the *Davida*, a yacht owned by one of Gilbert Beale's friends. He immediately became involved in royalist movements, which caused an outcry in some sections of the press. After spending the summer in Cannes, he moved into the royal palace in Athens as principal ADC to King George.

Another diplomatic row ensued when Andrew, again sailing on the *Davida*, entered Cypriot waters. In government circles, the prince was not at all welcome.

In November 1937, tragedy struck Andrew's family. On 16 November, Cécile, her husband George Donatus, sons six-year-old Louis and four-year-old Alexander, together with the widowed Grand Duchess Eleonore, boarded a Sabena aeroplane at Darmstadt, leaving their baby daughter Johanna at home. They were bound for England for the wedding of George Donatus's brother Louis to Margaret Geddes, which had been rescheduled because of the recent death of Grand Duke Ernest Louis of Hesse, father of George Donatus and Louis. The plane was due to land in Ostend to pick up two more passengers.

As their plane approached Steene aerodrome in heavy fog it hit the chimney of a brickworks, causing a wing and one of the engines to break off. It hit the ground and burst into flames. There were no survivors.[43]

Andrew and Alice were briefly reunited at the funeral on 23 November. It was their first meeting since 1931. Although they appeared to get on well together, and Alice hoped to make a fresh start with Andrew, the marriage was over.

Cécile was Andrew's favourite daughter. Her loss hit him very hard, and he developed a growing reliance on alcohol. Fears for Alice's health, meanwhile, were misplaced. The shock of Cécile's death appears to have cured her. Soon afterwards she returned to live in a flat in Athens. Andrew, who was consulted by the family, had seemingly agreed that this would be a good idea.

In early January 1938, Andrew travelled to Athens to attend the wedding of Crown Prince Paul and Princess Frederica of Hanover. Philip had been summoned from England and Margarita and Theodora would also be at the ceremony. Andrew was glad of his children's company; he did not want to go alone.

Also among the party was his nephew Grand Duke Dmitri Pavlovich of Russia. It will be recalled that Dmitri had been banished to the Persian front by Nicholas II for his part in the murder of Rasputin. With the revolution and the end of the war, he finally made his way to London, before settling in Paris in 1921. After becoming the lover of Coco Chanel, he married the heiress Audrey Emery in 1926. They had a son, Paul, but she obtained a divorce in 1937 in order to remarry. Dmitri was devastated and sought an escape through travel, making frequent journeys to Italy, Greece, England, Scotland and Monte Carlo, where his compulsive gambling continued. Forty-six-year-old Dmitri enjoyed spending time with his uncle Andrew and cousin Philip. Andrew and Dmitri were close and were photographed together at places such as the swimming pool at the Monte-Carlo Beach hotel.

Andrew and Dmitri left Monte Carlo by train on New Year's Eve, arriving the following morning in Rome, where Christopher greeted them at the station and they met up with Philip. The following day they all boarded a steamer at Brindisi ('a horrible place' according to Dmitri) and, after sailing through the 'remarkably beautiful' Corinth Canal, reached Piraeus the following day. In Athens Andrew was given a car and an Evzone officer. That night there was a formal dinner at the palace, but 'after dinner, Andrea [*sic*] got terribly drunk'.[44]

The wedding day, Sunday 9 January, dawned wet. The marriage service in the cathedral was 'a splendid scene' although 'the old metropolitan was terribly muddled'. It was followed by several days of family reunions. Andrew, Dmitri, Philip, his sisters and Christopher had lunch at the golf course ('really just a big puddle covered in sludge') and attended a party at the British Embassy. Andrew's niece Princess Marina and her husband Prince George, Duke of Kent were there representing the British royal family. Andrew was frequently visited by Dmitri for lunch or dinner but elsewhere there was concern about Andrew's conduct. Dmitri recorded that at lunch with King George of Greece on 15 January, 'Georgie [Prince George of Greece] made several angry comments to Andria [*sic*] about drunkenness. Poor Andria.'[45] That evening

Andrew, Christopher and Dmitri attended a cocktail party. Dmitri made no further comment about his uncle.

In September 1939, the Second World War broke out.

At the end of October, Andrew arrived in Athens and rented a small flat. He saw Alice occasionally but left after three weeks. They never met again.

Andrew returned to Athens for the funeral of his brother Christopher, who died suddenly on 21 January 1940. He had already lost his brother Nicholas, who died in February 1938, leaving Elena in a terrible state emotionally. The death of Andrew's sister Marie (the former Grand Duchess George) in 1940 left just him and George from Queen Olga's large family.

After the fall of France, Andrew was stuck on the Riviera. He told Alice's sister that food was scarce, his radio had been confiscated and he felt cut off. He wished he was in Greece but felt he was too old to be much use. He lived between Cannes and Monte Carlo, often on board the *Davida* after Gerald Beale gave his own yachts to the British navy. With him was Andrée de la Bigne. In 1940 he purchased the *Davida* for a nominal sum. It remained in the South of France, although Andrew transferred ownership to the Société Maritime Suisse.

In April 1941, Axis forces occupied Athens and most of the royal family went into exile again. Alice remained in Prince George's house in the centre of Athens with her widowed sister-in-law Elena. In 1943 she courageously sheltered a Jewish family, the Cohens, from the Nazis.[46]

Andrew applied to leave for neutral Portugal in June 1943 but was either refused or could not obtain a visa. Instead, his Danish cousin Erik, Count of Rosenborg, spent three months with him on board the *Davida*.

Andrew maintained a tenuous contact with his children via Victoria Milford Haven and Alice's sister Louise, who had married the Crown Prince of neutral Sweden in 1923. When the Allies landed in the South of France in August 1944, he was able to hear from Philip who, as we shall see, was serving in the Royal Navy.

By now Andrew was more or less a permanent resident of the Villa Alexandra belonging to the Hotel Metropole in Monte Carlo. Andrée de la Bigne remained with him until the end. On 1 December 1944 he attended a party in Marseille but remained overnight in Nice because he was tired. He returned to Villa Alexandra the following day, put on a dressing gown and, unusually, went to bed early.

For some while he had been suffering from 'premature arterial sclerosis' and an 'irregular pulsation of the heart'.[47] At around 4.00 a.m. on 3 December he woke, sweating. About an hour later he complained of a pain in his heart. A moment later he died. He was sixty-two.

A French army escort accompanied his coffin to the Russian Orthodox Cathedral of St Nicholas in Nice, which was constructed on the site of the villa where Tsarevich Nicholas, son of Alexander II, died in 1865. In Athens, Alice and Elena held a *panikhida* (prayer for the dead) for Andrew in the Orthodox Church, which a few of his friends were able to attend.

On 4 June 1946, the Greek cruiser *Averoff* conveyed his coffin to the port of Piraeus, where it was covered with a Greek flag and a 'flag with the greater royal coat of arms', with his military cap, sword and a laurel wreath on top. From there it was taken on a military vehicle to Tatoi, joined along the route by Alice and Elena in a car. When they arrived at the royal burial ground the prepared grave was too small, so the coffin was placed temporarily inside the small chapel.[48]

Some months later Andrew was buried alongside other members of the family. The inscription on his tomb says: 'Andrea *Vasilopais*, Prince of Greece, Prince of Denmark 1882-1944.' *Vasilopais* means son of a king.[49]

His will was in a bank vault in Athens. It left nothing to Andrée de la Bigne but Alice gave her his car (to save garage expenses) and allowed her the choice of some personal items. Alice described her as 'the friend who looked after Papa so touchingly to the end'. Victoria Milford Haven came to the conclusion that Andrew had been 'sucked dry'.[50]

To her dying day Andrée maintained a 'swanky apartment on the Avenue Georges V in Paris, as well as a country house in the Calvados area of France'. She died in hospital at Esquemauville on 3 October 1989.[51]

It was said that Andrew's money in Greece had been spent on purchasing uniforms when the monarchy was restored in 1935, but there was some money in Germany and a small sum in France after his large debts and the funeral expenses had been paid. 'All that was left was a capital sum of £23,525 – roughly £600,000 in today's money.' Even the diamonds from his Star of the Order of the Redeemer (the highest decoration awarded in Greece) had been replaced by paste and sold.[52]

It was 1947 before his estate was resolved and the large debts settled, some by Sir Harold Wernher, whose wife Countess Anastasia de Torby, Andrew's second cousin, was one of the daughters of Grand Duke Michael Michaelovich of Russia.[53]

Princess Alice survived her husband by twenty-five years. In 1949, inspired by her aunt Ella, she founded the Christian Sisterhood of Martha and Mary on the Island of Tinos, and from then on wore an austere grey nun's habit. She returned to London for the coronation of her daughter-in-law Elizabeth II in 1953, an incongruous figure in her grey habit amid the splendour of Westminster Abbey. Alice continued to travel and receive visits from Philip and other relatives but in 1967, faced with the turbulent state of Greek politics and her own failing health, she accepted an invitation from the queen to come and live at Buckingham Palace.

Alice died in the palace on 5 December 1969. After a funeral at St George's Chapel, her coffin was placed in the royal vault. She had requested that her body be taken to Jerusalem to be buried near her Aunt Ella on the Mount of Olives, but for political reasons it was August 1988 before this could be achieved.[54]

12

'I just had to get on with it'

The Early Years of Prince Philip of Greece, Charles's Father

Prince Philip of Greece and Denmark was born on the dining room table at Mon Repos.

His birthdate, recorded as entry no. 49 in the Corfu Register of Births, was 28 May 1921 according to the Gregorian calendar used in Greece at the time. According to the western Julian Calendar (which Greece did not adopt until 1923), he was born on 10 June. Alice had an easy delivery and the baby was sturdy and healthy. He was the fifth child of Prince Andrew and Princess Alice, sixth in line to the Greek throne.

Unluckily, the day before the birth Andrew had to return to the front, where he was commanding a division in the Asia Minor campaign against Turkey. It was several months before he saw his long-awaited son.

Philip paid his first visit to England that September when he was around three months old, after Princess Alice received the sad news that her sixty-seven-year-old father the Marquess of Milford Haven had died suddenly. She left immediately with Philip but they were unable to reach England in time for the funeral on the Isle of Wight.

They stayed at Fishponds, near Southampton, where Alice's widowed mother Victoria Milford Haven saw Philip before Andrew did. When they all returned to London, Prince Christopher's wife Nancy lent Alice Spencer House, which she had rented.

When Philip and his mother returned to Athens, they found Andrew there on leave.

According to the official record, on 24 October 1921 Prince Andrew appeared before the vicar of the Church of Our Christ the Saviour located in the grounds of Mon Repos and stated that his son was born on 28 May 1921 [OS] at 10 a.m. at Mon Repos. He was given the name of Philippos (Philip). His godparents were Queen Olga (who was represented by Princess Olga, eldest daughter of Prince Nicholas of Greece) and the Municipality of Corfiates, who were represented by the mayor Alexandros Kokotos and the president of the municipal council Stylianos Maniarizis. The act of registration was legally signed and witnessed by a doctor and a lawyer, both from Corfu.[1]

According to Alice's sister Louise a few months later, baby Philip looked very much like his father. He was sturdy, advanced for his age and cheerful all day long.

Philip went to London again in July 1922, when his sisters were bridesmaids at the wedding of his uncle Dickie Mountbatten and the heiress Edwina Ashley. This time Philip was left behind at Spencer House.

The young prince's experience of living in his native Greece was short. In December 1922, the family had to pack hurriedly and leave when Prince Andrew was banished after being arrested and tried on trumped-up charges. It was a tense moment as they left Mon Repos for the last time and boarded the *Calypso* with Gerald Talbot, who would take them to safety. An improvised cot made from an orange box served as Philip's bed that night as they sailed towards Brindisi.

After a brief stop in London, Alice and Andrew took Philip, Cécile and Sophie to Paris, leaving Margarita and Theodora to follow later. For the next seven years Philip's home was 5 rue du Mont-Valérian at Saint-Cloud, lent to them by his wealthy aunt Princess Marie. Alice's sister Louise described blue-eyed, blond-haired Philip in July 1923 as 'too adorable for words, a perfect pet, so grown up & speaks a lot & uses grand phrases'.[2] His days were enlivened by excursions in his father's motor car, walking in the Bois de Boulogne and watching his sisters play tennis on the court nearby. When he paid his third visit to London in 1924 he was excited to see policemen and buses, just like any other small boy.

In Paris other members of the family were living nearby and Philip had plenty of playmates. Their near neighbours were Andrew's cousin Princess Margrethe of Denmark, her husband Prince René of Bourbon-Parma and their four children Jacques, Anne (later queen of Romania), Michael and André. Also living at Saint-Cloud were Philip's uncle Nicholas, his wife Elena and their daughters Olga, Elizabeth and Marina.

There were also visits to other relatives. Philip's Russian-born grandmother Queen Olga once took him to see his great-aunt Dowager Empress Marie Feodorovna at Hvidøre, her Danish home in exile. Young Philip, usually so lively and mischievous, was 'rather subdued' in the dowager's presence.[3]

There were holidays at Panker, the summer home of the Landgrave of Hesse on the Baltic coast, where Philip met his aunt Queen Sophie of Greece and his cousin Princess Alexandra, the posthumous daughter of King Alexander of Greece who had died in 1920. Then there were his great-aunt Irene and her husband Prince Henry of Prussia at Hemmelmark, where Philip once broke a front tooth jumping from a hay wagon.

There were wealthy Greek friends like the Foufounis family in Marseille with whom Philip spent a lot of time, even going on holiday with them to their large villa near Le Touquet. The widowed Mme Foufounis had three children – Ria, Ianni and Hélène, the latter of whom was four years Philip's senior. At home they spoke English, a language Alice wanted her son to master, although conversations often reverted to French and sometimes to German.

In the summer of 1926, Philip and his English nanny Emily Roose went to Adsdean, near Chichester, to stay with his uncle and aunt Dickie and Edwina Mountbatten. They then went on to Fishponds to stay with Nona Kerr (Mrs Richard Crighton), who had been lady-in-waiting to Victoria Milford Haven. Philip enjoyed his stay, becoming fond of Nona and nicknaming her Mrs Good because, according to him, that was what she was.

In 1927, six-year-old Philip was enrolled in the American-owned MacJannet Country Day and Boarding School housed in The Elms, in Avenue Eugenie, Saint-Cloud. He introduced himself to classmates as 'just Philip' before finally admitting he was Prince Philip of Greece. The fees were paid by Prince Christopher, whose wife Nancy, who died in 1923, left some money for Andrew's children to cover such expenses.[4]

In 1928, Philip, Margarita and Theodora were sent to stay with their cousin Princess Helen of Romania at Sinaia in the Carpathians. Helen, a daughter of King Constantine and Queen Sophie of Greece, had married Crown Prince Carol of Romania in 1921 but he renounced his rights to the throne and they divorced in 1928. She had a young son named Michael, four months Philip's junior, who became king under a regency on the death of his grandfather in July 1927. When they were together at Mamaia on the Black Sea, where Helen had a villa, the boys enjoyed sea bathing and riding on the beach.

From the time Philip's mother entered the sanitorium in Kreuzlingen in 1930 when he was nine he had little contact with her for some years. There were occasional visits and he was also urged to write and let Alice know what he was doing, but after his father closed the family home Philip led an itinerant life in the care of his relatives.

In June 1930 he stayed at Wolfsgarten, the hunting lodge owned by the Hesse family south of Frankfurt, with his great-uncle Grand Duke Ernest Louis and his wife Eleonore, known as Uncle Ernie and Aunt Onor. Philip spent his birthday there and was thoroughly spoilt with presents, including a bicycle.

By the end of 1931, all Philip's sisters were married. He was sent to his grandmother Victoria Milford Haven at Kensington Palace, although his actual guardian was her elder son George Mountbatten, Marquess of Milford Haven, whose wife Nada was a rather Bohemian second cousin of Prince Andrew. Born Countess Nadejda de Torby, her father was Grand Duke Michael Michaelovich of Russia; her mother was a granddaughter of the poet Alexander Pushkin.

Andrew wanted his son to be educated in England, hoping to spare the boy the strict martial regime he had endured. George chose his own old school, Cheam, a prep school in Surrey which his son David, Earl of Medina, two years Philip's senior, was also attending. Philip and David were soon close friends. During holidays at George's home, the thirteenth-century Lynden Manor at Holyport in Berkshire, they played hockey on roller skates, rode on motorbikes and once cycled to Dover, hitching a ride back along the Thames on a barge. George Milford Haven's brilliant mathematical and inventive mind sparked Philip's interest in science and engineering.

Every summer Philip spent part of the holiday with his father, but most holidays were spent with friends or relatives – George and Nada, the Hesse family at Wolfsgarten, Nona at Fishponds, or Theodora and her husband Berthold of Baden at Schloss Salem near Lake Constance. Berthold was another major influence, teaching him to fish for trout and also to drive.

Victoria always had to consult Andrew about his son's movements but this frequently proved difficult, especially when he delayed his return, throwing Philip's schedule into limbo. Andrew 'was interested in his son, and proud of his son, but not very hands-on – or reliable – when it came to his care of him'. With his father living in the South of France, his mother ill and his sisters all starting families of their own, as Prince Philip said, 'I just had to get on with it.'[5]

In 1933 it was decided that Philip would enrol at Dr Kurt Hahn's boarding school at Schloss Salem, with the financial support of Theodora and Berthold, whose father had founded it. Philip lived with them in the schloss while the other boys occupied a wing of the school. Hitler had by now come to power in Germany, and after a struggle to defend the school against Nazi intolerance (there was much heel clicking and compulsory shouts of '*Heil Hitler*') Dr Hahn, who was of Jewish origin and had spoken out against Hitler, was arrested. On his release he moved the school to Scotland.

Philip, who had mocked the goose-step and compared the Nazi salute to schoolboys putting up their hand asking to be excused to go to the lavatory, followed in the autumn of 1934. Theodora and Berthold thought it for the best as they struggled against the Nazi takeover of the school.

Aged thirteen, Philip started at Gordonstoun School near the Moray Firth. The bleak-looking grey-stone Gordonstoun House had been leased by Hahn from the Gordon-Cumming family and had fallen into disrepair. As well as educational studies, Hahn therefore required the boys to help with farming, gardening, building, decorating the classrooms, domestic chores and any other jobs that needed doing on the estate. Sometimes intolerant and impatient, Philip was often naughty but never nasty.

The day started with a cold shower followed by a run. Lessons were broken mid-morning for exercise. After lunch the boys rested while someone more senior read to them. They learned seamanship twice a week. Other afternoons were taken up by games or different projects. Supper was at 6.30 p.m. and lights out at 9.30 p.m.

Gordonstoun was the beginning of Philip's lifelong love of sailing. The boys took part in expeditions, even going as far afield as Norway or the Shetland Islands, and as Philip never seemed to be seasick he was often given the job of cook. He proved 'thoroughly trustworthy and not afraid of dirty and arduous work'.[6] Philip thrived at Gordonstoun, and during his last term he was head boy, or 'guardian' of the school.

At that time Philip often spent Christmas with the millionaire Sir Harold Wernher and his wife Lady Zia at Thorpe Lubenham Hall in Leicestershire. Lady Zia, born Countess Anastasia de Torby, was the sister of Nada, wife of George Milford Haven. Philip regarded the Wernhers as an 'honorary uncle and aunt' and enjoyed long discussions with Harold, whom he later regarded as 'one of the early influences of his life', always arriving with a long list of questions for him to answer. He became close to their son Alex and daughters Georgina (Gina) and Myra, who were of a similar age. Locally, he was remembered as 'fair-haired, boisterous and very polite and handsome'.[7]

Royal events continued to impinge on his life, some happy, others sad. In 1934 he attended the Westminster Abbey wedding of his cousin Princess Marina of Greece to Prince George, Duke of Kent, the thirty-one-year-old fourth son of King George V and Queen Mary. Among the young bridesmaids was the Duke of Kent's eight-year-old niece, Princess Elizabeth of York. Unbeknown to Philip, he had just set eyes on his future wife.

The following year he returned briefly to Athens, where the monarchy had been restored under his cousin King George II, for the lying-in-state of the repatriated remains of Queen Olga, King Constantine and Queen Sophie. According to his cousin Alexandra, later Queen of Yugoslavia, Philip felt sick during the service. He grabbed his top hat just in time and, on leaving the cathedral, thrust it quickly into the hands of an unsuspecting equerry.[8]

He continued to spend occasional holidays with Helen of Romania and her son Michael, who had been deposed by his father King Carol in 1930. He spent Christmas 1936 with them at Villa Sparta in Florence.

In November 1937, Philip was at Gordonstoun when he was told the shocking news of the death of Cécile and her family in a plane crash in Ostend. At the funeral in Darmstadt on 23 November, sixteen-year-old Philip walked behind the coffins in civilian clothes, flanked by Dickie Mountbatten in Royal Naval uniform, Sophie's husband Prince Christoph of Hesse in SS uniform and *his* brother Prince Philipp of Hesse in his SA Brownshirt, as the crowd saluted with shouts of *Heil Hitler*. Both Philip's parents were present, briefly united in their shared grief. He spent that sad Christmas at Lubenham with the Wernhers.

In January 1938 Philip's father summoned him to Rome, where he met up with his glamorous forty-six-year-old cousin Grand Duke Dmitri Pavlovich of Russia. They were all to travel to Athens for the wedding of Crown Prince Paul and Princess Frederica of Hanover.

'Spent the day with Philip in Rome. Left at 12.30 for Brindisi,' Dmitri recorded in his diary on New Year's Day. At the wedding on 9 January, Philip, Dmitri and Michael of Romania were among those who held golden crowns over the couple's heads. Afterwards there were dinners and family reunions to attend before Philip returned to school. Dmitri 'was around a lot when I was a boy,' Prince Philip told author Robert Hardman. 'He was a hugely entertaining chap. I remember him with great affection.'[9]

In April, George Milford Haven died of cancer. Prince Andrew then asked Philip's other uncle, Dickie Mountbatten, who was on active service in the Royal Navy, to take over his guardianship. At Easter 1939, Philip left Gordonstoun after taking his final exams.

Soon after Cécile's funeral, Princess Alice, now quite her old self, returned to Athens and took a two-bedroomed flat for her and Philip at 8 rue Coumbari. She felt strongly that her son should get to know his country and countrymen. She arranged for Captain Nicky Merlin from the Greek navy to be seconded to look after Philip and accompany him on social occasions as what Alice called 'a paternal eye'. When in Greece Philip could live with her, but he also maintained his previous arrangements with Victoria Milford Haven at Kensington Palace and Dickie Mountbatten in London or Adsdean. Alice asked Dickie for another copy of his private code book so that they could all communicate in secret.

Philip started having Greek lessons alongside German-born Crown Princess Frederica when he stayed in Greece for the holidays. '[The lessons] became so hilarious that we had to give them up, we laughed too much,' she recalled.[10]

Despite pressure from King George of Greece to enter Philip into the Greek Nautical College, Andrew insisted that after finishing his education Philip would take the examination for entry into the Royal Naval College at Dartmouth, Devon. Philip had originally expressed an interest in joining the Royal Air Force but bowed to the family tradition of naval service. He passed the entry examination sixteenth out of thirty-four. It was intended that he do a term at the Royal Naval College followed by two terms on the training cruiser, then leave the navy after reaching sub-lieutenant's rank.

On 22 July 1939, the king and queen paid a visit to the Royal Naval College, which Philip had entered as a cadet in May with the approval of the British royal family.

King George V had died in 1936 and at the end of that year his eldest son, King Edward VIII, abdicated, leaving his brother the Duke of York to reign. It was therefore King George VI, his wife Queen Elizabeth and their daughters thirteen-year-old Elizabeth and nine-year-old Margaret who arrived at the Royal Naval College on the royal yacht, attended by Dickie Mountbatten. The king had once been a cadet there and wanted to hold an inspection and attend a special service in the chapel.

The college was in the grip of an outbreak of mumps and chickenpox, so it was thought advisable to send the princesses to the captain's house, where his seventeen-year-old son was asked to get out his clockwork railway and other childhood toys for them to play with. As Philip was uninfected by the outbreak, Dickie Mountbatten arranged for him to assist with the entertainment.

Philip had his father's good looks, height and sense of fun. The princesses' governess Marion Crawford recalled how 'a fair-haired boy, rather like a Viking, with a sharp face and piercing blue eyes', entered and knelt with them to play with the trains. They drank lemonade and ate ginger crackers and then, growing bored, Philip said, 'Let's go to the tennis courts and have some real fun jumping the nets.'[11]

Although Elizabeth was impressed by how high he could jump there was no indication that Philip was interested in this shy, solemn thirteen-year-old. When he came on board the royal yacht for dinner that evening she and her sister had already been sent to bed.

The next day she watched admiringly as he tucked into 'several platefuls of shrimps, and a banana split, among other trifles'.[12]

When the royal party left, the cadets arranged a flotilla of small boats to escort them out to sea. As they fell back one by one, a solitary blond oarsman remained, watched by Elizabeth through binoculars, until he was ordered through a megaphone to go back. It was, of course, Philip.

In July he left for Paris with his mother, going from there to Italy and sailing to Greece. They had barely arrived when, on 3 September, war was declared.

Philip now had to decide whether to be a prince of Greece and get to know the language and people or return to England and the Royal Navy. The naturalisation department had been suspended so he was unable to apply for British citizenship. He was also still in line to the Greek throne and moved even closer when his cousin Prince Peter disqualified himself by marrying a divorced Russian commoner. The decision was made by King George II of Greece, who instructed him to resume his naval training in England. After Dickie Mountbatten pulled some strings, the Admiralty gave permission.

On 21 September, Philip left Athens to finish his training at Dartmouth. He passed out of the college in early 1940, receiving the King's Dirk (a long-bladed dagger) for the best cadet of his year.

In January 1940, he was back in Greece. King George II told Princess Alice that he looked 'very well and happy'.[13]

Greece was neutral, so there was no chance of him seeing action. With the consent of King George VI and his own parents, Philip was appointed to HMS *Ramillies*, escorting ships from Australia to Egypt. This at least kept him out of harm's way. He then joined HMS *Kent* and HMS *Shropshire* in the Asia-Pacific region. He received news of his mother and sisters from his grandmother Victoria Milford Haven.

Then, in 1940, Italy invaded Greece. Philip was no longer a neutral.

He was appointed to HMS *Valiant* in the Mediterranean and mentioned in despatches at the victory over the Italian fleet at Cape Matapan in March 1941. His bravery and initiative in controlling the *Valiant*'s searchlights during the night action 'greatly contributed to the devastating results achieved' by the guns.[14]

In April 1941 the Germans attacked Greece and the British decided to evacuate the royal family. They were taken by Sunderland flying boat to Crete. A few days later German troops entered Athens. Alice remained there with her widowed sister-in-law Elena. Philip was able to correspond with his mother via his aunt Crown Princess Louise of neutral Sweden.

After passing his sub-lieutenant's examination he was posted to the destroyer HMS *Wallace* in 1942, escorting convoys off Britain's east coast. The following year HMS *Wallace* was sent to the Mediterranean to support the invasion of Sicily. Philip was described as an 'officer of unusual promise'.

On 7 October 1943, his sister Sophie's husband Prince Christoph of Hesse was killed on active service over Italy with the Luftwaffe. The following February Sophie gave birth to her fifth child, Clarissa. Philip heard the news from his mother, who had managed to get to Sophie's home near Frankfurt. Margarita gave birth to twins that April but Greece was freed from German occupation in October 1944, leaving Alice isolated from her daughters.

In February 1944, Philip was appointed First Lieutenant of HMS *Whelp*. He was present at the surrender of Japan in Tokyo Bay in September 1945.

While on leave in England, Philip stayed with his grandmother at Kensington Palace and sometimes spent weekends with the royal family at Windsor Castle.

To raise money for war charities, Princesses Elizabeth and Margaret had begun acting in pantomimes produced by Herbert Tanner, schoolmaster of the Royal School at Windsor, and involving pupils from the school. The first production was *Cinderella* in 1941, followed by *Sleeping Beauty* in 1942. Philip was in the audience on 18 December 1943 for *Aladdin*, when Elizabeth played Aladdin and Margaret was Princess Roxana. Their last performance was *Old Mother Red Riding Boots*, devised by the princesses in 1944.

It was noticed that Elizabeth was always more animated if Philip was attending.

There had been other girls, of course. In 1938, in Venice, Philip is believed to have 'fallen very heavily' for seventeen-year-old Cobina Wright,[15] a blond-haired, blue-eyed budding American actress he met in Harry's Bar. He was staying with his aunt Princess Aspasia of Greece (widow of King Alexander) and the bar was one of her favourite haunts. For three weeks Philip squired Cobina around Venice, dining, dancing and taking romantic gondola rides along the Grand Canal. He then followed her to London where they spent another week. He desperately wanted to marry her but she was not interested.

Then there was Osla Benning, whom he met in late 1939 through her flatmate Sarah Norton, a goddaughter of Dickie Mountbatten. Osla was two years Philip's junior and had come over from Canada after her mother's divorce. Sarah and her father Lord Grantley lived in a cottage near the Hawker Siddeley aircraft factory in Slough where Osla was working. Philip was among the many young men invited to their home for drinks. Soon they became closer, dancing at the 400 Club in Leicester Square or the Café de Paris until it was bombed. Osla wore a jewelled naval cipher as a brooch and reluctantly admitted to a friend that it was given to her by Philip of Greece. By 1941 her linguistic skills had secured her a job in the naval section at Bletchley Park and, after going out dancing, Philip took her to Paddington station to catch the milk train to Bletchley. Her daughter later said that Philip was her 'first love'.[16] By 1944 they had begun to drift apart, but they remained friends until Osla's death in 1974.

Gina Wernher, daughter of Sir Harold and Lady Zia, was another early girlfriend with whom Philip dined and danced. Although Gina's royal connections pleased Princess Alice, nothing came of this friendship.

Philip also stayed in touch with Hélène Foufounis (later Hélène Cordet), whose family had done so much for him in his childhood. When she married William Kirby in 1938, Philip gave her away. The marriage unfortunately ended in divorce and she next married Marcel Boisot, who deserted her. When their son Max was born in 1943 (before the couple's marriage), Philip was his godfather. A daughter, Louise, followed later. The friendship and help Philip gave this family was in recompense for the assistance he had received from them.

During the war he went out with other girls when on shore leave in Melbourne and Sydney but, according to his friend Mike Parker, there was nothing serious. Everyone on board ship knew he was corresponding regularly with Princess Elizabeth and had a photo of her in his cabin. In return, the princess had his photograph on her mantlepiece. Warned by her governess that it could lead to gossip, she substituted it for a photo of Philip with a beard, which she claimed made him unrecognisable.

By 1944, Dickie Mountbatten was angling King George VI to have Philip naturalised as a British subject so that he could continue with his career in the Royal Navy. Dickie did not believe there was any future for his nephew in the Greek navy. There were also additional considerations at play. Mountbatten and some of the family thought that naturalisation might help with what they tactfully called 'other matters'.

As far back as 1941, the diarist 'Chips' Channon recorded a meeting with Alice's sister-in-law Elena at a cocktail party in Athens. Philip was also present and Channon found him 'extraordinarily handsome'. Channon continued, 'He is to be our Prince Consort, and that is why he is serving in our Navy. He is charming, but I deplore such a marriage; he and Princess Elizabeth are too inter-related.'[17] They were both descendants of Queen Victoria, as well as Christian IX of Denmark.

In February 1945, Victoria Milford Haven told Dickie that King George of Greece wanted the naturalisation process to wait for a while. Perhaps as he had still not been restored to the throne after the war, he felt it would not look good if one of the Greek princes gave up his nationality.

While awaiting his appointment to HMS *Whelp*, Philip undertook a tactical training course. It was while serving on *Whelp* in the Mediterranean that he received a coded signal from Uncle Dickie informing him of his father's death on 3 December 1944 in Monte Carlo. Although he had not seen his father for five years, the news came as a shock. Mike Parker said that 'he really loved his father'. To his great grief, it was impossible for him to go to the Riviera to attend the funeral. Andrew's will left seven-tenths of his estate to Philip. He received the small sum of money left in France, which Alice informed him amounted to little more than pocket money, and a monogrammed silver service from Mon Repos which had been stored in Sweden with Crown Princess Louise.[18]

With the end of the war, Princess Alice was able to return to England. By this time Dickie Mountbatten, confident that his plans for Philip's naturalisation and hopes of his marriage to Princess Elizabeth were going well, was already researching the title of Prince Consort which had been given to Queen Victoria's husband Albert.

In April, Philip attended the marriage of his widowed sister Sophie and Prince George of Hanover in Salem, Germany. From there he went to the Café de Paris in Monte Carlo with Mike Parker to meet Andrée de la Bigne. She gave him Andrew's books and some personal effects, including an ivory shaving brush and his signet ring, the latter of which Philip wore from that time on. He also arranged for alterations to be made on any of his father's suits or jackets that he could wear himself.

Philip returned home from the Far East on 17 January 1946. He was given posts at various naval training establishments but these could not compete with the excitement of active service during the war. However, he was able to see more of Princess Elizabeth, and his MG sports car was frequently spotted at Buckingham Palace. He often spent leave with his widowed cousin Princess Marina, Duchess of Kent (whose husband Prince George had been killed on active service in 1942) at Coppins, near Iver in Buckinghamshire, where he was able to meet Elizabeth in private.

In October, the couple were photographed together at the wedding of Dickie Mountbatten's elder daughter Patricia and Captain Lord

Brabourne. The princess was a bridesmaid at the ceremony at Romsey Abbey in Hampshire, and as Philip helped Elizabeth remove her coat at the abbey door the press caught a loving look between them.

Following a plebiscite, King George II had returned to Athens in September but died suddenly the following April after a stroke. He was succeeded by his brother Crown Prince Paul, whose wife Frederica had once had Greek lessons with Philip.

On 28 February 1947, Philip became a naturalised British subject. He gave up his style and title of HRH Prince Philip of Greece and took the anglicised name of his mother's family, Mountbatten, although that had never been the name of either of his parents. From now on, he was known as Lieutenant Philip Mountbatten, R.N.

Princess Elizabeth was on a tour of South Africa with the king, queen and Princess Margaret. It is believed that she and Philip were already privately engaged but the king had asked them to wait until they returned home before any announcement was made.

On 9 July, the Court Circular made a proclamation:

> It is with the greatest of pleasure that the King and Queen announce the betrothal of their dearly beloved daughter the Princess Elizabeth to Lieutenant Philip Mountbatten, R.N., son of the late Prince Andrew of Greece and Princess Andrew (Princess Alice of Battenberg), to which union the King has gladly given his consent.

The newspapers made much of Philip's British education and his service in the Royal Navy during the war, building him up as the nephew of Dickie Mountbatten rather than as a foreign prince.

The following afternoon, the couple appeared at the garden party at Buckingham Palace where they were warmly greeted by the crowds. The engagement ring had been made by jewellers Philip Antrobus of Old Bond Street from stones given by Princess Alice, taken from a diamond and aquamarine tiara given to her as a wedding present by Nicholas II. Since 1930 her jewels had been in a bank vault at the National Westminster Bank in Paris in Prince Andrew's name. She had to obtain the signatures of Philip and his sisters to gain access to them. The tiara was dismantled to make a ring with a large central diamond with five smaller stones clustered around it. Antrobus also a made a diamond bracelet. Alice took the jewels to Antrobus herself, as they feared Philip being recognised and the press getting wind of the forthcoming engagement if he was spotted near a jeweller's shop.

There were more problems over jewels when it was discovered that the diamonds in Andrew's Star of the Order of the Redeemer, which Philip had planned to wear at the wedding, had been substituted for paste stones.

Philip was now given a detective, a secretary to organise his diary and, most importantly, a valet – John Dean, Dickie Mountbatten's former butler.

The wedding was set for Thursday 20 November in Westminster Abbey. Royal relatives from all over Europe were invited, although it was decided that Philip's sisters, all married to Germans, would be excluded from the invitation list. With the war having finished only two years earlier, it was felt too early to invite them when anti-German feelings still ran so high in the British public. Philip well understood the problems. 'I think that the difficulty with all royal families is they've always had to compromise between their family interests and their national interests,' he said many years later. 'This can be extremely unpleasant. I was serving in the British Navy and I had three brothers-in-law serving in the German army. You get swept up into these things. It was tragic.'[19]

His cousin David, Marquess of Milford Haven, was asked to be best man and moved into Kensington Palace, where Philip still stayed when in London. John Dean was astonished when he saw the pair living in modest attic rooms with worn-out rugs on the bare floorboards.

Philip had been baptised Greek Orthodox but was received into the Church of England in a private service at Lambeth Palace in early October. He was also given the Order of the Garter (a week after his fiancée received hers).

His official bachelor party was held at the Dorchester Hotel on the wedding eve. It was attended by Dickie Mountbatten (who had flown back from India with Edwina for the occasion) and Philip's comrades from the 27th Destroyer Flotilla. A few press photographers were permitted to take pictures before Philip left shortly after midnight to be ready for the big day ahead.

The wedding day dawned dull and cloudy. That morning, as the bride dressed at Buckingham Palace, the bridegroom and David

Milford Haven calmed their nerves with a gin and tonic. Philip left Kensington Palace wearing his naval uniform with the Garter insignia and the sword of his maternal grandfather, the former Prince Louis of Battenberg.

At the abbey David Milford Haven looked after the Welsh gold wedding ring fashioned from a nugget from the Clogau St David's mine in Snowdonia. Although the groom appeared on the order of service as Lieutenant Philip Mountbatten, R.N., the king had created him a Royal Highness with the titles of Baron Greenwich, Earl of Merioneth and Duke of Edinburgh. There would be no chance of Princess Elizabeth ever being known as just Mrs Mountbatten. The announcement came too late to be included on the order of service.

King George VI and his daughter arrived at Westminster Abbey in the Irish State Coach. Norman Hartnell had designed a romantic wedding gown based on a Botticelli painting. Made from ivory silk satin and decorated with more than 10,000 pearls forming garlands of star flowers, wheat ears and the white rose of York, it had an embroidered train 15 feet long and a veil to match. Like other post-war brides Princess Elizabeth had collected clothing coupons for her wedding dress, although the allowance had been supplemented by material previously purchased by both her mother and her grandmother Queen Mary.

Five kings, five queens and several European princes and princesses awaited them in the Abbey. The bride's uncle the Duke of Windsor (the former King Edward VIII) was not invited. The bridegroom's mother Princess Alice sat with her sister Crown Princess Louise of Sweden and their mother Victoria Milford Haven. Dickie and Edwina were nearby. Of Philip's father's siblings, only Prince George was still alive and attended with his wife Princess Marie, from whom he was now estranged. Among the eight bridesmaids was Princess Margaret.

As they stood before the Archbishop of Canterbury, Elizabeth promised to 'obey' her husband. Afterwards, in his address, the Archbishop of York said that the ceremony was essentially the same as it would be for any cottager in a remote village. The service was broadcast by radio in forty-two languages and, although television cameras were not permitted to film the wedding ceremony, newsreels around the world showed film of the bridal party leaving the abbey.

The Duke and Duchess of Edinburgh returned to Buckingham Palace escorted by the Household Cavalry, who were wearing full ceremonial dress for the first time in six years. The king had suggested an austerity wedding in keeping with the times as so many people were suffering after the war. Although in a nod to austerity the street decorations were few, the wedding was described by Winston Churchill as 'a flash of colour on the hard road we have to travel'.

At the wedding breakfast, bunches of white Balmoral heather decorated the tables and the speeches were kept short at the king's request. With rationing still in force, ingredients for the 9-foot-high official wedding cake, made by McVitie and Price, had been sent as gifts from overseas.

As dusk fell the couple drove out of the palace courtyard in an open carriage pursued by laughing guests showering them with confetti.

The first part of the honeymoon was spent at Dickie and Edwina's Hampshire home, Broadlands. A few photographers were allowed into the grounds to take pictures but sightseers hovered everywhere hoping for the slightest glimpse of the famous newlyweds. When they went to Sunday morning service at Romsey Abbey, people used chairs, ladders or even tombstones to climb up and peer through the windows for a better view. After a few days the couple left for Birkhall on the Balmoral estate in Scotland, where amid the winter snow they finally found solitude.

Like many young couples at that time, they had no home of their own. Even the country home that the king had designated for them, Sunninghill Park in Windsor Great Park, burnt down before they could occupy it.

Philip was working at the Admiralty. Their London home was to be Clarence House but, with refurbishment work still ongoing, they moved into Elizabeth's former rooms at Buckingham Palace. Philip was given a bedroom, with a sitting room between his room and Elizabeth's. It was not ideal and there was some friction between the somewhat brash Philip and the stuffy (in his opinion) courtiers. To enliven the atmosphere, he asked Mike Parker to become his equerry. Nevertheless, life was not easy for Philip. He was frustrated with his job at the Admiralty and frustrated with life at the palace. When one of the courtiers told him that he would like Windsor Castle once he got to know it, Philip replied, 'Yes, my mother was born there.'[20]

Life was made a little easier by the appointment of General Sir Frederick 'Boy' Browning, husband of the novelist Daphne du Maurier. Browning, a former Guards officer, was appointed treasurer and comptroller to the Edinburghs' household and was able to stand up to the other former Guards officers in the royal household who were too fond of telling the young couple what they should, or should not, do.

Within three months of the wedding the princess discovered she was pregnant. Despite this, in May 1948 the Duke and Duchess of Edinburgh undertook their first official visit abroad, a four-day trip to Paris. Against the background of the Cold War, with communism now the main enemy, the trip was engineered to stress Anglo-French solidarity. The visit followed a pattern which would later become familiar – the opening of an exhibition, a reception to meet prominent dignitaries and a dinner at the British embassy.

Elizabeth was shy. It was the more outgoing Philip, who was expert at making witty speeches without notes, who suggested phrasing for her speeches and took the lead in any potentially awkward situations.

Despite suffering from food poisoning (reputedly brought on by the food at the British embassy), Philip insisted on going through with the whole arranged programme. Elizabeth, in the early stages of pregnancy, tired easily and Philip had to insist she rest. Nevertheless, the glamorous couple took Paris by storm and by the time they left cries of '*Vive la Princesse*' were heard everywhere.

At 9.14 p.m. on 14 November 1948, Princess Elizabeth gave birth to a son at Buckingham Palace. The happy news was greeted with gun salutes, bells, bonfires and fountains running 'blue for a boy' all week. Letters Patent been hastily issued to give the child the style, title or attribute of Royal Highness and the titular dignity of prince or princess. The king had also abolished the centuries-old custom of the Home Secretary being in attendance during the birth.

Prince Charles Philip Arthur George was christened on 15 December in the Music Room of the palace (the chapel had been bombed). The choice of the name Charles caused some surprise in royal circles because of its association with the unlucky Stuarts, but the couple chose the name simply because they liked it. At his birth he was Duke of Cornwall.

The Romanov blood had now entered the direct line of the British royal family.

In May 1949, Elizabeth and Philip finally moved into Clarence House. The duke, who had not experienced a settled home life since he was nine years old, threw himself into the project with gusto, installing many modern labour-saving devices. For a country home they rented Windlesham Moor, a five-bedroomed, four reception-roomed house within easy reach of Windsor. Philip enjoyed rearranging furniture or buying gadgets like an electric mixer or a washing machine from the Ideal Home Exhibition. On Sundays they drove over to Royal Lodge to join the king and queen for a service in the private chapel in the grounds. Yet there was concern.

The fifty-four-year-old king had been suffering from cramp in his legs, which developed into arteriosclerosis. It was feared that his right leg might have to be amputated, although thankfully this did not prove necessary. Reluctantly he was forced to postpone a planned tour of Australia and New Zealand. Early in March 1949 a lumbar sympathectomy was successfully performed at Buckingham Palace and at the sovereign's Birthday Parade that June the king rode in a carriage. Princess Elizabeth rode side-saddle at the head of the parade.

Philip still longed to go back to sea. In the autumn his wish was granted when he was appointed first lieutenant of HMS *Chequers*, part of the Mediterranean Fleet based on the tiny island of Malta. Also based there were Philip's uncle Dickie and aunt Edwina, now Earl and Countess Mountbatten of Burma, who had leased the villa at 49 Guardamangia Hill, Pietà, on the outskirts of Valletta while the earl was serving as flag officer of the First Cruiser Squadron.

After celebrating her son's first birthday, Elizabeth flew out to join her husband for their second wedding anniversary. Prince Charles was left at home in the care of his nanny and his grandparents.

The couple led a fairly normal life on Malta. They were often seen dining and dancing at the Hotel Phoenicia, although the princess had an ever-present detective and a lady-in-waiting and was addressed as ma'am. She left the island reluctantly just before Christmas.

She returned to Villa Guardamangia at the end of March 1950. Lord Mountbatten had been recalled home but recommended Joe Micallef, one of his former crew members, as the couple's butler. It was, Mr Micallef said, a happy household, 'like working with a family of your own'.[21]

The eighteen-roomed villa had six bedrooms and three bathrooms. Chief Petty Officer Herbert Hicks was employed as a driver and handyman, responsible for unpacking all the household effects transported to Malta and handing responsibility for them to Micallef. According to the princess, Hicks was 'in charge of the technical side and will be responsible for all repairs inside and out ... Any breakages or replacement in that line will be attended to by him on our instructions. He should also see that everything is in working order (bells, telephones, plumbing, cupboards etc) before I arrive.' Above all, though, she sincerely hoped 'that full co-operation will exist between all members ... so as to create a happy atmosphere at the Villa Guardamangia'.[22]

Housekeeper Josephine Grech (known as 'Sergeant Major Jessie' because of her firm attitude) often brought her five-year-old daughter Elizabeth along. Years later Elizabeth Pulé recalled how the Duke of Edinburgh, enticed by the smell of cooking, came into the kitchen and asked Jessie if he could taste the Maltese black pudding she was making. 'He was very friendly, she said.'[23]

In the warm Mediterranean weather the royal couple swam, enjoyed picnics and explored the island's beaches and coves in small boats. Philip played polo, a sport at which he was rapidly becoming accomplished, and went water-skiing.

The princess returned to Clarence House in May to await the birth of Princess Anne on 15 August. Philip joined her in time for the happy event before returning to Malta to take up his first command on HMS *Magpie*. In December, Elizabeth re-joined him and they resumed their life under the Mediterranean sun.

From Malta HMS *Magpie* was sent on several ceremonial exercises to fly the British flag in Mediterranean ports. In December 1950 it was the turn of Greece, which Philip was anxious to show to his wife. Elizabeth travelled on HMS *Surprise* as the commander-in-chief decided there was no suitable accommodation for her aboard *Magpie*. This arrangement caused a lively exchange of signals between the vessels:

> *Surprise* to *Magpie*: Princess full of beans.
> *Magpie* to *Surprise*: Is that the best you can give her for breakfast?[24]

After a state drive through Athens with Philip's cousins King Paul and Queen Frederica, Elizabeth inspected a guard of honour of the Evzones, the presidential guard, in their traditional red toques, embroidered tunics and white pleated kilts. They later saw the floodlit Parthenon and attended a state dinner at the royal palace, where Frederica wore a lace dress which had belonged to Philip's grandmother Queen Olga.

Accompanied by the king and queen, their daughters Sophia and Irene (Crown Prince Constantine was at school) and Philip's sister Sophie and her husband George, they toured the Acropolis and other sights.

There were also some more informal moments. Lady Norton, the British ambassador's wife, had given Philip the key to her husband's beach house so that they could cook a late-night feast. Unfortunately, she forgot to tell the ambassador. As the lively party, cutlasses in their teeth, scaled the cliffs to the house, Sir Clifford Norton was heard to roar from an upstairs window, 'Who's there?' Later he changed out of his pyjamas and joined them as they cooked sausages.

They spent six days at Tatoi, driving round in a jeep without giving notice of their route, causing a headache for their security men. Before leaving Greece on 12 December, they also visited the grave of Philip's father in the royal burial ground.

Back in Malta, on 2 April 1951 they made an excursion to the neighbouring island of Gozo – but their idyll was soon to end.

By the spring of 1951 the king was again ill. There was a shadow on his lung and the doctors suspected that he had cancer, although the royal family were not informed. Since the previous summer, Princess Elizabeth had been allowed access to cabinet papers and memoranda in order to broaden her experience of state matters.

In April, Elizabeth and Philip embarked on an official visit to Rome, where they made a courtesy call at the Vatican. This sparked protests from Protestant groups in England, unhappy that the heiress presumptive had been received in audience by the Pope.

King George's health had declined further and Princess Elizabeth was needed to take over some of his duties. In July Philip was given indefinite leave from the navy and they returned from Malta for good.

A planned visit by the king and queen to Canada and the United States was postponed and instead, in September, the king underwent a bronchoscopy after a tumour was found on his lung. The doctors' worst fears were confirmed when they found that the tumour was malignant. On 23 September his left lung was removed and a cautious bulletin was issued, but by now it was obvious that the king would not survive much longer.

It had been decided that the Duke and Duchess of Edinburgh would undertake the postponed state visit to Canada and the United States. On 7 October, Elizabeth therefore became the first member of the royal family to fly across the Atlantic when she and Philip boarded a British Overseas Airways Corporation jet for the seventeen-hour flight to Montreal. As the king's life hung by a thread, among the piles of luggage were black mourning clothes and a sealed envelope containing the draft Accession Declaration.

In Canada they covered a distance of 10,000 miles, taking in every province in the dominion. A crowd of 25,000 people greeted them at Montreal's airport – half a million thronged the streets of Ottawa alone – but it was not all plain sailing. Philip referred to Canada as 'a good investment', a remark which to some smacked of colonialism and caused offence. Yet there were moments of relaxation and sheer enjoyment. In Ottawa they threw themselves with gusto into a traditional square dance and were photographed spinning arm in arm, Elizabeth in a full skirt, Philip in a chequered shirt and jeans. At Niagara Falls they donned protective clothing and went down to the viewing platform at the foot of the falls where, as *The Times* reported, 'they stood amid the thunder of the water with the spray drifting over them'.

Elizabeth was naturally anxious about her father, but on the long train journeys across Canada Philip attempted to lighten the mood by playing practical jokes, surprising her with a booby-trapped tin of nuts and chasing her down the corridor wearing a set of false teeth.

Washington, where they arrived by air on 31 October, was easier. As the White House was being redecorated they stayed at Blair House with President Truman, whose deaf, bedridden mother lived on the top floor.

'Mother, I've brought Princess Elizabeth to see you!' the president informed her.

Having just heard that Churchill had been returned to power in the general election, the confused old lady told the princess, 'I'm so glad your father's been re-elected.'[25]

On their return to England in November, the king created them both privy councillors. They were not reassured by his appearance. Nevertheless, on 2 December a day of national thanksgiving for the king's recovery was celebrated before the entire royal family gathered at Sandringham as usual for Christmas.

On 29 January, the king returned to London for a consultation with his doctors and the following evening the royal family ('us four and

Philip' as the king called them) attended a performance of the musical *South Pacific* at the Drury Lane Theatre.

The next day Elizabeth and Philip left London Airport for the tour of East Africa, Australia and New Zealand which the king had postponed in 1948. It would take them away for six months. The king stood on the tarmac, waving goodbye until his daughter's plane disappeared from view. Newsreel films showed him hatless in the cold wind, looking tired and drawn.

Their first stop was Nairobi, where they were driven through cheering crowds to Government House for a few days of official engagements, including a visit to Nairobi National Park where they photographed the wildlife. They were also officially presented with the key to Sagana Lodge, a cedarwood hunting lodge in the Aberdare Forest game reserve at Nyeri. The lodge was a wedding present from the Kenyan people and on 3 February Elizabeth and Philip drove 100 miles over dusty roads to spend a few days resting there before the next stage of the tour.

On 5 February they decided to spend the night at nearby Treetops Hotel, set in the branches of a giant fig tree. It had only three bedrooms, a dining room and a room for the hunter but a specially constructed platform formed a perfect place from which to watch the wildlife. Although the hotel had recently been redecorated, baboons had since forced their way inside and eaten some of the new lampshades. With Philip's equerry Mike Parker and cousin Lady Pamela Mountbatten, who acted as Elizabeth's lady-in-waiting, they spent a fascinating night watching, and filming, the elephants, baboons and rhinos at the watering hole and saltlick below. It was almost dawn before Elizabeth went to bed.

Back at Sandringham, at some time during the early hours of 6 February, the king died peacefully in his sleep from thrombosis. Elizabeth had climbed up to Treetops as a princess but, unknowingly, she climbed down as queen.

After breakfast, unaware of what had occurred, Elizabeth and Philip drove back to Sagana Lodge to spend a few hours fishing before they left for Mombasa.

News of the king's death took a while to reach Kenya. The king's private secretary had sent a telegram to Elizabeth's private secretary, Martin Charteris, with the agreed code 'Hyde Park Corner' but it never arrived. Meanwhile, an unconfirmed Reuters newsflash arrived at the press headquarters for the royal visit, the Outspan Hotel in Nyeri, where Martin Charteris was having lunch. Informed by a local journalist, he quickly telephoned Mike Parker, who found a radio and tuned in to the BBC. They were playing sombre music but there was no news. As Charteris drove back to Sagana Lodge, Parker made frantic telephone calls to obtain official confirmation.

With the sad news confirmed, he attracted Philip's attention and beckoned him outside onto the lawn. 'He looked as if you'd dropped half the world on him,' Parker recalled later.[26] It was 2.45 p.m. in Kenya, 11.45 a.m. in London.

Philip found Elizabeth and took her outside towards the river, where they walked slowly up and down for a long time, trying to come to terms with what had happened.

As Mike Parker made hasty arrangements for their immediate return to London, Martin Charteris opened the accession documents and asked by what name she wanted to be known as queen. Twenty-five-year-old Elizabeth showed no hesitation. 'My own name, of course,' she replied. 'What else?'

On 7 February, they arrived back at London Airport. In a symbolic moment, as Queen Elizabeth II came down the aircraft steps dressed all in black, Prince Philip waited behind until she had stepped onto British soil.

For the next sixty-five years the Duke of Edinburgh walked slightly behind his wife, playing a supporting role to the queen until his retirement from public life in 2017. He truly became her liege man, as he had sworn to be at the coronation in 1953.

Two more children were born: Andrew in 1960 and Edward in 1964. They, and all their descendants, also have Romanov blood.

The penniless prince, initially known by his detractors as 'Phil the Greek' or even 'the Hun', made his mark on all aspects of British life. His list of patronages and interests, if printed, would cover volumes. His contribution to Britain was enormous.

He died on 9 April 2021, just short of his one-hundredth birthday, and is buried at St George's Chapel, Windsor.

On the death of Queen Elizabeth II on 8 September 2022, Charles became the fifth monarch of the House of Windsor. The Romanov blood runs from him to Princes William and Harry, as well as their children and future descendants.

The chain of events which started with the marriage of Tsar Ivan IV and Anastasia Romanov in 1547 will continue to have an impact on the direct line of the British royal family for years to come.

13

'Prints Waleski's Visits to Russia'

King Charles has visited the lands of his ancestors several times. Although members of the royal family had been there unofficially and Princess Anne paid a two-week official visit in 1990, when Charles arrived in St Petersburg in 1994 he was the first Prince of Wales to visit Russia for a hundred years.

The last to do so was Albert Edward, eldest son of Queen Victoria, who as Prince of Wales came for the funeral of Emperor Alexander III and the wedding of Nicholas II in November 1894. After he became King Edward VII he paid a state visit in 1908 but, for security reasons, he and Queen Alexandra remained on board their yacht and never set foot on land.

Prince Charles arrived on 16 May 1994 for a three-day official visit to St Petersburg. During his stay he laid a wreath in the Piskarevskoye cemetery, which holds the remains of 450,000 victims from the 872-day siege of Leningrad, which lasted from September 1941 to January 1944. At the bronze statue of Mother Russia he stood alone for some time, his head bowed. From his base at the Grand Hotel Europe he toured the Maryinskaya Hospital, where most of the equipment still dated from the 1930s; visited Littlewoods, the first big western retailer to open a store in Russia; and toured a farm about 20 miles from St Petersburg.

Perhaps the most poignant part of his trip was a visit to the SS Peter and Paul Cathedral, where many of his ancestors are buried in white marble sarcophagi.

On 4 November 1996, 'Prints Waleski', as the Russian press called Charles, arrived in Kiev at the invitation of President Leonid Kuchma.

At Boryspil International Airport he was met by the Minister of Foreign Affairs and greeted with the traditional bread and salt by women wearing national costume. Then there was a meeting with President Kuchma. At a joint interview Prince Charles said he was very touched at the kind welcome and expressed how pleased he was to have a brief opportunity to see something of this remarkable country.

During his stay in Kiev the prince laid a wreath at the Tomb of the Unknown Soldier in the Eternal Glory Park to commemorate the Ukrainians who died in the Second World War fighting the Nazis. He visited a care centre, addressed Ukrainian and international entrepreneurs at a Prince of Wales Business Forum at the Kiev Mohyla University, and visited St Sophia's Cathedral, whose frescoes date from the eleventh century. It has been a UNESCO World Heritage site since 1990.

The day ended with a dinner given by President Kuchma at the seventeenth-century blue-and-white Maryinsky Palace. From 1916 until the revolution in 1917, this had been the residence of Charles's great-great-great-aunt the Dowager Empress Marie Feodorovna of Russia, mother of Nicholas II and sister of Britain's Queen Alexandra.

The following day the Prince of Wales travelled south to the Crimea, which at that time was part of Ukraine.

At Bakhchisaray, the old capital of the Crimea, he toured the 500-year-old palace of the ruling khans and admired the Fountain of Tears immortalised by Pushkin's poem. In the Tatar village he learnt about Crimean Tatar culture from the Osmanov family, who offered him a cup of traditional Tatar black coffee. Later Emine Osmanova told a reporter from *Vesti Krym* that a street in Bakhchisaray had been named Prince of Wales Street after their eminent visitor. 'He came to our house, by the way. Grandma made him coffee. He really liked it,' she said. 'He promised to come again.'

Charles then continued south to Sevastopol. Until recently it had been a closed city, and the city leadership were now anxious to build relations with both western and post-Soviet countries. As part of this initiative the Duke and Duchess of Gloucester were welcomed to the Crimea in September 1994. This paved the way for the official visit of the Prince of Wales, as part of a trip to five former Soviet republics.

The visit to Sevastopol was a chance to see the battlefields of the Crimean War and lay a wreath to remember the 23,000 British soldiers who perished at Sevastopol and Balaklava. The prince was accompanied by the British Ambassador Extraordinary and Plenipotentiary Robert Reeve, and the Military Attaché in Ukraine

Captain Lee Merrick of the Royal Navy, as well as the head of the Presidential Administration of Ukraine D. V. Tabachnick and the Ukrainian Ambassador Extraordinary and Plenipotentiary to the United Kingdom C. V. Komissarenko. Prince Charles's visit took place a few days before Remembrance Sunday in Britain, so he wore a poppy in his lapel.

The prince's first stop was the observation platform on Sapun Hill, where Colonel Valery B. Ivanov told the prince about the battles in which the British soldiers participated and showed him maps, graphics, photos and lithographs. Both Light and Heavy Brigades had been stationed at Balaklava Valley and hundreds of British soldiers lost their lives in the ill-fated Charge of the Light Brigade, when Lord Cardigan's cavalry was decimated. Prince Charles was told that Sevastopol had accrued vast amounts of information about the British participants and there was a computer database recording the fallen British soldiers in Crimea.

Accompanied by a crowd of dignitaries and journalists, the prince then climbed the steps to the British Memorial Complex of 1854–56 at Cathcart Hill, named after General Sir George Cathcart who was killed in action on that spot. He silently viewed the memorial plaques all around, bearing the name of regiments, ships and units which took part in the battles. It was explained to the prince that the cast-iron plaques were salvaged from shipwrecked vessels found near the Kacha shores outside Sevastopol. Not only naval items were salvaged; even bottles of old whisky were recovered from the wrecks. (Some of this old whisky was tasted by former British prime minister Lord Callaghan on a visit in 1992.)

As a band played sombre music, the prince laid a wreath before the British and Ukrainian national anthems were performed. Then Prince Charles and Victor M. Semenov, chairman of the Sevastopol City Administration, each planted a juniper tree nearby.

This idea had caused some concern among Ukrainian officials at the meeting of the protocol department. The Ministry of Foreign Affairs was opposed to such a plan.

'Are you going to give a spade in the hands of the heir to the British throne to plant some tree?' an official asked incredulously.

'Okay, we won't,' replied Semenov.

As soon as the protocol chiefs had left, however, he instructed Mikhail Yurlov, head of the Department for External Affairs, to 'prepare two trees and dig holes'.

Mikhail Yurlov, who acted as interpreter, later provided his personal impression of the Prince of Wales. 'Despite the fact that Charles could also joke during brief conversations with officials, he seemed to me a very reserved person,' he said. Sevastopol had received many high-ranking visitors at that time, yet Yurlov said he had never felt 'such restraint, even a certain coolness, as from Prince Charles'. Others were amazed by his 'calmness and unexpected simplicity'.

On signing the visitor's book in the Foreign History Museum the prince was surprised to see other eminent names, among them a descendant of Lord Cardigan, who commanded the cavalry in 1854.

After meeting local leaders and representatives of the navy the prince chatted with children from School No. 3 and their teacher. The conversations were in English, so there was no need for Mikhail Yurlov's services.

The Prince of Wales spent the night at the Zarya facility. This modern dacha, situated roughly a mile from the village of Foros, was once the holiday home of Soviet president Mikhail Gorbachev. The red-roofed dacha, built in 1988 near the Sevastopol–Yalta highway, looked out over the sea and provided every modern luxury from a gym to a helipad and an escalator down to the private beach.

The Prince of Wales left from Belbek Airport near Sevastopol, where things did not go quite according to plan. The technicians had forgotten to remove the 'chocks' – the blocks of wood placed under the wheels to prevent the plane from moving. As the plane began to taxi forward it suddenly stopped, to the dismay of airport staff. The watching officials continued to wave goodbye to the prince for what seemed like hours but, try as they might, the technicians were unable to remove the chocks. Suddenly, Captain Merrick appeared with a hammer. He knocked the chocks out and the plane took off.[1]

Charles returned to St Petersburg between 13 and 16 July 2003 to mark the 300th anniversary of the founding of the city by Peter the Great.

He returned to the Piskarevskoye cemetery for another wreath-laying ceremony, toured the spectacular Peterhof Palace, where he was impressed by the famous fountains in the grounds, and gave the training ship the *Adventure* to the Russian navy as a gift from the British Navy.

Back in St Petersburg he visited the tombs of Nicholas II and Empress Alexandra. Since his previous visit their remains had been buried in the SS Peter & Paul Cathedral.

On the last day he went north to the Russian Solovki Islands in the White Sea, near the Arctic circle. Charles, who has an interest in the Orthodox religion into which his father was baptised, always dreamed of visiting the fifteenth-century Solovetsky Monastery, an Orthodox shrine which Stalin had turned into a gulag but which was now restored to the church. He commemorated the victims of the gulag memorialised in the monastery walls and planted fir saplings in the memorial alley. Through his International Business Leaders Forum, he was helping to restore the monastery to its former glory.

Poignantly, in the Arboretum at Highgrove, the king's private home in Gloucestershire, there is a bronze statue called *The Daughters of Odessa: Martyrs of Modernism* by the American sculptor Frederick Hart. It is dedicated to all the oppressed people in the world. Presented to Charles in 1997, it represents the four martyred daughters of Nicholas II – Grand Duchesses Olga, Tatiana, Marie and Anastasia – and their qualities of Faith, Hope, Innocence and Beauty.[2]

The girls were his second cousins once removed.

14

'The bastards murdered half my family'

King Charles III has other links to the Russian imperial family, specifically to the ill-fated last tsar and tsarina, Nicholas II and Alexandra, who were his great-great-uncle and aunt. (The older title 'tsar' will be used in connection with Nicholas II, who preferred it to that of emperor.)

Although Charles's maternal great-grandfather King George V was the first cousin of Nicholas (their mothers were sisters), he had no Romanov blood. It was Prince Philip who provided Charles's other Russian link.

Philip's maternal great-grandmother Princess Alice was the second daughter of Queen Victoria and wife of Grand Duke Louis IV of Hesse and By Rhine. Alice and Louis had four surviving daughters. The eldest, Victoria, as we have seen, married Prince Louis of Battenberg in 1885 and became Marchioness of Milford Haven in 1917; Elisabeth (Ella) married Grand Duke Sergei Alexandrovich, a younger brother of Alexander III and uncle to the future Nicholas II. The next sister, Irene, married Prince Henry of Prussia, brother of Kaiser William II; and Alix married Nicholas II of Russia in 1894 and became Empress Alexandra Feodorovna. Ella and Alix were killed by the Bolsheviks.

On the paternal side, Prince Philip's grandfather King George I of Greece had a Romanov wife, Grand Duchess Olga Constantinovna, but he was also the brother of Empress Marie Feodorovna, wife of Alexander III. Some of Philip's Greek relatives also married Russians: his uncle Prince Nicholas married Grand Duchess Elena Vladimirovna.[1] His aunt Princess Alexandra married Grand Duke Paul Alexandrovich and another aunt, Princess Marie, married Grand Duke George Michaelovich. Both grand dukes were shot in the environs of the SS Peter & Paul Cathedral in 1919, along with Grand Dukes Dmitri Constantinovich (Philip's great-uncle) and Nicholas Michaelovich. Their bodies were thrown into a common grave. Dmitri's body was removed by his former adjutant the next day and buried in the garden of a private house, where it remains.[2]

Prince Philip also had four Russian first cousins: Grand Duke Dmitri Pavlovich (who we have seen was with Philip in Rome in 1938) and his sister Grand Duchess Marie Pavlovna, who escaped the revolution; and Princesses Nina and Xenia Georgievna, who were in England with their mother Grand Duchess George when the revolution occurred.

Altogether, seventeen of Prince Philip's close relatives were killed during the Russian revolution. It is little wonder, then, that when asked by an interviewer in 1967 whether he would like to go to Russia, Philip was quoted as saying 'that he would like to go to Russia very much, although the bastards had murdered half his family'.[3]

His relationship to the Romanovs proved useful, though, when it came to identifying putative imperial remains.

On 17 July 1918, Nicholas II, Empress Alexandra, their five children and four retainers were shot in the Ipatiev House in Ekaterinburg. When the White Army took Ekaterinburg eight days later, the house was empty. There was only the sinister ground-floor room, with blood on the floor and bullet holes in the walls. The imperial family had completely disappeared. For more than sixty years nobody knew what had happened to them.

Then, in 1989, the *Moscow News* announced that 'the grave of the tsar and his family' had been secretly found ten years earlier in Koptyaki Forest near Ekaterinburg.

That same month President Mikhail Gorbachev was received at Windsor by Queen Elizabeth II. The Russians were anxious for the monarch to pay a return visit to Russia (which British newspapers were already reporting would go ahead within a year), but the fate of Prince Philip's great-uncle and aunt needed to be clarified first.[4]

After the break-up of the Soviet Union in 1991, President Boris Yeltsin (who as regional first secretary had ordered the demolition of the Ipatiev House in 1977) ordered the grave to be opened. Almost 1,000 bone fragments were discovered and assembled into a total of nine bodies – but were they the Romanovs?

After extensive work by Russian forensic experts, which included facial recognition technology, in 1992 bone specimens were examined by a forensic team from the University of Florida led by Dr William Maples. He concluded that there were five members of the imperial family and four retainers. Two bodies were missing – Tsarevich Alexei and one of his sisters, either Anastasia (according to the Americans) or Marie (according to the Russians). The news caused a media sensation and reignited stories of the escape of one of the tsar's daughters.

Then, in what at the time was a new scientific breakthrough, the chief forensic medical examiner of the Russian Ministry of Health approached the British Home Office and requested an official Anglo-Russian investigation using DNA-based techniques.

On 15 September 1992, Dr Pavel Ivanov of the Moscow Forensic Institute arrived at Heathrow Airport with a bag containing 'a few discoloured bones'.[5] He was welcomed by Nigel McCrery, a BBC television producer who had studied Russian history and was active in efforts to have the bones brought to England for testing. Thinking it 'inappropriate to carry the Russian imperial family in the boot of my Volvo', he hired a limousine from a funeral company to transport himself, Ivanov and the bones to Aldermaston, where a small laboratory was used by the Forensic Science Service (FSS).[6]

Dr Ivanov joined Dr Peter Gill, director of the Molecular Research Centre of the FSS, and his team in a project lasting six months. It is here that the Duke of Edinburgh entered the picture.

The pieces from the femurs and tibias of the nine skeletons, which had been buried in the ground for over seventy-five years, had obviously deteriorated and were too degraded to be subjected to standard genetic testing.[7] Gill, Ivanov and the team therefore used mitochondrial DNA (mtDNA), which comes exclusively from the mother. They consequently needed relatives who were closely related to Nicholas and Alexandra through the female line. Prince Philip's mother Princess Alice of Greece was the daughter of Victoria, Marchioness of Milford Haven, the elder sister of Empress Alexandra. Prince Philip was therefore one of the closest living relatives of the last Empress of Russia. Although mtDNA cannot prove identity, it *could* refute a genetic relationship.

In around September 1992, Dr Janet Thomson, director of the FSS, wrote to Prince Philip at Buckingham Palace to ask if he would be willing to provide a sample for testing. He was said to be 'delighted to assist the research'.[8] The blood sample he provided in a test tube was used to map his mtDNA sequence, which was then compared with mtDNA samples taken from the bones. He was 'the first living relative of the Romanovs to provide a sample for DNA analysis'.[9]

The paper later published by Dr Gill and his team confirmed a complete match. 'Analysis of mitochondrial (mt) DNA reveals an exact sequence match between the putative Tsarina and the three children with a living maternal relative.'[10] Alexandra's mtDNA was shared by her sister Victoria, passed down to her daughter Alice and then to Prince Philip. In the same way, Alexandra's mtDNA was passed to her children Olga, Tatiana, Marie, Anastasia and Alexei. The bodies of the three children in the grave were therefore offspring of Alexandra.

Nicholas II's case proved slightly more difficult, and here the Duke of Edinburgh was unable to help. Although his father was a first cousin of Nicholas it was through the *paternal*, not maternal, line. Two maternal relatives were tested, including Madame Xenia Sfiris, whose mother Princess Irina was the daughter of Nicholas's elder sister, Grand Duchess Xenia. Although they had identical mtDNA, Nicholas 'had a single mutation [alteration] not present in relatives'.[11] Nicholas's mother Empress Marie Feodorovna was buried in Roskilde Cathedral in Denmark, but it was not possible to take any sample from her. Even when she was taken to St Petersburg for reburial in the SS Peter & Paul Cathedral in 2006, it was on the strict condition that her coffin remained unopened and no DNA samples were taken.[12]

None of Grand Duchess Xenia's children were now alive. However, Nicholas's mtDNA was shared by Tihon Kulikovsky, elder son of his other sister, Grand Duchess Olga. Although he was the tsar's closest living relative, he declined to help, believing the whole episode was a hoax organised by the KGB. Nor would he have anything to do with the British testing, firstly because George V had refused asylum to the imperial family in 1917 and secondly 'because he believed the British royal family had personally swindled his mother out of hundreds of thousands of dollars following the sale of certain jewellery to Queen Mary'.[13]

In a 2016 exhibition at Amalienborg Palace in Copenhagen entitled 'From the Attics' there was a box of paper packets containing locks of hair from the children and grandchildren of Queen Louise of Denmark, Nicholas II's maternal grandmother. Among them were packets containing the hair of Empress Marie Feodorovna and her daughter Grand Duchess Olga. Whether these locks of hair were known about in 1993 (and whether they would have been of any use for DNA testing if they were) is unknown.[14]

Instead, in May 1993 the burial vault of Nicholas's brother Grand Duke George (who died in 1899) in the SS Peter and Paul Cathedral was opened and samples were sent to the Armed Forces Institute of Pathology in Washington. 'The mtDNA sequence of George Romanov matched that of the putative Tsar, and was heteroplasmic [more than one gene type] at the same position,' the report stated. It was powerful evidence.[15]

The tests determined that there was a probability of 98.5 per cent that the bones were those of the imperial family. Still, there were thousands of missing bones and nothing corresponding to Alexei, nor to one of his sisters.

Through the decades, stories had persisted that Nicholas and Alexandra's youngest daughter Anastasia survived the massacre at Ekaterinburg. Here Prince Philip's mtDNA could also be of assistance – but first there were obstacles to overcome.

There had been numerous pretenders but the most famous was the woman later known as Anna Anderson, who was pulled from the Landwehr Canal in Berlin in 1920 after attempting suicide. She carried no identification, refused to answer questions and her body bore marks of violence. It was thought she was Russian. After six weeks in hospital, she was sent to an asylum as 'Miss Unknown'. Gradually, she befriended the nurses. Then, during the autumn of 1921, the woman confided that she was Anastasia, sole survivor of the tsar's family.

The resulting investigations divided the Russian émigré community and the surviving Romanovs for decades. Maurice Philip Remy, a German television producer from a wealthy aristocratic family, was determined to solve the mystery once and for all and began making a film about Anastasia. In alliance with members of what was loosely termed the Hesse family (descendants of the siblings of Empress Alexandra), he intended to prove that Anna Anderson was an imposter.[16]

Opposing him were Richard and Marina Schweitzer. Marina's grandfather Dr Eugene Botkin had died with the imperial family in 1918, and they firmly believed in Anna Anderson's identity as Anastasia.

A sample of Anna Anderson's tissue existed in the Martha Jefferson Hospital in Charlottesville, Virginia. They had retained it after a biopsy when she underwent a bowel operation in 1979. The relatives of Anderson's husband Jack Manahan (who died in 1990) could not grant access as they were not her blood relatives. The hospital needed a court order to release the specimen.

In September 1993, a petition was filed with a Virginia court on behalf of Marina Schweitzer asking that Dr Peter Gill be granted access to a small sample for testing purposes. The hearing began on 1 November but, because of legal challenges by Remy and the Russian Nobility Association, litigation dragged on for seventeen months.

For several years Remy had attempted to block the Schweitzers' access to the sample and to do this he tried to involve the Hesse family in his challenges to the Virginia court. He had already obtained a blood sample from Prince Philip's sister Princess Sophie of Hanover. He then tried to involve Princess Margaret of Hesse, the widowed daughter-in-law of Empress Alexandra's brother Ernest Louis (it was her London wedding that Cécile and her family were travelling to in 1937 when they were killed in a plane crash), and Prince Moritz of Hesse, adopted heir of Margaret's late husband. In the summer of 1994, Prince Philip thwarted these efforts.

Having already provided a blood sample for Peter Gill, Philip had no objection to his sister Sophie being approached. 'When Remy went further and tried to draw Sophie, Margaret and Moritz into the Charlottesville litigation,' however, the prince's private secretary Sir Brian McGrath, speaking on behalf of Prince Philip, 'sternly "advised" these royal relatives to stay away'.[17]

Philip and the royal advisers were worried that the controversy over Anna Anderson's identity 'and the resulting lawsuits in Charlottesville' could compromise the state visit the queen was to make to the Russian Federation that October.[18]

There was also another source of material. Following the death of Jack Manahan, much of his library was sold at a North Carolina bookstore. Among the books were several envelopes marked 'Anastasia's hair'. Some were strands or cut locks but there was 'a large clump' dated 1979 which appeared to have come from a hairbrush. Some of it still had follicles attached at the roots. This was purchased by Mrs Susan Burkhart, whose husband, a molecular biologist, prepared the sample to ensure there was no contamination. Then, with the assistance of historians Marlene Eilers Koenig and Peter Kurth, arrangements were made for the hair to be tested.[19]

It was hoped that the question of identity would be solved before the queen and duke left London. For the royal family the fate of the Romanovs 'was part of family folklore', Prince Philip explained. 'But I don't look at this [state visit] as a family occasion.'[20]

On 19 June 1994, Peter Gill collected samples of Anna Anderson's tissue from the Martha Jefferson Hospital and took them back to

England. Prince Philip's mtDNA was then tested against the samples. If she was Anastasia, her mtDNA would match that of Philip. It did not. Tests against the remains of Nicholas, Alexandra and the other daughters confirmed this, and two further tests by independent scientific institutions obtained the same result.[21] Additional confirmation later came from tests on the strands of hair.

On 5 October, Peter Gill announced his findings at a press conference. Anna Anderson was not Anastasia. Prince Philip was not surprised. 'There was a general consensus that the family couldn't allow her to claim who she was unless she had very much better credentials than she had,' he told the *Daily Telegraph*. 'When the results came through it was a great relief.' Sir Brian McGrath, who was at Sandringham with Prince Philip, rejoiced over the 'scuppering of the pro-Anna party'.[22]

On 17 October 1994, Queen Elizabeth II and the Duke of Edinburgh flew into Vnukovo Airport in Moscow to begin a state visit to the Russian Federation. As they entered Russian airspace, they were escorted by four Russian Air Force fighter jets doing aerobatics.

Although King Edward VII and Queen Alexandra had visited Russia in June 1908, for security reasons they did not set foot on the mainland. All the meetings were conducted on board the yachts *Victoria and Albert* and *Standardt*, which were moored at Reval (now Tallinn) on the Baltic Coast. Elizabeth II was therefore the first reigning British monarch to set foot on Russian territory.

After the queen inspected a guard of honoùr, the royal couple drove to the Kremlin in a Rolls-Royce sent specially from England.

At the Great Kremlin Palace. the queen and duke ascended the grand ceremonial staircase, lined by soldiers of the new Presidential Guard in royal blue and gold unforms, whose cap badge had a double-headed eagle and a crown. They then entered St George's Hall (part of the new palace built by Philip's great-great-grandfather Nicholas I in 1849) through massive gold doors and walked down the red carpet of the 200-foot-long hall 'with its gold finish and stunning chandeliers'. President and Mrs Yeltsin entered from the opposite end, while up in the gallery a symphony orchestra provided a fanfare and a drumroll before playing both national anthems. The couples met at the midway point. The welcome was warm.[23]

The queen and duke stayed in the Kremlin (she was the first monarch to do so since Nicholas II), scene of so many dramatic incidents in the lives of Philip's ancestors. The ten-roomed guest apartment had been hastily redecorated, but Prince Philip was disappointed at not being able to tune the radio to the BBC World Service.

Early that evening at the Bolshoi Theatre they sat in what was still called the Tsar's Box for a performance of *Giselle*. This was followed by a reception at the British embassy.

The next day, after a tour of the Kremlin's historical apartments and a wreath-laying ceremony at the Tomb of the Unknown Soldier, there was supposed to be a chance for the royal visitors to meet ordinary Russians in Red Square – but it did not go according to plan. There were few people there, and most were British. As the Duke of Edinburgh approached one young man he was told, 'You will be surprised to learn I'm from London.' 'No, I won't,' Philip replied. 'I've just met a whole group of people from Birmingham.' He approached another, bearded young man. 'Are you Russian?' 'No, I'm just visiting,' replied the Bristolian student. 'Well, you are halfway to being Russian with that beard,' the duke joked. It transpired that the Russian authorities feared the event would be spoiled by protests against President Yeltsin.

During a tour of the Kremlin they visited the Uspensky Sobor, where so many of Philip's direct ancestors had been crowned, and were blessed by Patriarch Alexei II of Moscow and All Russians. Prince Philip, who was originally baptised into the Orthodox faith, had earlier told the *Daily Telegraph* that 'he believed the Church had a strong role to play in the modernisation of the country'. Later he visited the Russian Academy of Sciences where he discussed environmental issues.

That evening a state banquet was given in the historic Palace of Facets, the former location of the coronation feasts. Caviar, pike, perch, beef, salmon, chicken and raspberry parfait were washed down with, among other vintages, 'Tsar wine'. This was the first time dinner jackets had been seen in the Kremlin since the reign of the last tsar (lounge suits had been customary in communist times) and many guests had a real panic to get hold of one. Newspapers reported that some men had borrowed suits from waiters in local restaurants.

On the following morning Prince Philip had the chance to visit the Moscow convent of his great-aunt Ella, Grand Duchess Elisabeth Feodorovna, a place very dear to his heart as his mother had attended the laying of the foundation stone.

After her husband Grand Duke Sergei was blown to bits by a terrorist's bomb in 1905, Ella divested herself of all her worldly goods to fund the building of a convent of which she became abbess. The

Martha and Mary Convent of Mercy began its activities in 1909. The sisters were deaconesses employed in works of mercy, something between a monastic order and a nursing institution. Besides their spiritual duties they took food to the poor and could render immediate medical aid when necessary. In 1918 Ella was arrested, imprisoned with Princes Ioann, Constantine and Igor Constantinovich, cousins of Prince Philip's father, and two of his more distant cousins. As Prince Philip explained, Ella was 'eventually taken and thrown down a mineshaft in Siberia ... They lobbed some hand grenades on top of her.' In October 1918, her body was recovered from the mineshaft by the White Army and taken overland to Beijing. In 1921 her sisters and brother arranged for her coffin to be taken to Jerusalem for burial in the Russian Orthodox Church of St Mary Magdalene on the Mount of Olives.[24] Grand Duchess Elisabeth Feodorovna was later canonised by the Russian Orthodox Church. On 9 July 1998, the queen and Prince Philip were present when the statue of Ella, along with those of nine other twentieth-century martyrs, was unveiled above the west door of Westminster Abbey.

It was Ella's work with the sick and poor in her Moscow convent that inspired Prince Philip's mother to found her own sisterhood on the Greek island of Tinos. Princess Alice is also buried on the Mount of Olives. In June 2018, Prince William visited Jerusalem and laid flowers on her tomb.

After visiting the convent, the duke called on Patriarch Alexei II.

That afternoon the queen and duke flew to St Petersburg, where the royal yacht *Britannia* awaited them at the newly renamed English Embankment.

At the Catherine Palace at Tsarskoe Selo (at that time still called by its communist name of Pushkin), the old imperial flag was flying for the queen and duke's visit. The palace had literally risen from the ashes after the Second World War and was currently being restored, although the panels in the famed Amber Room, which were removed by the Nazis, had disappeared.

That evening there was a concert and reception in the Youssoupov Palace, once the home of Prince Felix Youssoupov and the scene of Rasputin's murder in 1916. Felix's wife Princess Irina had been Prince Philip's second cousin.

The Hermitage Museum, founded by another of Philip's ancestors, Catherine the Great, posed its own challenges the following day. With more than 3 million items on display, it is currently estimated that eleven years would be needed to view every item for just one minute;

with only just over an hour to see some paintings and artefacts, they avoided the special exhibition on Nicholas II and Alexandra.

As church bells rang out along the shoreline, they then travelled by royal barge across the River Neva to the fortress and cathedral of SS Peter & Paul. The cathedral, with its golden spire gleaming in the sunlight, was the burial place of the Russian emperors since Peter the Great. They viewed the tombs of Prince Philip's ancestors – but there were still no sarcophagi for his great-uncle and great-aunt. Although their identities had been confirmed, Nicholas and Alexandra remained unburied.

'I think he ought to be buried anyway,' the duke told the *Daily Telegraph* before he and the queen left London. 'Just to leave the bones in a polythene bag somewhere on a scientist's table is rather undignified.'[25]

Lunch was served in the Maryinsky Palace, home of Nicholas I's daughter Grand Duchess Maria Nicolaievna (Philip's great-great-aunt) and her husband the Duke of Leuchtenberg, before a wreath-laying ceremony at the memorial to the victims of the siege of Leningrad in the Piskarevskoye Cemetery.

After a return banquet for the Russian president that evening on board the *Britannia*, the royal yacht made a dramatic departure from St Petersburg beneath a display of fireworks.[26]

The reburial of the tsar and his family was postponed several times as discussions continued as to where, and how, they should be interred.

Then, on 16 July 1998, the coffins of Nicholas, Alexandra, three of their children and four retainers arrived at St Petersburg's Pulkovo Airport. The flags of Russia and St Petersburg, complete with black mourning ribbons, hung from lamp posts and the route was lined with troops as they were driven to the SS Peter & Paul Cathedral. Many Russians mingled with the tourists to see the dark green hearses pass.[27] At the fortress the child-sized coffins were carried in by soldiers, escorted by pipers from the Royal Scots Dragoon Guards (formerly the Scots Greys, of whom Nicholas had been colonel-in-chief).

On 17 July, eighty years to the day after their murder, the remains of Nicholas II, Empress Alexandra, Olga, Tatiana, Anastasia (at the insistence of the Russians) and their four retainers were finally laid to rest in a side chapel of the cathedral. Yet the Orthodox Church remained sceptical. Neither Patriarch Alexei II nor the Metropolitan of St Petersburg attended the burial, and it was left to Archpriest Boris

Glebov to conduct a service for 'Christian victims of the revolution', during which the names of the deceased were not even mentioned. As Nicholas's coffin was lowered into the ground last of all, a nineteen-gun salute was fired from the banks of the Neva.

In 2000 the Russian Orthodox Church canonised Nicholas II and his family as passion bearers. The Orthodox Church Outside Russia canonised them in 1981.

In July 2007, members of the Military Historical Club in Ekaterinburg discovered forty-four partial, very damaged bone fragments buried about 50 feet from where the other Romanov remains were found in Koptyaki Forest. They had apparently been covered in acid and burnt, then thoroughly smashed with spades. Initial tests indicated that they are the bones of Alexei and his sister. At the time of writing, they remain unburied.

Prince Philip's Romanov blood helped solve one of the greatest mysteries of the twentieth century. Yet it is an eerie coincidence that the Romanov dynasty which began in the Ipatiev Monastery in Kostroma ended in the Ipatiev House in Ekaterinburg.

Notes

Introduction

1. *The Guardian*, 26 April 2004.
2. *The Guardian*, 26 April 2004; *The New York Times*, 3 September 1973.
3. Prince Philip's visit to the Crimea is taken from A. Sedov's article 'A Horn was Heard – Mute Witness of the War' in *Slava Sevastopolya*, 27 October 2004.
4. *Daily Telegraph*, 17 October 1994; Hardman, p. 446.

1 Game of Thrones

1. Hughes, *Romanovs*, p. 12.
2. The house was built for Nikita Romanov, Tsar Michael's grandfather. After becoming extremely dilapidated it underwent drastic restoration in the reign of Alexander II and afterwards, so its appearance now bears little relationship to its original design. There is no proof that Michael was actually born there. Warnes, p. 54; Greg King, 'The Romanov Boyar House in Moscow', in www.atlantismagazine.substack.com
3. Andrei Ivanovich Kobyla was created a boyar in 1347 and served the grand princes. His fourth son Feodor was known as Feodor Koshkin (after his nickname *koshka*, meaning cat). Feodor's son Ivan was the father of Zakhary Ivanovich Koshkin, who died in 1461. Zakhary's second son Yuri Koshkin-Zakharin became a boyar in 1493 and died in 1504. He was the father of Roman Yurevich Zakharin (1490-1543), who transformed the family name into Romanov. See Hughes, *Romanovs*, pp. 7/8; Tourtchine, pp. 118/9; Montefiore, *Romanovs*, p. 15.
4. Montefiore, *Romanovs*, pp. 3/4.
5. Qtd. in Lincoln, *Romanovs*, p. 26.
6. Bergamini, p. 25.
7. Bergamini, p. 20.
8. Merridale, p. 142.
9. Riasanovsky, pp. 196 & 104.
10. It was 1616 before a decent set of rooms was ready for Michael but the Kremlin was gutted by fire twice before 1626 and the Terem was rebuilt in 1635.

11. Merridale, p. 144.
12. Almedingen, *Romanovs*, p. 47.
13. Lincoln, *Romanovs*, p. 31.
14. Lincoln, *Romanovs*, p. 31; 'In medieval Russia the terms crown and cap were synonymous.' See *The Regalia of Russian Sovereigns*, p. 8; Later other precious stones were added to the core and a gold cap and smooth gold cross with pearls on the points was added and the pendants of pearls and gold on the edge were replaced by sable. See Polynina, *Regalia*, p. 31. The tradition of trimming the royal crowns with sable goes back many centuries. The crown was used until 1682.
15. Montefiore, *Romanovs*, p. 27. The orb and sceptre had survived the Time of Troubles.
16. Warnes, p. 66.
17. Montefiore, *Romanovs*, p. 32.
18. Montefiore, *Romanovs*, p. 32.
19. For Easter see Montefiore, *Romanovs*, p. 33 footnote, & Warnes, p. 65.
20. Merridale, p. 145. It was known as the Frolovskaya Tower until 1658.

2 The Young Monk

1. Almedingen, *Romanovs*, p. 48; S. Massie, *Firebird*, p. 189.
2. Lincoln, *Romanovs*, p. 40.
3. S. Massie, *Firebird*, p. 287. See also Montefiore, *Romanovs*, pp. 47/48 footnote.
4. *The Russian Chronicles*, p. 137.
5. Bergamini, p. 63.
6. Warnes, p. 75.
7. Hughes, *Romanovs*, p. 34.
8. Montefiore, *Romanovs*, p. 51.
9. Warnes, p. 77.
10. Montefiore, *Romanovs*, p. 56.
11. Lincoln, *Romanovs*, p. 56; Hughes, *Romanovs*, p. 44.
12. Hughes, *Romanovs*, p. 44; Riasanovsky, p. 178.
13. Almedingen *Romanovs*, pp. 51/2.
14. Polynina, p. 101.
15. Merridale, p. 162; Warnes, p. 83.
16. S. Massie, *Firebird*, p. 86; Warnes, p. 83. Most of it was demolished by Catherine the Great but the gatehouse and a detailed model of the palace survive.
17. Hughes, *Romanovs*, p. 46.

3 From Moscow to St Petersburg

1. Warnes, p. 86.
2. Hughes, *Peter*, p. 9.
3. Polynina, pp. 103/4 & 90; *The Regalia of Russian Sovereigns*, p. 36.
4. R. Massie, *Peter*, p. 52.

5. Hughes, *Romanovs*, p. 50.
6. Lincoln, *Romanovs*, p. 142; R. Massie, *Peter*, pp. 114/5.
7. R. Massie, *Peter*, p. 111.
8. R. Massie, *Peter*, p116.
9. Lincoln, *Romanovs*, p. 145.
10. Lincoln, *Romanovs*, p. 146.
11. Montefiore, *Romanovs*, p. 74; Hughes, *Romanovs*, p. 50.
12. Hughes, *Romanovs*, p. 58.
13. Hughes, *Peter*, p. 23.
14. Emerson, p. 18.
15. Warnes, p. 95. In Dresden King Augustus, known as 'the Strong', founded the Kunstkammer to house his art collection and the famous Green Vault to house his collection of glittering jewelled artifacts. It was robbed in 2019 but much of the collection was recovered and is now back on public display. Dominic Sandbrook, *The Times*, 17 Aug. 2024.
16. S. Massie, *Firebird*, pp. 95 & 96.
17. S. Massie, *Firebird*, pp. 360 & 368; Hall, *Little Mother*, p. 128.
18. Warnes, p. 99.
19. Peter had given the title of Prince of Russia and Izhora to Menshikov in 1707 for defeating the Swedes in Poland. With the title went large estates. Menshikov obtained the rank of Count (1702) and then Prince of the Holy Roman Empire (1709) from the Holy Roman Emperor, because by tradition the tsars did not award titles. The emperor would always grant them at the request of the tsar. See Hughes, *Peter*, p. 436; Montefiore, *Romanovs*, p. 92 footnote.
20. Hughes, *Romanovs*, p. 72.
21. See Hughes, *Romanovs*, p. 73 & *Peter*, p. 397.
22. Lincoln, *Romanovs*, p. 240.
23. Hughes, *Peter*, p. 40.
24. Lincoln, *Romanovs*, p. 159.
25. R. Massie, *Peter*, p. 678.
26. Lincoln, *Romanovs*, p. 161.
27. She remained there until her grandson Peter II ascended the throne in 1727. She died in 1731.
28. Lincoln, *Romanovs*, p. 162.
29. In 1750 Empress Elizabeth's architect Francesco Bartolomeo Rastrelli extended the palace and in 1755 constructed the famous Amber Room, using the panels from an unfinished amber chamber presented to Peter the Great by King Frederick William I of Prussia in 1716. (Peter's craftsmen had been unable to reassemble them.) Catherine the Great ordered new panels to replace some fake sections and the resulting room was one of the wonders of the world. The walls were inlaid with amber panels from top to bottom and even the furniture was amber. Scott-Clark & Levy, pp. 27/8 & 53/6.
30. See Emerson, p. 23. 'The use of the title tsar is incorrect, although, even today, in current usage.'

31. Merridale, p. 187.
32. According to Lindsey Hughes, this story appears in only one contemporary memoir, by a retainer of the Duke of Holstein. He may have been trying to show that Peter intended the crown to go to Anna, the Duke of Holstein's fiancée, thereby founding a new male line with the couple's children. See Hughes, *Romanovs*, p. 80.
33. Gendrikov & Sen'ko, p. 38.

4 The Heir from Holstein

1. R. Massie, *Peter*, p. 833.
2. Qtd. in R. Massie, *Peter*, p. 806.
3. Hughes, *Peter*, pp. 413/4.
4. Longworth, p. 43.
5. R. Massie, *Peter*, p. 833; Hughes, *Peter*, pp. 413/4.
6. Qtd. in Montefiore, *Romanovs*, p. 142.
7. Peter II and the deposed Ivan VI were the only post-Petrine emperors to be buried in the Archangel Cathedral in Moscow. The so-called curse of the Dolgorukys continued. On 6 July 1880 Alexander II married (morganatically) his mistress Princess Catherine Dolgoruky. In March 1881 he was assassinated.
8. Hughes, *Romanovs*, p. 101.
9. Sources variously give her date of death as 4 or 5 May 1728 in Kiel. She was reburied in the SS Peter & Paul Cathedral on 6 February 1826 after an unmarked grave, believed to be hers, was discovered while preparing for the interment of Alexander I. See Gendrikov & Sen'ko, p. 57.
10. Anna and her husband were exiled to the north of Russia in 1744. She gave birth to two daughters and two more sons and died in 1746. Ivan VI grew up separated from his family. See my next chapter. Also Warnes, p. 119; Hughes, *Romanovs*, p. 90.
11. Bergamini, p. 173.
12. See S. Massie, *Firebird*, pp. 112 & 127.
13. Longworth, p. 180.
14. R. Massie, *Catherine*, p. 48.
15. R. Massie, *Catherine*, p. 11.
16. Catherine the Great's *Memoirs*, qtd in R. Massie, *Catherine*, p. 51.
17. The Church of the Nativity of the Theotokos was founded in 1733 and consecrated in 1737 in the presence of the Empress Anna Ivanovna. It was considered a 'court church' and had an icon of Our Lady of Kazan. During the reign of Empress Elizabeth it officially became a cathedral and was called the Kazan Cathedral, but apparently was still mainly called by its previous name. 'Such confusions are typical for the Russian Orthodox Church.' The present 1801-11 building designed by Voronikhin replaced the Church of the Nativity of Theotokos where Catherine and Peter were married. I am indebted to The Tsarskoe Selo Museum and Heritage site for this information.
18. R. Massie, *Catherine*, p. 106.
19. *Memoirs*, qtd. in R. Massie, *Catherine*, p. 112.
20. See Emerson, p. 35; Hughes, *Romanovs*, p. 102.

21. Hughes, *Romanovs*, p. 105.
22. Bergamini, p. 213; Massie, p. 202.
23. Hughes, *Romanovs*, p. 261, note 6.

5 Exit Peter III – Enter Catherine II

1. Bergamini, p. 216, qtg. Bain, *Peter III* (1902); R. Massie, *Catherine*, p. 240.
2. Qtd. in R. Massie, *Catherine*, p. 224.
3. Emerson, p. 35.
4. Montefiore, *Romanovs*, p. 194.
5. Bergamini, p. 222.
6. R. Massie, *Catherine*, p. 264.
7. Montefiore, *Romanovs*, pp. 199/200.
8. Qtd. in Lincoln, *Romanovs*, p. 212.
9. Montefiore, *Romanovs*, p. 202.
10. His letter is in Oldenburg, p. 204.

6 Catherine II and the Expansion of Empire

1. Later in her reign the 193-carat Orlov diamond, the fourth largest in the world, was given to Catherine by Gregory Orlov and added to her sceptre. Legend says that a French soldier stole it from the eye of a Hindu god's statue in a temple in India. It passed through several hands before an Armenian merchant sold it to Orlov for 400,000 roubles. Orlov apparently only paid the first instalment for this 'diamond the size of an egg' and the remainder of the money came 'from the state coffers'. Jacques, p. 133. Suzanne Massie says it was bought from an Amsterdam bank for 460,000 roubles. *Firebird*, pp. 132/3.
2. Qtd. in Alexander, p. 110.
3. Warnes, p. 133. For the full story of the commission see Alexander, pp. 107/20.
4. Easter & Vorhees, p. 95.
5. Easter & Vorhees, pp. 88/92.
6. Easter & Vorhees, p. 125. For the whole fascinating story of the efforts to find and salvage the *Vrouw Maria* see Easter and Vorhees.
7. Easter & Vorhees, p. 92.
8. Alexander, p. 74.
9. Hughes, *Romanovs*, p. 113.
10. Alexander, p. 139.
11. Montefiore, *Potemkin*, p. 71. The story goes that the beating damaged his eye, he had treatment by a quack doctor for an infection and it turned septic. Simon Sebag Montefiore thinks the beating is unlikely, as Gregory Orlov always behaved decently to Potemkin. However it happened, Potemkin certainly lost an eye.
12. Bergamini, p. 248.
13. Bergamini, p. 248.
14. Montefiore, *Romanovs*, p. 219.

15. For a full discussion of this see Montefiore, *Potemkin*, pp. 137/41 & *Romanovs*, p. 223 footnote; and R. Massie, *Catherine*, pp. 429/30. There is also a legend that on 13/24 July 1775 Catherine secretly gave birth to Potemkin's daughter, known as Elizabeth Grigorievna Temkina (a truncation of Potemkin). Most historians think this unlikely, as Catherine acknowledged her other illegitimate children. Elizabeth grew up in the household of Potemkin's nephew Alexander Samoilov and in 1794 married Ivan Kalageorgi, who had been hired to teach Greek to Catherine's grandson Grand Duke Constantine Pavlovich. The couple had ten children and Elizabeth died in 1854. Her great-grandson, the San Francisco-born actor Andrey Kalageorgi, who certainly believes the story, has recently been granted Russian citizenship. Montefiore pp. 146 & 528 and information from Tatyana Bukharina.
16. R. Massie, *Catherine*, p. 474.
17. R. Massie, *Catherine*, p. 564.
18. Qtd in R. Massie, *Catherine*, p. 444.
19. Qtd in R. Massie, *Catherine*, p. 498.
20. Obolensky, p. 79; R. Massie, *Nicholas & Alexandra*, p. 163.
21. The Fountain of Tears was built in memory of a beautiful girl in the khan's harem, with whom he had fallen in love. When she died young, the heartbroken khan commissioned an Italian architect to build a fountain with a flower from which the water flowed, representing the tears flowing from his eyes. Pushkin visited in 1820 and placed roses on the fountain. When we visited in 1999 fresh roses were still being placed in the same position.
22. Qtd. in R. Massie, *Catherine*, p. 502.
23. King, Greg. 'The Russian Riviera.' In *Atlantis*, Vol. 3, No. 1, p. 24. See Montefiore, *Potemkin*, pp. 380/83 for a full discussion of this.
24. Montefiore, *Potemkin*, p. 488.
25. Montefiore, *Romanovs*, p. 242.
26. Juliane was the aunt of Queen Victoria. For the story of this disastrous marriage and Juliane's later life see Hall, *Queen Victoria and the Romanovs.*
27. Alexander, p. 322.
28. Qtd. in Montefiore, *Romanovs*, p. 254.
29. The list is in Oldenburg, p. 272.

7 *Murder in the Castle*

1. See Hughes, *Romanovs*, p. 106.
2. S. Massie, *Pavlovsk*, p. 6.
3. S. Massie, *Pavlovsk*, pp. 24/5.
4. Lincoln, *Romanovs*, p. 375.
5. Hughes, *Romanovs*, pp. 137/8.
6. See Hughes, *Romanovs*, p. 137. In 1886, with the number of grand dukes and grand duchesses ever-increasing, Alexander III issued a new statute limiting the rank of grand duke/duchess and the income that went with it. See Hall, *Little Mother of Russia*, p. 119.
7. Warnes, p. 147; Swedish ambassador, qtd. in Hughes, *Romanovs*, p. 140.

8. Descendants of this marriage include the current Duke of Kent, Princess Alexandra and Prince Michael of Kent. Elena died in childbirth in 1803 aged 19.
9. Warnes, p. 150.
10. Qtd. in Montefiore, *Romanovs*, p. 268.
11. Montefiore, *Romanovs*, p. 268.
12. Montefiore, *Romanovs*, p. 271.
13. Montefiore, *Romanovs*, p. 274.
14. Qtd. in Montefiore, *Romanovs*, p. 276.
15. Gendrikov & Sen'ko, p. 112.
16. Montefiore, *Romanovs*, p. 278 footnote. On 11/23 March 1998 a prayer service was conducted at Paul's grave and an evening was held in his memory. ITAR-TASS/Pravoslavie v Rossi 23 March 1998.

8 'Tomorrow morning I shall be either emperor or dead'

1. Lincoln, *Nicholas*, p. 52.
2. Sorel & Ruud, p. 28.
3. Zeepvat, *Autumn*, p. 2; Emperor Nicholas, qtd. in Lincoln, *Nicholas*, p. 53.
4. Sorel & Ruud, p. 30.
5. Sorel & Ruud, p. 29.
6. Lincoln, *Nicholas*, p. 59.
7. Sorel & Ruud, p. 32.
8. Qtd. in Montefiore, *Romanovs*, p. 329.
9. Qtd. in Lincoln, *Nicholas*, pp. 67/8.
10. Zeepvat, *Autumn*, p. 27.
11. Charlotte Zeepvat mentions the loss of another baby before 1824. See *Autumn*, page 3.
12. Jackman, *Relations*, p. 190.
13. Qtd. in Montefiore, *Romanovs*, p. 330.
14. Empress Elizabeth did not long survive her husband. She died on 15 May 1826. For many years a legend persisted that Alexander I faked his own death and lived as a holy man under the name of Feodor Kuzmich. He was said to speak fluent French and be familiar with the Russian court. Kuzmich refused to reveal his past to the police and died in Tomsk in 1864.
15. Jackman, *Relations*, p. 116.
16. For the insurrection of 1825 and events leading up to it: Soroka & Ruud, pp. 72/7; Lincoln, *Nicholas*, pp. 31/47; Lincoln, *Romanovs*, pp. 407/10; Hughes, *Romanovs*, pp. 159/60; Bergamini, pp. 305/7; Montefiore, pp. 343/7. According to legend, the night before the uprising Nicholas wandered the corridors of the Winter Palace racked by insomnia. By the light of the moon in the White Ballroom he froze in terror as he spotted a figure in a white nightgown. It was his father Paul, who instantly vanished through the wall. Radzinsky, *Alexander II*, p. 27.
17. Jackman, *Annette*, p. 120.
18. Hall, *Queen Victoria and the Romanovs*, p. 57.

19. Lincoln, *Romanovs*, p. 415.
20. S. Massie, *Firebird*, pp. 234/5.
21. Soroka & Ruud, p. 92.
22. Ashton, in *Atlantis*, Vol. 6, p. 163.
23. Soroka & Rudd, p. 92.
24. S. Massie, *Firebird*, p. 369.
25. Seaman & Sewell, pp. 53 & 82.
26. Lincoln, *Nicholas*, p. 135; Soroka and Rudd, p. 99.
27. Qtd. in S. Massie, *Firebird*, p. 147.
28. Christopher of Greece, p. 50. It is ironic that when a similar fire damaged Windsor Castle in 1992, one of the items that survived was a giant malachite vase in the Grand Reception Room, presented to Queen Victoria by Nicholas I in 1839. It was too heavy to move.
29. Merridale, p. 229. In Stalin's time the St Andrew's and the St Alexander's halls were joined together to make one large hall which housed the Supreme Soviet of the U.S.S.R.
30. *The Alexander Palace, Pages from History*, p. 8.
31. Jackman, *Relations*, pp. 312/3; *The Alexander Palace, Pages*, p. 15.
32. Queen Victoria's diary. RA VIC/MAIN/QVJ (W), 2 June 1844. Qtd. in Hall, *Queen Victoria and the Romanovs*, p. 52.
33. Hall, *Queen Victoria and the Romanovs*, pp. 55/6. For full details of the emperor's 1844 visit see pages 50/59.
34. Lincoln, *Nicholas*, pp. 313 & 318.
35. Bergamini, p. 327.
36. Lincoln, *Nicholas*, p. 350.
37. Jackman, *Stranger*, p. 159.

9 *'I want shipwrights and sailors, not clerks'*

1. Jackman, *Annette*, pp. 144/5; Jackman, *Relations*, p. 145. Although Nicholas called his wife Mouffy, the Empress Maria always called her Alexandrine.
2. Jackman, *Annette*, p. 155.
3. Zoia Belyakova in Beéche (ed), *The Grand Dukes*, p. 54.
4. Ashton, in *Atlantis*, Vol. 6, p. 146.
5. Jackman, *Annette*, p. 252.
6. Zoia Belyakova in Beéche (ed,) *The Grand Dukes*, p. 54.
7. King & Wilson, in *Atlantis*, Vol 6, p. 5.
8. Ashton, in *Atlantis*, Vol. 6, p. 153; Radzinsky, p. 128. According to Radzinsky, *zhinka* is a Russian folk expression.
9. Wilson, 'Oreanda.' In *Atlantis*, Vol 3. No. 1, p. 122.
10. Zoia Belyakova in Beéche (ed), *The Grand Dukes*, p. 56. Although officially it was called the Constantinovsky Palace, it was more usually called the Marble Palace.
11. Warnes, p. 171. The concerts were still going on in 1914, when they were mentioned by Baedeker.
12. Zeepvat, *Autumn*, p. 68.

13. Jackman, *Stranger*, pp. 159/60; Soroka & Ruud, p. 198.
14. Almedingen, *Alexander*, p. 109.
15. For the story of Constantine's visit see Hall, *Queen Victoria and the Romanovs*, pp. 74/5.
16. Almedingen, *Alexander*, p. 120.
17. Soroka & Ruud, pp. 254/5.
18. Almedingen, *Alexander*, p. 151.
19. Qtd. in Soroka & Ruud, pp. 270 & 272.
20. Radzinsky, *Alexander*, p. 131.
21. Anna Tyutcheva's diary, qtd. in Radzinsky, *Alexander*, pp. 120/1.
22. Belyakova in Beéche (ed), *The Grand Dukes*, p. 60.
23. Qtd. by Ashton in *Atlantis*, Vol 6, p. 165.
24. Kleinmichel, pp. 25/6.
25. Jackman, *Stranger*, p. 239.
26. Zeepvat, *Camera*, p. 89.
27. Zoia Belyakova in Beéche (ed), *The Grand Dukes*, p. 61.
28. Mossolov, p. 75.
29. Zoia Belyakova in Beéche (ed), *The Grand Dukes*, p. 62.
30. Ferrand, *Descendances Naturelles*, pp. 352/6. It should be noted that Ferrand was disinclined to believe this story.
31. Meisner, p. 112.
32. Ferrand, *Descendances Naturelles*, pp. 344/50. Marina and Anna both left descendants; Zoia Belyakova in Beéche (ed), *The Grand Dukes*, p. 62; See also Ashton, in *Atlantis*, Vol. 6, p. 176.
33. Chavchavadze, p. 62.
34. For the full story see King & Wilson, 'The Grand Duke and Mrs Blackford' in *Atlantis* Vol. 6, pp. 23/41.
35. King & Wilson, 'The Grand Duke and Mrs Blackford.' *Atlantis* Vol. 6, p. 30.
36. King & Wilson, 'The Grand Duke and Mrs Blackford.' *Atlantis* Vol. 6, p. 31.
37. Radzinsky, p. 246.
38. Qtd. in Lincoln, *Romanovs*, p. 240.
39. Qtd. in Radzinsky, p. 348.
40. This granted her request of 5 December 1891 which related only to the attribution of the name Kniazev. See Ferrand, *Descendances Naturelles*, p. 344.
41. Zeepvat, *Autumn*, p. 154.
42. Christopher, p. 22. This story must have been told to Christopher, as the prince was only four years old when his grandfather died.
43. Christopher, pp. 22/3. According to Ashton, *Atlantis*, Vol. 6, p. 173, she then forbade Kuznetsova and her daughters from living at Pavlovsk or Oreanda. They moved to Dubein on the Baltic and relied on loyal friends to take letters to Constantine.
44. Ashton, in *Atlantis*, Vol 6, p. 176; Anna Kuznetsova died in Moscow at the end of December 1922. Marina died in 1941 and Anna died in 1978. Ferrand, *Descendances Naturelles*, pp. 344/5.

45. Christopher, p. 22.
46. Buxhoeveden, *Before the Storm*, p. 153.
47. Zoia Belyakova in Beéche (ed), *The Grand Dukes*, p. 64; Zeepvat, *Autumn*, p. 75.

10 *'I fell in love with the man, not with the king'*

1. Qtd. in Gelardi, p. 15.
2. RA VIC/MAIN/QVJ (W), 7 November 1861; Nicholas of Greece, p. 101.
3. Kleinmichel, p. 19.
4. Van der Kiste, *Hellenes*, p. 13.
5. Van der Kiste, *Hellenes*, p. 25.
6. Klausen, *Tak for Dansen*, p. 148. Olga had apparently been present at the betrothal ceremonies for Tsarevich Alexander and Princess Dagmar of Denmark in Denmark in 1866. King George noticed her at the picnic, playing with her dolls. Grand Duke Constantine had visited Denmark in 1865. See Klausen, *Tak for Dansen*, p. 108.
7. Grand Duchess George, p. 1.
8. Details of Olga's wedding and honeymoon journey are in Klausen, *Tak for Dansen*, pp. 152/6.
9. Gelardi, p. 31.
10. Prince Michael & Alan Palmer, p. 19.
11. Van der Kiste, *Hellenes*, p. 39.
12. Grand Duchess George, p. 3.
13. Nicholas, p. 12; 'The Costume of the Ladies-in-Waiting to Queen Olga: Court Elegance Using Local Materials,' by Xenia Politou. In *Patterns of Magnificence. Tradition and Reinvention in Greek Women's Costume.* Exhibition catalogue. Ioanna Papantoniou (Ed). (The Hellenic Centre, 2014), p. 63.
14. Christopher, p. 44.
15. Nicholas, p. 27.
16. Grand Duchess George, p. 30.
17. Gelardi, p. 119.
18. King & Wilson, 'The Grand Duke & Mrs Blackford.' In *Atlantis*, Vol. 6, pp. 38/9.
19. Letter of January 1905 in *Kejserlige Gaver*, p. 146. In 1895 Nicholas bought Daria Chassovitin for 100 roubles so that he could spend nights with her and live with his wife during the day. Daria bore him three children – Daria, Sviatislav and Nikolai. In 1901 he bigamously married Varvara Khmelnitskaya, a fifteen-year-old grammar schoolgirl, but this marriage was annulled and Varvara and her family were exiled from Tashkent. King & Wilson, *Atlantis*, Vol. 6, p. 39.
20. Gelardi, p. 114.
21. Her daughter Marie believed that one morning in September Alexandra jumped into a boat moored by the landing stage and collapsed into a convulsive fit. Other versions state that the following evening she fainted

during a ball and was carried to her room, where she suffered severe labour pains. There was no doctor for miles and the only help that could be obtained was from the old village midwife. See Mager, p. 142; Zeepvat, *Autumn*, p. 140; Bodenhoff, p. 43; Hall, *Little Mother*, pp. 147/8. For the full story of Alexandra's labour and death, see 'A Tragedy at Ilinskoye' by Penny Wilson. An autopsy revealed that she also had advanced kidney disease. www.atlantismagazine.substack.com

22. RA/PRIV/AA46/49 qtd. in Gelardi, p. 122.
23. RA/PRIV/AA46/49 qtd. in Gelardi, p. 122. In 1939, after Stalin agreed to send the remains back in exchange for 'a large bulldozer or a pair of tram cars', Alexandra's body was brought back to Tatoi. It remained in the Church of the Prophet Elijah until January 1940, when it was interred at the same time Prince Christopher was buried. See 'A Tragedy at Ilinskoye' by Penny Wilson. www.atlantismagazine.substack.com
24. Qtd. in Perry & Pleshakov, p. 63.
25. Van der Kiste, *Hellenes*, p. 59. For Queen Olga and Crown Princess Sophie's nursing activities, see Hall, *Princesses on the Wards*, pp. 43/7.
26. *Kejserlige Gaver*, p. 74.
27. Van der Kiste & Hall, p. 73.
28. Gelardi, p. 183/4.
29. Sofia Baltazzi, born in 1858, was the daughter of Aristide Baltazzi (1830-1887) and his wife Wilhelmina von Reineck. Aristide 'was at times the municipal head of the Büyükdere neighbourhood on the Bosphorus, the general head of the forestry commission, vice-minister of finance and the president of the Société General company. He was honoured by the title of "Bey" and the order of Mecidiye.' See Levantine Testimony 44, www.levantineheritage.com Through her father, Sofia was a second cousin of Mary Vetsera whose mother was also a Baltazzi.
30. Garshin, *The Hellenes Queen Olga Constantinovna* (Prague: Para, 1937) chapter 1, qtd. in Gelardi, p. 302.
31. Nicholas, *Political Memoirs*, p. 167.
32. Ioulia N. Karolou, *Olga, Queen of the Greeks*. (Athens: Hestia, 1934) chapter 14, qtd in Gelardi, p. 303.
33. For the full story of Rasputin's murder and the involvement of the British see Hall, *Rasputin's Killer and His Romanov Princess*. (Amberley, 2023)
34. Kudrina, *Mother and Son*, p. 115.
35. Klausen, *Dagmar*, pp. 309/10.
36. Van der Kiste & Hall, p. 116.
37. Garshin, chapter 1, qtd. in Gelardi, p. 338.
38. S. Massie, *Pavlovsk*, p. 140.
39. Garshin, chapter 1, qtd. in Gelardi, p. 339.
40. Garshin, chapter 1, qtd. in Gelardi, p. 337.
41. RA/GV/PRIV/AA 46/94. 7 July 1918. Qtd. in Gelardi, p. 360.
42. Karolou, qtd. in Gelardi, p. 346; RA GV/PRIV/AA 46/95, 2 December 1918, qtd in Gelardi, p. 349. Grand Duke Paul had made a second, morganatic,

marriage to Olga von Pistolkors, by whom he had three more children: Vladimir, Irene and Natalie Paley. Vladimir was killed by the bolsheviks in 1918, Olga and her daughters escaped via Finland. See Hall, *To Free the Romanovs*.

43. Garshin, chapter 1, qtd in Gelardi, p. 350.
44. Dimitrakis, p. 13. FO 608/38. Letter to Lord Acton, 28 June 1919.
45. Grand Duchess George, pp. 248/9.
46. TNA. FO 800/154. Lord Curzon to Sir Arthur Davidson, 28 June 1921. Lord Stamfordham to Lord Curzon, 27 June 1921.
47. TNA. FO 800/154. Memo to Sir Sydney Waterlow, 13 September 1921.
48. Olga's daughter Grand Duchess George had reverted to her former name Princess Marie of Greece. In 1923 she married Admiral Pericles Ioannides.
49. Karolou, chapter 17, qtd in Gelardi, p. 377.
50. Van der Kiste & Hall, p. 170.

11 *In and out of Exile*

1. Marie, *Story*, Vol. 1, p. 216; Van der Kiste, *Hellenes*, p. 37.
2. Nicholas, p. 64.
3. Vickers, p. 56.
4. Boothroyd, p. 68.
5. Vickers, p. 26.
6. Vickers, p. 52.
7. Duff, p. 274. The icon screen (Iconostasis) before which they were married, was brought to the Russian church from Clarence House, where it had formed part of the Orthodox chapel of Grand Duchess Marie Alexandrovna of Russia, wife of Queen Victoria's son Prince Alfred.
8. Michael of Greece & Alan Palmer, p. 33; Hawkins, p. 183. Empress Alexandra to Marie Feodorovna, 6 October 1903.
9. Duff, pp. 275/6.
10. Victoria, *Recollections*, p. 157.
11. Qtd. in Ede, p. 16.
12. Van der Kiste, *Hellenes*, p. 69.
13. Victoria, *Recollections*, p. 182.
14. Victoria, *Recollections*, p. 182; Vickers, p. 92.
15. Judd, p. 44; For the full story of Alice's nursing career see Hugo Vickers, *Alice;* and Coryne Hall, *Princesses on the Wards*.
16. Vickers, p. 101.
17. Vickers, p. 106; Pimlott, p. 87.
18. Vickers, p. 119.
19. Grand Duchess George, p. 198.
20. Vickers, p. 122.
21. Qtd. in Hall, *Princesses on the Wards*, p. 107.
22. FO 371/1920 4681, qtd. in Vickers, p. 147.
23. See next chapter.
24. Van der Kiste, *Hellenes*, p. 133.

25. Llewellyn Smith, p. 245.
26. Van der Kiste, *Hellenes*, p. 136.
27. Van der Kiste, *Hellenes*, p. 137.
28. Christopher of Greece, p. 173.
29. Talbot always maintained that he had acted on the instructions of Sir William Tyrell, adviser to the Foreign Secretary Lord Curzon. See Vickers, p. 171, & Ede, p. 36.
30. FO 286/802, qtd in Dimitrakis, p. 15.
31. FO 286/802, qtd in Dimitrakis, p. 15; Rose, pp. 347/8; Vickers, p. 171.
32. Vickers, pp. 165 & 170; Ede, p. 37.
33. Heald, pp. 11/12.
34. Ede, p. 39.
35. Boothroyd, p. 64.
36. Judd, p. 59; Alexandra of Yugoslavia, p. 37; Vickers, p. 178.
37. Victoria Milford Haven to Nona Kerr, qtd. in Vickers, p. 202.
38. Christopher Wilson, in the *Daily Express* online, 11 June 2019; Alexandra of Yugoslavia, pp. 24/5.
39. Christopher Wilson, in the *Daily Express* online, 11 June 2019.
40. Ede, p. 166; Vickers, p. 308.
41. Ede, pp. 166/7; Liane de Pougy, *My Blue Notebooks*. (André Deutsch, 1979), p. 104; Victoria Milford Haven to Dickie Mountbatten, qtd in Vickers, p. 308.
42. Christopher Wilson, in the *Daily Express* online, 11 June 2019.
43. Cécile had been pregnant. The remains of a premature infant were found in the plane's wreckage. Louis and Margaret married quietly in London the following day and adopted baby Johanna. Tragically, she died aged two.
44. Diary of Grand Duke Dmitri Pavlovich, 2 and 3 January 1938. Trans. by Dr William Lee.
45. Diary of Grand Duke Dmitri Pavlovich, 9, 10 & 15 January 1938. Trans. by Dr William Lee.
46. On 11 April 1993 Alice was given a posthumous award as Righteous Among the Nations for risking her own life to save persecuted Jews. Prince Philip and his sister Sophie went to Jerusalem to visit the Holocaust Memorial and receive the award on behalf of their late mother. See Vickers, p. 397.
47. Vickers, p. 309.
48. Horbury, 'Queen Elizabeth II and Greece.' In *Royalty Digest Quarterly*, Vol 1, 2024, p. 60.
49. Boothroyd, p. 74.
50. Ede, p. 166; Vickers, p. 308.
51. Christopher Wilson, in the *Daily Express* online, 11 June 2019.
52. Christopher Wilson, in the *Daily Express* online, 11 June 2019.
53. See Vickers, p. 316. Sir Harold and Lady Zia Wernher provide another link with Romanov blood. In 2024 their great-grandson Hugh Grosvenor, 7th Duke of Westminster, married Olivia Henson in Chester in what was called

the society wedding of the year. Hugh and King Charles III are fourth cousins once removed, through their descent from Emperor Nicholas I.

54. For the full story, see Vickers, pp. 399/405.

12 *'I just had to get on with it'*

1. Birth registration, Corfu, in Judd, p. 51.
2. Ede, p. 48.
3. Hall, *Little Mother of Russia*, p. 348. Ian Vorres said Philip was six but Queen Olga died in June 1926 so he must have been younger. (See *The Last Grand Duchess*, Hutchinson, 1964, p. 172.)
4. Heald, p. 34; Ede, p. 52; Seward, p. 26.
5. Brandreth, p. 63; Seward, p. 35.
6. Report of 14 December 1938 in the school archives, qtd. in Ede, p. 99.
7. Trevelyan, p. 339.
8. Alexandra of Yugoslavia, pp. 51/2.
9. Diary of Grand Duke Dmitri Pavlovich, 1 January 1938; 'Prince Philip's Links with the Russian Imperial court,' by Robert Hardman. *The Spectator*, 19 March 2022.
10. Frederica, p. 22.
11. Crawford, p. 101.
12. Crawford, p. 102.
13. Qtd. in Vickers, p. 290.
14. Qtd. in Ede, p. 137.
15. Ede, p. 121. Cobina Beudette died in California in 2011 aged 90. She is said to have always kept a photo of Philip on her bedside table. *The Daily Mail*, 5 September 2011.
16. Ede, p. 147.
17. Rhodes-James, pp. 286/7.
18. Pimlott, p. 89; Vickers, p. 315.
19. *The Daily Telegraph*. 17 October 1994.
20. Vickers, p. 345.
21. www.guidememalta.com
22. 'Queen's letter shows her aim to have happy atmosphere at Villa Guardamangia,' by Claudia Calleja. *The Times of Malta*, 5 June 2022.
23. *Point de Vue*, No. 3850. 1-7 June 2022; 'A "Normal" Existence,' by Coryne Hall. In *Majesty*, October 2022.
24. Alexandra of Yugoslavia, p. 123.
25. Boothroyd, p. 148.
26. Heald, p. 99.

13 *'Prints Waleski's Visits to Russia*

1. Charles's visit to the Crimea is taken from: *ForPost* online newspaper, 12 September 2022; 'His Royal Highness on the Land Where his Ancestors Fought' by Elizaveta Yurzditskaya. In *Slava Sevastopolya*, 9 November 1996;

Secrets of Sevastopol, Book 6. Secrets of Diplomacy by Valery Borisovich Ivanov. (Russia: 2008); *Vesti Krym*, 24 September 2023. According to Valery Ivanov, there was very little coverage of Charles's visit to the Crimea in the British press because of a financial problem. It appears that £175,000 had been raised in the U.K. to build a British war memorial in Sevastopol but only £18,000 reached the Crimea. What happened to the rest remains a mystery. The office of Queen Elizabeth II donated £3,000 towards the completion of a memorial.
2. *Daily Mail*, 6 April 2014. With thanks to Katrina Warne for pointing this out to me.

14 *'The bastards murdered half my family'*

1. Nicholas and Elena were the grandparents of the Duke of Kent, Princess Alexandra and Prince Michael of Kent.
2. Penny Wilson, in Beéche (ed), *The Other Grand Dukes*, p. 132.
3. Qtd. in *The Daily Mail*, 28 April 2000.
4. For the full story of the search and excavation of the grave see Hall, *To Free the Romanovs*. The *Daily Mail* reported on 8 April 1989 that 'the Queen is going to Russia. A year from now she could be in Moscow…' The queen's visit to Russia was finally announced in the summer of 1994.
5. *The Times*, 18 September 1992.
6. *Nature Genetics*, Vol 12, April 1996; R. Massie, *Final Chapter*, p. 82.
7. King & Wilson, *Fate*, pp. 444/5.
8. *The Daily Mail*, 11 December 1992.
9. *The Times*, 11 December 1992.
10. 'Identification of the remains of the Romanov family by DNA analysis,' by Peter Gill and others. In *Nature Genetics*, Vol 6, February 1994, p. 130.
11. Home Office Press Release, 9 July 1993.
12. Private information to the author, 2006.
13. King & Wilson, *Fate*, p. 446; See also Hall, *Little Mother of Russia*, pp. 354/5. Queen Mary paid the full valuation figure.
14. *From the Royal Attics*, pp. 100/101 and personal visit to the exhibition.
15. Nature Genetics, Vol 12, April 1996, p. 419; Press release, Armed Forces Institute of Pathology, 30 August 1995; *The Washington Post*, 1 September 1995.
16. R. Massie, *Final Chapter*, p. 216. A German court had already rejected her claim to be Grand Duchess Anastasia in 1970.
17. R. Massie, *Final Chapter*, pp. 235/6.
18. R. Massie, *Final Chapter*, p. 236.
19. King & Wilson, *Resurrection*, p. 263; *The Daily Progress*, Charlottesville, Virginia, 30 July 1993.
20. *The Daily Telegraph*, 17 October 1994.
21. *The Sunday Times*, 9 October 1994; King & Wilson, *Resurrection*, pp. 263/4.
22. *The Daily Telegraph*, 17 October 1994; Massie, *Final Chapter*, p. 242. DNA tests in 1994 further proved that she was, as many had suspected, a Polish woman called Franziska Schanzkowska. See King & Wilson, *Resurrection*.

23. *The Daily Express*, 18 October 1994; *The Times*, 18 October 1994. Contemporary newspaper accounts variously give the size of St George's Hall as 300 feet or 400 feet but the 1914 Baedeker and the official Kremlin Guide book both say 200 feet/61 metres.
24. *The Daily Telegraph*, 17 October 1994. Latest research in Russia has disproved many of the myths around Ella's death. See https://tsarnicholas.org/2024/07/18/there-are-still-many-conjectures-surrounding-the-death-of-grand-duchess-elizabeth-feodorovna/ by Paul Gilbert. 18 July 2024.
25. *The Daily Telegraph*, 17 October 1994.
26. The visit to Russia is taken from the Court Circular in the *Daily Telegraph* for 17-20 October, newspaper reports in *The Times*, *Daily Telegraph*, *Daily Express*, *Daily Mail*, *Independent*, *Sunday Times* and Robert Hardman's *Queen of the World*, pp. 441/53.
27. I was among the tourists watching the procession as it passed the Winter Palace.

Bibliography

Aldrich, Richard J. & Cormac, Rory. *The Secret Royals.* (Atlantic Books, 2021)
Alexander, John T. *Catherine the Great. Life and Legend.* (Oxford University Press, 1989)
Alexandra, Queen of Yugoslavia. *Prince Philip. A Family Portrait.* (Hodder & Stoughton, 1959)
Almedingen, E.M. *The Emperor Alexander II.* (The Bodley Head, 1962)
Almedingen, E.M. *The Romanovs.* (The Bodley Head, 1966)
Beeché, Arturo (ed). *The Grand Dukes.* (California: Eurohistory.com, 2010)
Beeché, Arturo (ed). *The Other Grand Dukes.* (California: Eurohistory.com, 2012)
Belyakova, Zoia. 'Grand Duke Constantine Nicolaievich', in *The Grand Dukes.* (California: Eurohistory.com, 2010)
Bergamini, John. *The Tragic Dynasty.* (Constable, 1970)
Bodenhoff, Willie. *Den Gamle Kammerherre.* (Copenhagen: H. Hagerup, 1935)
Boland, Terry. *Death of a Romanov Prince.* (California: Eurohistory.com, 2018)
Boothroyd, Basil. *Philip. An Informal Biography.* (Longman, 1971)
Brandreth, Gyles. *Philip. The Final Portrait.* (Coronet Books, 2021)
Buxhoeveden, Baroness Sophie. *Before the Storm.* (Macmillan, 1938)
Chavchavadze, David. *The Grand Dukes.* (New York: Atlantic International Publications, 1990)
Christense, Svend Aage & Gottlieb, Henning (ed). *Danmark og Rusland i 500 år.* (Copenhagen: SNU 1993)
Christopher, Prince of Greece. *Memoirs.* (Hurst & Blackett Ltd, 1938)
Crawford, Marion. *The Little Princesses.* Foreword by Jennie Bond. (Orion, 2002)
Dimitrakis, Panagiotis. *Greece and the English.* (N.Y: Tauris Academic Studies, 2009)
Dimond, Frances. *Queen Alexandra. Loyalty and Love.* (History & Heritage Publishing, 2022)
Duff, David. *Hessian Tapestry.* (Frederick Muller, 1967)
Eade, Philip. *Young Prince Philip.* (Harper Press, 2011)

Easter, Gerald & Vorhees, Maria. *The Tsarina's Lost Treasure.* (N.Y: Pegasus Books, 2020)

Emerson, Barbara. *The First Cold War.* (Hurst & Co, 2024)

Ferrand, Jacques. *Descendances Naturelles des Souverains et Grands-Ducs de Russie de 1762 à 1910.* (Paris: 1995)

Figes, Orlando. *Crimea.* (Allen Lane, 2010)

Frederica, Queen of the Hellenes. *A Measure of Understanding.* (Macmillan, 1971)

From the Royal Attics. Exhibition Catalogue. (Copenhagen: The Royal Danish Collection, 2016)

Gelardi, Julia. *From Splendour to Revolution.* (St Martin's Press, 2005)

Gendrikov, Vladimir, & Sen'ko, Sergei. *The Cathedral of SS Peter & Paul.* (St Petersburg: Liki Rossii, 1998)

George, Grand Duchess of Russia. *A Romanov Diary.* (New York: Atlantic International Publications, 1988)

Gould Lee, Arthur S. *The Royal House of Greece.* (Ward Lock & Co., 1948)

Hall, Coryne. *Little Mother of Russia. A Biography of the Empress Marie Feodorovna 1847-1928.* (Shepherd Walwyn, 1999)

Hall, Coryne. *Princesses on the Wards. Royal Women in Nursing Through Wars and Revolutions.* (The History Press, 2014)

Hall, Coryne. *Queen Victoria and the Romanovs. Sixty Years of Mutual Distrust.* (Amberley Publishing, 2020)

Hall, Coryne. *Rasputin's Killer and his Romanov Princess.* (Amberley Publishing, 2023)

Hall, Coryne. *To Free the Romanovs.* (Amberley Publishing, 2018)

Hardman, Robert. *Queen of the World.* (Century, 2018)

Hawkins, George (ed). *Alexandra Feodorovna, Diaries & Correspondence. Vol. 3, The Young Empress, 1895-1905.* (Printed by Amazon, 2024)

Heald, Tim. *The Duke. A Portrait of Prince Philip.* (Hodder & Stoughton, 1991)

Hughes, Lindsey. *Russia in the Age of Peter the Great.* (Yale University Press, 1998)

Hughes, Lindsey. *The Romanovs. Ruling Russia 1613-1917.* (Continuum, 2008)

Jackman, S.W. *A Stranger in The Hague.* (North Carolina: Duke University Press, 1989)

Jackman, S.W. *Chère Annette.* (Alan Sutton, 1994)

Jackman, S. W. *Romanov Relations.* (Macmillan, 1969)

Jacques, Susan. *The Empress of Art.* (N.Y: Pegasus Books, 2016)

Jenkins, Michael. *Arakcheev. Grand Vizier of the Russian Empire.* (Faber & Faber, 1969)

Judd, Denis. *Prince Philip, a Biography.* (Michael Joseph, 1980)

King, Greg & Wilson, Penny. *The Fate of the Romanovs.* (Hoboken, New Jersey: John Wiley, 2003)

King, Greg & Wilson, Penny. *The Resurrection of the Romanovs.* (Hoboken, New Jersey: John Wiley, 2011)

Klausen, Inger-Lise. *Dagmar, Zarina fra Danmark* (Copenhagen: Lindhardt & Ringhof, 1997)

Klausen, Inger-Lise. *Tak for Dansen, Louise.* (Copenhagen: Ashehoug, 2003)
Kleinmichel, Countess. *Memories of a Shipwrecked World.* (Brentano's, 1923)
Klier, John & Mingay, Helen. *The Quest for Anastasia.* (Smith Gryphon, 1995)
Kudrina, Yulia. *Mother and Son.* (Russia: Glagol, 2004)
Lincoln, W. Bruce. *Nicholas I.* (Allen Lane, 1978)
Lincoln, W. Bruce. *The Romanovs.* (Weidenfeld & Nicolson, 1981)
Llewellyn Smith, Michael. *Ionian Vision.* (Allen Lane 1973)
Longworth, Philip. *The Three Empresses.* (Constable, 1972)
Maclean, Fitzroy. *Holy Russia.* (Weidenfeld & Nicolson, 1978)
Mager, Hugo. *Elizabeth, Grand Duchess of Russia.* (N.Y: Carroll & Graf, 1998)
Marie Feodorovna, Empress of Russia exhibition catalogue. (Copenhagen: Christiansborg Slot, 1997)
Marie, Queen of Romania. *The Story of My Life.* Vol. 1. (Cassell, 1934)
Massie, Robert. *Catherine the Great.* (Head of Zeus, 2012)
Massie, Robert. *Nicholas and Alexandra.* (Victor Gollancz, 1968)
Massie, Robert. *Peter the Great.* (Victor Gollancz, 1981)
Massie, Robert. *The Romanovs. The Final Chapter.* (Jonathan Cape, 1995)
Massie, Suzanne. *Land of the Firebird.* (Hamish Hamilton, 1980)
Massie, Suzanne. *Pavlovsk: The Life of a Russian Palace.* (Hodder & Stoughton, 1990)
Meisner, Nadine. *Marius Petipa. The Emperor's Ballet Master.* (Oxford University Press, 2019)
Merridale, Catherine. *Red Fortress.* (Allen Lane, 2013)
Michael, Prince of Greece & Palmer, Alan. *The Royal House of Greece.* (Weidenfeld & Nicolson, 1990)
Miller, Ilana. *The Four Graces.* (California: Eurohistory.com, 2011)
Moncreiffe, Sir Iain of that Ilk, Bt. *Royal Highness.* (Hamish Hamilton, 1982)
Montefiore, Simon Sebag. *Prince of Princes. The Life of Potemkin.* (Weidenfeld & Nicolson, 2000)
Montefiore, Simon Sebag. *The Romanovs.* (Weidenfeld & Nicolson, 2016)
Mossolov, Alexander. *At the Court of the Last Tsar.* (Methuen, 1935)
Nicholas, Prince of Greece. *Erindringer fra et Halvt Aarhundrede.* (Denmark: Gyldendal, 1929)
Nicholas, Prince of Greece. *My Political Memoirs, 1914-1917.* (Hutchinson, 1928)
Obolensky, Serge. *One Man in His Time.* (Hutchinson, 1960)
Oldenburg, Zoe. *Catherine the Great.* (William Heinemann Ltd, 1965)
Petropoulos, Jonathan. *Royals and the Reich.* (Oxford University Press, 2006)
Pimlott, Ben. *The Queen.* (Harper Collins, 1996)
Polynina, Irina & Rakhmanov, Nicolai. *The Regalia of the Russian Empire.* (Moscow: Red Square Publishers, 1994)
Radzinsky, Edvard. *Alexander II. The Last Great Tsar.* (First Free Press paperback, 2006)
Rhodes James, Robert (ed). *The Diaries of Sir Henry Channon.* (Weidenfeld & Nicolson, 1967)

Riasanovsky, Nicholas. *A History of Russia.* (Oxford University Press, 1993)

Rose, Kenneth. *King George V.* (Weidenfeld & Nicolson, 1983)

Ruslands Skatte – Kejserlige Gaver. Exhibition catalogue. (Copenhagen: The Royal Silver Room, 2002)

Scott-Clark, Catherine & Levy, Adrian. *The Amber Room.* (Atlantic Books, 2004)

Seaman, W.A.L, & Sewell, J.R. (ed). *The Russian Diary of Lady Londonderry. 1836-37.* (John Murray, 1973)

Seward, Ingrid. *Prince Philip Revealed.* (Simon & Schuster, 2020)

Shchutskaya, G.K. *Palaty boyar Romanovich.* (Moscow: 2000)

Soroka, Marina & Ruud, Charles A. *Becoming a Romanov. Grand Duchess Elena and Her World. (1808-1873)* (Routledge, 2016)

The Alexander Palace, Pages from the History. (St Petersburg: Alfa-Colour Art Publishers, 2008)

The Regalia of Russian Sovereigns. (Moscow: The Moscow Kremlin, 1997)

The Russian Chronicles. (Random Century Group, 1990)

Tourtchine, Jean-Fred. *Les Manuscrits du Cedre. L'Empire de Russie*, Vol. 2. (France: Lamorlaye. No date.)

Trevelyan, Raleigh. *Grand Dukes and Diamonds.* (Secker & Warburg, 1991)

Troyat, Henri, *Alexander of Russia.* (New English Library, 1984)

Van der Kiste, John. *Kings of the Hellenes.* (Alan Sutton, 1994)

Van der Kiste, John & Hall, Coryne. *Once a Grand Duchess.* (Sutton Publishing, 2002)

Vickers, Hugo. *Alice, Princess Andrew of Greece.* (Hamish Hamilton, 2000)

Victoria, Marchioness of Milford Haven. *Recollections.* Edited & expanded by Arturo E. Beéche & Ilana D. Miller. (Eurohistory.com, 2020)

Warnes, David. *Chronicle of the Russian Tsars.* (Thames & Hudson, 1999)

Zeepvat, Charlotte, *Romanov Autumn.* (Sutton Publishing, 2000)

Zeepvat, Charlotte. *The Camera and the Tsars.* (Sutton Publishing, 2004)

Articles

Ashton, Janet. 'Daring to Emphasize his Independence. Konstantin Nikolaievich, the Radical Grand Duke.' In *Atlantis*, Vol. 6.

Horbury, David. 'Queen Elizabeth II and Greece.' In *Royalty Digest Quarterly*, Vol 1, 2024.

King, Greg. 'The Russian Riviera. A Short History of the Crimea.' In *Atlantis*, Vol. 3, No. 1.

King, Greg & Wilson, Penny. 'Grand Duchess Alexandra Josifovna.' In *Atlantis*, Vol. 6.

King, Greg & Wilson, Penny. 'The Grand Duke and Mrs Blackford.' In *Atlantis*, Vol. 6.

Martin, R. 'Choreographing the Tsar's Happy Occasion.' *Slavic Review*, 63. 2004.

Mogensen, Ove. 'Tatoi and its Royal Burial Ground.' In *Royalty Digest Quarterly*, Vol. 4, 2012.

Warne, Katrina. 'A Surfeit of Sophias'. In *Royalty Digest Quarterly*, Vol.4, 2023.

Wilson, Christopher. 'Prince Philip: the untold story of the Duke of Edinburgh's stepmother who spent his money.' *Daily Express online*, 11 June 2019.
Wilson, Penny. 'Oreanda. The Spirit of the Mountains.' In *Atlantis*. Vol. 3, No. 1.
Zeepvat, Charlotte. 'The Only Lady Admiral in the World.' In *Royalty Digest*, Dec. 2001 & Jan. 2002.

Guidebooks

Gatchina Palace and Park (St Petersburg: P2 Art Publications, 1997)
Pavlovsk Palace and Park (St Petersburg: P2 Art Publications, 1996)
Petrodvorets. The Cottage Palace. (Leningrad: 1990)
The Moscow Kremlin. An Album. (Moscow: Art-Ridnik, 2001)

Magazines and Newspapers

Atlantis. In the Courts of Memory
Majesty
Royalty Digest
Royalty Digest Quarterly
The Daily Mail
The European Royal History Journal
The Sunday Times
The Times

Internet

www.atlantismagazine.substack.com

Index